STORYING MENTAL ILLNESS AND PERSONAL RECOVERY

This book contains excerpts of life stories from 118 individuals diagnosed with schizophrenia, bipolar disorder, borderline personality disorder, and major depressive disorder. This library of personal narratives, heavily reproduced and quoted throughout the text, presents a composite image of the ways in which narrative identity can be affected by mental illness while also being a resource for personal recovery. Those researching, studying, or practicing in mental health professions will find a wealth of humanizing first-person perspectives on mental illness that foster perspective-taking and aid patient-centered treatment and study. Researchers of narrative psychology will find a unique set of life stories synthesized with existing literature on identity and recovery. Moving toward intervention, the authors include a "guide for narrative repair" with the aim of healing narrative identity damage and fostering growth of adaptive narrative identity.

DORTHE KIRKEGAARD THOMSEN is a professor of psychology at Aarhus University, Denmark. She is a prominent scholar in narrative identity, which she has studied extensively over the past decade. She has authored more than 60 scientific papers and has received several grants and awards in recognition of her work.

TINE HOLM completed her PhD on life stories in schizophrenia, then received funding to examine trauma within psychiatric settings particularly in relation to force treatment. In parallel with her research, she works as a clinical psychologist at an outpatient unit for individuals with severe mental illness and co-occurring substance use disorder.

RIKKE AMALIE AGERGAARD JENSEN received her Ph.D. in psychology in 2020 from Aarhus University, Denmark. As an assistant professor at the University of Southern Denmark, she continues to study stories about the lived experience of mental illness. Specifically, she concentrates on children of parents with mental illness and family stories to aid the development of family-centered treatment and to mitigate social inequalities and stigmatization in mental healthcare.

MAJSE LIND is an assistant professor at Aalborg University, Denmark. She is a prominent scholar in research on life stories and psychopathology, particularly in the subarea of personality disorders, and has received several awards for this work.

ANNE MAI PEDERSEN received her MSc in psychology from Aarhus University, Denmark, where she is now pursuing a PhD degree. Her primary field of research is life stories in people with mental and somatic illness, with a focus on narrative identity in psychopathology and specifically in bipolar disorder.

STORYING MENTAL ILLNESS AND PERSONAL RECOVERY

DORTHE KIRKEGAARD THOMSEN
Aarhus University

TINE HOLM
Aarhus University

RIKKE AMALIE AGERGAARD JENSEN
University of Southern Denmark
Mental Health Services Region of Southern Denmark

MAJSE LIND
Aalborg University

ANNE MAI PEDERSEN
Aarhus University

Shaftesbury Road, Cambridge CB2 8EA, United Kingdom

One Liberty Plaza, 20th Floor, New York, NY 10006, USA

477 Williamstown Road, Port Melbourne, VIC 3207, Australia

314–321, 3rd Floor, Plot 3, Splendor Forum, Jasola District Centre, New Delhi – 110025, India

103 Penang Road, #05–06/07, Visioncrest Commercial, Singapore 238467

Cambridge University Press is part of Cambridge University Press & Assessment, a department of the University of Cambridge.

We share the University's mission to contribute to society through the pursuit of education, learning and research at the highest international levels of excellence.

www.cambridge.org
Information on this title: www.cambridge.org/9781009301138

DOI: 10.1017/9781108907606

© Dorthe Kirkegaard Thomsen, Tine Holm, Rikke Amalie Agergaard Jensen, Majse Lind, and Anne Mai Pedersen 2023

This publication is in copyright. Subject to statutory exception and to the provisions of relevant collective licensing agreements, no reproduction of any part may take place without the written permission of Cambridge University Press & Assessment.

First published 2023
First paperback edition 2025

A catalogue record for this publication is available from the British Library

Library of Congress Cataloging-in-Publication data
NAMES: Thomsen, Dorthe Kirkegaard, 1974- author. | Holm, Tine, 1985-author. | Jensen, Rikke, 1988- author. | Lind, Majse, 1989- author. | Pedersen, Anne Mai, 1988- author.
TITLE: Storying mental illness and personal recovery / Dorthe Kirkegaard Thomsen, Tine Holm, Rikke Jensen, Majse Lind, Anne Mai Pedersen.
DESCRIPTION: Cambridge ; New York, NY : Cambridge University Press, 2023. | Includes bibliographical references and index.
IDENTIFIERS: LCCN 2022025743 (print) | LCCN 2022025744 (ebook) | ISBN 9781108830454 (hardback) | ISBN 9781009301138 (paperback) | ISBN 9781108907606 (epub)
SUBJECTS: LCSH: Psychology–Biographical methods. | Psychiatry–Research–Methodology. | Psychology–Qualitative research. | Mentally ill–Biography. | Narrative therapy. | Identity (Psychology)
CLASSIFICATION: LCC BF39.4 .T46 2023 (print) | LCC BF39.4 (ebook) | DDC 155.2–dc23/eng/20220716
LC record available at https://lccn.loc.gov/2022025743
LC ebook record available at https://lccn.loc.gov/2022025744

ISBN   978-1-108-83045-4   Hardback
ISBN   978-1-009-30113-8   Paperback

Cambridge University Press & Assessment has no responsibility for the persistence or accuracy of URLs for external or third-party internet websites referred to in this publication and does not guarantee that any content on such websites is, or will remain, accurate or appropriate.

Contents

List of Figures		*page* vii
List of Tables		viii
Acknowledgments		ix
Chapter 1	Introducing the Book	1
Chapter 2	The Science of Mental Illness	15
Chapter 3	Vulnerability, Stress, and Burden in Mental Illness	28
Chapter 4	Recovery and Mental Illness	41
Chapter 5	Narrative Identity	53
Chapter 6	Narrative Identity, Illness, and Well-Being	68
Chapter 7	How Did We Collect and Analyze the Life Stories?	85
Chapter 8	Overview of Narrative Identity Themes from the Initial Analyses	100
Chapter 9	Relationship Themes in Narrative Identity	114
Chapter 10	Self Themes in Narrative Identity	133
Chapter 11	Functional-Level Themes in Narrative Identity	156
Chapter 12	Treatment Themes in Narrative Identity	168
Chapter 13	Summary and Synthesis	180
Chapter 14	Understanding the Interplay between Narrative Identity and Mental Illness: A Framework	188
Chapter 15	Tools for Narrative Repair	198
Conclusion		229

Appendix 1 My Personal Story of Mental Illness	231
Appendix 2 The Alternative View of Personality Disorders	232
Appendix 3 Life Story Chapters	233
Appendix 4 Methodological Details on Studies	235
Appendix 5 Detailed Description of Analyses	249
Appendix 6 Coding Manual	255
Appendix 7 Worksheets for Chapters	262
Appendix 8 The Guide for Narrative Repair in Practice: A Case Story	265
References	274
Index	293

Figures

3.1	How the life story analyses complement diathesis-stress models	page 36
7.1	Overview of the analyses	93
9.1	Consequences of mental illness for narrative identity: relationship themes	115
9.2	Well-being, value, and meaning in narrative identity: relationship themes	123
10.1	Consequences of mental illness for narrative identity: self themes	135
10.2	Well-being, value, and meaning in narrative identity: self themes	145
11.1	Consequences of mental illness for narrative identity: functional-level themes	157
11.2	Well-being, value, and meaning in narrative identity: functional-level themes	158
12.1	Consequences of mental illness for narrative identity: treatment themes	169
12.2	Well-being, value, and meaning in narrative identity: treatment themes	170
13.1	Consequences of mental illness for narrative identity: an overview of themes	181
13.2	Well-being, value, and meaning in narrative identity: an overview of themes	182
15.1	Overview of tasks in the guide for narrative repair	204
A3.1	Illustration of chapters in a life story	234
A8.1	Illustration of past chapters in the case story	272
A8.2	Illustration of future chapters in the case story	273

Tables

2.1 DSM-5 diagnostic criteria for schizophrenia, manic episode, hypomanic episode, major depressive disorder, and borderline personality disorder — page 19
7.1 Overview of samples and methods in the four projects — 87
7.2 Themes extracted under each of the three focus areas — 94
7.3 Superordinate themes, themes, and subthemes in narrative identity — 96
8.1 Percentages (frequencies) for negative consequences of mental illness from a narrative identity perspective — 101
8.2 Percentages (frequencies) for positive consequences of mental illness from a narrative identity perspective — 105
8.3 Percentages (frequencies) for sources of well-being from a narrative identity perspective — 108

Acknowledgments

First and foremost, we are deeply grateful to the participants who agreed to share their life stories. Thank you for your time and openness.

Many people assisted with the collection of the life stories, contributing with clinical knowledge of patient groups and practical help with recruiting participants: Vibeke Fuglsang Bliksted (senior researcher, the Psychosis Research Unit), Rikke Bøye (chief clinical psychologist, the Unit for Personality Disorders), Nicolai Ladegaard (clinical psychologist, the Depression and Anxiety Research Unit), and Krista Nielsen Straarup (clinical psychologist, the Unit for Mania and Depression) – all from Aarhus University Hospital Skejby; clinical psychologist Sebastian Simonsen and chief physician Torben Heinskou, the Psychotherapeutic Center Stolpegård; and Professor Carsten René Jørgensen, the Department of Psychology and Behavioural Sciences, Aarhus University.

Our colleagues at the Centre of Excellence for Autobiographical Memory Research (CON AMORE) and the Department of Psychology and Behavioural Sciences reacted with great enthusiasm when we shared our ideas about the book. The memories of their reactions kept us going. Thank you in particular to Professor David B. Pillemer for his continued support and his insightful comments on the book, and to chief clinical psychologist Torben Østergaard Christensen for engaging in discussions about the book's contribution to psychiatric care and for sharing his extensive knowledge on psychiatric research, which improved the book tremendously. Several people pointed us to relevant research, read drafts of the book, and provided thoughtful feedback: Tilmann Habermas, Lynn Ann Watson, Carsten René Jørgensen, William L. Dunlop, Katherine Panattoni, Krista Nielsen Straarup, Klaus Nielsen, Esben Hougaard, and two anonymous reviewers. Also thank you to Annie Dolmer Kristensen for her assistance with proofreading the book, to Marie Tranberg Hansen and Julie Hauballe Klinke for their help with content coding of the life stories, to Mark Røn for preparing the figures, and to Gina Bay for assistance with references.

The Carlsberg Foundation generously funded Dorthe Kirkegaard Thomsen while writing the book (CF18–0150). The study conducted by Rikke Amalie Agergaard Jensen was supported by a grant from the Velux foundation (VELUX33266). Majse Lind was funded by a grant from the Independent Research Fund Denmark (8023-00029B) while working on the book. Tine Holm was employed at the Psychosis Research Unit, Aarhus University Hospital, during the writing of this book. Note that the coauthors Tine Holm, Rikke Amalie Agergaard Jensen, Majse Lind, and Anne Mai Pedersen appear in alphabetical order.

Finally, Susanne Kirkegaard Thomsen and her family lent us their beach house where we wrote most of the book. Days with no emails, no phone calls, and walks by the seafront made space for reflection and creativity. Annika, Esther, Alfred, and Jan: Thank you for your limitless support, patience, and sound advice ("take your time, don't hurry").

CHAPTER I

Introducing the Book

The Aim of the Book

We would like to start with a quote from Elyn Saks,[1] who suffers from schizophrenia: "*While medication had kept me alive, it had been psychoanalysis that had helped me find a life worth living*" (p. 298).

Elyn Saks studied at world-leading universities. She pursued a career in academia and presently holds a position as professor at the University of Southern California, where she founded the Saks Institute for Mental Health Law, Policy, and Ethics. In her autobiography, *The Center Cannot Hold – My Journey through Madness*, she tells her story of struggling with delusions, resisting medication, and years of psychoanalysis. The opening quote is deeply touching, and it captures important insights that deserve more attention. Let us unpack it a little bit. First, the quote clarifies that although medication is lifesaving, it has limits. Psychopharmacological drugs may relieve symptoms, prevent suicide, and be a crucial part of treatment. Even then, problems remain. Individuals need more than medication to recover from mental disorder and find well-being.[2] Second, the quote also reveals that Elyn Saks interprets her schizophrenia as costing her a life worth living, a life that had to be restored. She perceived psychoanalysis as helping her gain value in life, but psychoanalysis may not work for everyone. What other experiences do individuals with psychiatric disorders narrate as propelling them toward well-being, happiness, and thriving? Toward a satisfying life with meaning, joy, and other positive emotions? These reflections drove us to formulate the central questions that this book will seek to answer:

1. What do life stories reveal about subjective consequences of suffering from mental illness?
2. What do life stories reveal about experiences bringing well-being when living with mental illness?

Throughout the book, we use diverse terms, including mental illness, psychiatric disturbance, mental disorder, psychopathology, and others. Each term comes with its own associations and understandings of the central phenomenon.[3-5] For example, the terms illness and pathology signify (brain) disease, but not all researchers agree that disease is involved. Rather, they comprehend mental disorder as the severe end of a spectrum of psychological problems or as a disability. We will return to these varying models later in the book. Views also vary with the type of diagnosis considered. For example, current understandings of schizophrenia emphasize pathological brain processes,[6] whereas this is less the case for other types of psychopathology, such as personality disorders.[7] Given that there are no clear-cut answers about the validity of these conceptualizations, we adopt the perspective that the different frameworks and their associated terms all capture part of the picture concerning mental disorder. As such, we embrace the view that psychopathology is complex and that we may gain insights about mental illness through the lens of diverse models. Whether we comprehend mental disorder following a disease model, as the severe end of a psychological problems dimension, or as disability, afflicted individuals will experience costs. These costs may hinder well-being and our book will foster ideas about how to support individuals with mental illness in recovering a good life.

Broadly speaking, we examine whether personal stories, like Elyn Saks', provide unique insights into mental illness not captured by traditional medical and psychological research. Systematic research on narratives has emerged over the last decades as scientists began to recognize the power of stories.[8-11] Personal stories capture the richness of subjective experience, the meaning individuals imbue their lives with, and impact how they act. Examining how individuals with mental disorder story the costs of their illness and sources of well-being can yield knowledge crucial for tailoring interventions to support recovery from psychopathology. In later chapters, we elaborate on the nature of personal stories and analyze life stories told by 118 individuals living with psychiatric disorders. First, we consider autobiographies by authors struggling with mental illness as these provide cues for answering our two questions. These authors differ from many other people with mental disorder since not everyone can publish their memoires. Their stories have surely been adapted to become widely read, but they may still inspire our thinking about how individuals interpret the consequences of their illness and create possibilities for happiness.

Mental Illness Portrayed in Autobiographies

Elyn Saks is one of many people who have shared their experiences of living with psychopathology. Others include Kay Redfield Jamison (who wrote about her life with bipolar disorder), Susanna Kaysen (narrating her hospitalization for borderline personality disorder), and Matt Haig and Elizabeth Wurtzel who both disclosed their stories of depression. If you have read any of these books, they probably moved you. They certainly moved us. We think this is what good books can do. They move people, change their attitudes, and transform their view of themselves and other people.

Autobiographies about psychiatric disturbance vary in many ways. This is natural as the authors are very different people who suffer from distinct mental illnesses. At the same time, common threads run through the stories. We read the autobiographies paying close attention to how psychopathology impacted the authors' lives and found convergence on some themes. The writers talk about fundamental issues like loss of time, loss of future, and loss of life. They depict difficulties with accepting their mental illness. They share stories about keeping their disorder secret, about pretending, in fear of stigmatization. Further, they portray the pain of abandoning hopes for work and relationships and the loss of a "normal life." Finally, most of the narratives feature a frightening loss of self and describe how selfhood is damaged and tainted.

Elizabeth Wurtzel was a young and gifted student at Harvard University when depression hit her: "*No matter if I ever got out of this depression alive, it made no difference because it had already fundamentally changed me. There had been permanent damage*" (p. 84).[12]

Matt Haig also talks about how mental illness affected his sense of self. After finishing his university studies, he was putting off adulthood by working a last summer job in Spain. First, panic swallowed Matt, then depression: "*I can remember the day the old me died. It started with a thought. Something was going wrong .... And then my heart started to go. And then I started to go. I sank, fast, falling into a new claustrophobic and suffocating reality. And it would be over a year before I would feel anything like even half-normal again*" (p. 9).[13]

Kay Redfield Jamison, an accomplished psychologist and researcher suffering from bipolar disorder, echoes this loss of self: "*I was confused and frightened and terribly shattered in all of my notions of myself; my self-confidence, which had permeated every aspect of my life for as long as I could remember, had taken a very long and disquieting holiday . . . . I had a horrible sense of loss for who I had been and where I had been*" (pp. 85 and 91).[14]

These quotes illustrate the harm to selfhood sometimes accompanying mental illness. The autobiographies display a multitude of devastating losses flowing from mental illness. However, although most of the consequences are negative, there are reflections about the silver linings. These are tiny bits in the overall stories, but we found some.

Matt Haig, who is very explicit about the costs of his anxiety and depression, states:

> *Depression, for me, wasn't a dulling but a sharpening, an intensifying, as though I had been living my life in a shell and now the shell wasn't there. It was total exposure. A red-raw, naked mind . . . . You know, before the age of twenty-four I hadn't known how bad things could be, but I hadn't realized how good they could feel either. That shell might be protecting you, but it's also stopping you feeling the full force of that good stuff.* (pp. 126–127)[13]

Kay Redfield Jamison expresses a similar theme. She notes that some of her milder manias came with increased creativity and work productivity: "*So why would I want anything to do with this illness? Because I honestly believe that as a result of it I have felt more things, more deeply; had more experiences, more intensely*" (p. 218).[14]

What do the writers have to say about experiences important to well-being? They emphasize stable, loving relationships with partners, friends, and parents who do not shy away as the authors fall into darkness. They focus on working with therapists who respect their autonomy and go out of their way to care for them. Not that all close others and therapists are viewed as guardian angels. In fact, the writers often describe unhelpful behaviors by others and therapists. Nevertheless, other people are often depicted as crucial to thriving. Some authors also vividly describe how well-being resulted from accepting their mental disorder and speaking openly about it. Below, we present two exemplar quotes illustrating this point.

Early in her autobiography, Elyn Saks uses the metaphor of a riptide to understand her relationship with her illness and explains how you cannot resist a riptide. If you do, it will pull you under. Still, throughout much of her book, she describes fighting the idea that she had schizophrenia, trying to get off medication, which would soon leave her psychotic again. However, at some point, she starts a new type of medication and things change:

> *The most profound effect of the new drug was to convince me, once and for all, that I actually had a real illness . . . . There's no way to overstate the thunderclap this revelation was to me. And with it, my final and most profound resistance to*

> the idea that I was mentally ill began to give way. Ironically, the more I accepted I had a mental illness, the less the illness defined me – at which point the riptide set me free. (p. 304)[1]

Matt Haig's book, *Reasons to Stay Alive*, reached a wide audience and made it to the top of the *Sunday Times* bestseller list. However, for a long time, he kept his disorder very private. In the book, he describes the realization that openness about the illness brought him hope: "*It took me more than a decade to be able to talk openly, properly, to everyone, about my experience. I soon discovered the act of talking is in itself a therapy. Where talk exists, so does hope*" (p. 68).[13]

What we can learn from these autobiographies is that across a range of psychopathologies, individuals story their illness as having profound consequences for their lives, some good, but mostly bad. Although some of these perceived outcomes are unique to the individual, to the particular circumstances of the author's life, there are convergent themes. Similarly, the authors agree to some extent about which experiences they narrate as helping them gain well-being despite the costs of mental illness. Some of the themes emerging from these autobiographies foreshadow what our participants describe in their life stories. They may not be as verbally fluent nor as vivid in their descriptions. After all, they did not publish their life stories as memoires. Our participants represent a broader spectrum of people living with psychiatric disturbance and examining their narratives systematically will expand our knowledge about how people make meaning of mental illness and pursue personal recovery.

How the Book Complements Existing Research in Mental Illness

Answering questions about the personal impact of mental illness and pathways to thriving is important for a broader perspective on mental illness. However, the scientific study of psychopathology has tended to focus on etiology and treatment, that is, examining causal mechanisms behind a given disturbance, such as schizophrenia or bipolar disorder, and employing this knowledge to design effective treatments. The basic idea is that if therapy can reverse the causal mechanism, it will alleviate mental illness. For each disorder, scientists have put forward theories explaining the biological, psychological, and social processes leading to the eruption of psychopathology. Grounded in these theories, psychologists and psychiatrists have developed treatments to remedy the faulty processes and cure mental illness. Let us illustrate this general idea with an example. Established theories hold that schizophrenia is caused by genetic vulnerability leading to altered brain functioning.[15,16] This vulnerability combined with environmental stress leads individuals toward psychotic episodes. Following this theory, treatment includes medication to restore normal brain functioning and psychotherapy to reduce stressors. For other mental illnesses, the logic is similar. We are presenting a simplified picture here; research has begun to illuminate mental illness from a broader perspective (see Chapter 4). Nevertheless, this picture captures a central truth about the scientific framework for psychopathology. For many years, it has centered on understanding the objective causes of mental illness and developing treatments to target these causes.

The perspective of this book complements such etiology-driven understandings. We need to pay more attention to the subjective experience of mental disorder. What personal consequences of psychiatric disturbance emerge when individuals make sense of their lives through narrative? And which experiences are storied as helping well-being in the face of the losses flowing from mental illness? These questions focus our attention on what happens *after* mental illness, rather than what happened *before* the illness and caused it. They emphasize first-person narratives, rather than objective events. Answering these questions is important because it will broaden our scope in efforts to support individuals with psychopathology. As a case in point, listen to one of our participants, a 26-year-old woman, who was diagnosed with bipolar disorder when she was 21:

> *Those years are characterized by mood swings: Three depressions/mixed episodes and hypomania. I feel like I lack a stable core/personality, and there is no consistency .... I am "hospitalized" at home for three summers and cared for by my parents. It provides safety, but it feels like a step back compared to my "independent" peers. I cannot complete an education; behave embarrassingly dramatic half of the time and the rest of the time I cannot deal with other people. It feels like there is no hope, as the mania/depression pattern repeats itself three years in a row.*

The narrative illustrates a cascade of negative outcomes following from her disorder, including loss of self, lack of independent living, missing out on education and relationships, just to name a few. However, later she writes about how starting a new study program had positive effects: "*I start a new study program, which offers stability and purpose. I feel a bit more like myself before I became ill .... I have hope for my future.*" Such narratives drive home the point that supporting individuals with psychopathology in gaining well-being is about restoring the massive losses of self, relationships, future, meaning, and purpose.

We are not arguing that professionals should abandon efforts to understand the causes of psychiatric disturbance and the development of treatment grounded in such causal models. We are simply suggesting that we, as researchers, healthcare professionals, and individuals with mental illness, focus more on addressing the massive personal costs that stand in the way of well-being. We are arguing that researchers should conduct more studies examining the subjective consequences of mental illness, so we can support recovery from the losses associated with the illness and foster well-being. This could be an especially valuable perspective on severe psychopathology with periodic relapse, where afflicted individuals may profit from efforts to attain thriving not driven by symptom remission.

While most research on psychopathology has traditionally emphasized etiology and treatment, scientists have also identified the costs of mental illness. Studies addressing this issue paint a bleak picture. Having a mental disorder is associated with costs across a range of areas, such as lower educational attainment, unemployment, and higher mortality.[17–19] Turning to research on the psychosocial outcomes of mental illness, studies show reduced well-being and stigmatization.[20,21] However, these studies do not address how individuals with psychopathology interpret the consequences of mental illness and they leave us in the dark concerning experiences narrated as restoring well-being. In other words, how do people make meaning of mental disorder and construct their personal recovery?

Why Life Stories?

Life stories are precisely the tool we need to understand the subjective side of psychopathology. Human beings are natural born storytellers.[9,10] We understand events in our lives by forming stories, connecting events to their causes and consequences. We remember life in storied forms.[22–24] We process emotions by contextualizing them in narratives.[11] We share stories when connecting with friends, when falling in love, and when conveying lessons to our children.[25,26] We gain identity through crafting narratives.[27–29] When we use a life story perspective to understand mental illness, we read personal tales and examine them for insights about how individuals view the devastating impact of illness and their paths to well-being. Because our participants told their stories in an open-ended manner, often spanning decades of their lives, the narratives portray a broad range of identity-salient consequences and well-being sources.

Individuals interpret the significance of their experiences for identity through constructing life stories, also termed narrative identity.[8] Therefore, our analyses yield insights about how identity is impacted by mental illness and is involved in attaining well-being and personal recovery. Given that narrative identity shapes how individuals engage with the world and direct future action, our analyses concern the consequences and well-being sources most likely to pervasively impact individuals with mental illness. The close interaction between experiences and narrative identity entails that our analyses provide answers at two levels. First, we explore what individuals experience as costs (e.g., relationship rupture), and paths to well-being (e.g., creative activities). Second, we address how these experiences color identity (e.g., identity conclusions such as "I am a burden to other people") and how identity is involved in thriving (e.g., identity conclusions such as "I am creative").

One could argue that life stories are so subjective and unique that we can learn nothing general from them. That is, insights will only apply to the individual who told the story. Based on extensive research, we disagree with this standpoint. While life narratives are unique and capture the particulars of each individual, they also share commonalities.[27,30,31] Although we are different, we are also similar, because we share nature as well as culture.[32] Analyzing a large number of life stories draws attention to similarities in the meaning of mental illness, while also showcasing different tales of the costs of mental illness and sources of thriving. Maybe you watched *A Beautiful Mind*, the movie depicting John Nash, who perceived patterns invisible to other people? We watched the movie and realized that John Nash, like Elyn Saks, needed more than psychopharmacological drugs to get well. A brilliant scientist and Nobel Prize winner, Nash developed a delusional disorder early in adulthood. Gradually, delusions took over his life: his work, his marriage, and his role as a father. He lost his job, a primary source of value and meaning in his life. While medications helped, he still experienced symptoms along with side effects of the drugs. He spent most of his time sitting on the porch, smoking. Then things changed. In a salient scene, he goes to see the head of the mathematics department at Princeton, a former fellow student, seeking a teaching job. He explains that he and his wife believe that he needs to be with people. Soon after, he starts teaching and interacting with students who read his famous work. Although he still experiences symptoms, life is better. In the present context, the movie serves as an illustration that removal of symptoms and a good life are not the same thing. The symptoms of mental illness may be alleviated, but individuals will experience little well-being if lost sources of value and meaning cannot be restored. As such, the movie echoes themes expressed in autobiographies of psychopathology and testifies to shared experiences across individuals. In other words, although life stories are unique, we can use common themes as guidance in assisting individuals with mental disorders to thrive, even when symptoms remain, and relapse is likely.

Others would argue that the subjective interpretations captured in stories might simply be untrue. For example, a woman could talk about mental illness having cost her a job that she loved, but objectively speaking the job loss occurred because of downsizing at the workplace. The question is what does "objectively speaking" mean? For the woman who lost her job, her boss may identify downsizing as the reason for firing her and her former colleagues may accept this explanation. Nevertheless, the woman *experienced* the job loss as a direct result of her mental illness, and this *subjective* interpretation is what stories are all about. The interpretations feel true to the storyteller, and this subjective reality has important consequences. The woman who lost her job may blame her job loss on the illness and base future decisions on this interpretation. The point is that the subjective interpretations that form a key part of narrative identity matter.

A final reason for analyzing life stories from individuals living with psychiatric disorders is that first-person perspectives are valuable supplements to research,[5,16,33] which takes concepts and theories as the starting point. The recovery movement has argued that individuals have unique knowledge of their own mental illness, grounded in rich and contextualized experience, which can yield insights overlooked in scientific studies with a priori specification of concepts. Individuals with psychopathology have first-hand knowledge of the consequences of mental illness and sources of well-being and it simply makes sense to use their expertise in building a broader framework for how narrative identity and mental illness interact. Analyzing life stories to grasp the complexities of living with mental illness yields an understanding that is not limited to objectively established causes and does justice to the immense personal impact of psychopathology individuals need to recover from.

About Us

Before moving on, we would like to introduce ourselves. We have researched life stories for years and have been drawn to the question of how narratives can illuminate mental illness, in particular what life stories can tell us about how individuals suffering from psychopathology understand themselves. This fascination was fueled by four PhD projects. Tine Holm dedicated her PhD project to examining life stories in individuals with schizophrenia.[34–36] Rikke Amalie Agergaard Jensen followed up on Tine Holm's research by interviewing individuals with either schizophrenia or severe depression to understand similarities in past and future life story chapters from individuals with different diagnoses.[37,38] Majse Lind broadened the scope of our research by interviewing individuals with borderline personality disorder about both their own and their parents' life narratives.[39,40] Finally, Anne Mai Pedersen thought that narrative identity research was necessary to gain a deeper understanding of problems with selfhood in bipolar disorder.[41,42] Our most significant contributions to the field sprang out of these studies where we share our insights about relations between psychopathology and identity as represented in narratives. Furthermore, we have introduced the concept of vicarious life stories, that is, the stories of others (e.g., parents, peers) that individuals keep and use as guidance,[43,44] an idea we return to several places in the book.

Well-being and mental illness have always been topics close to our hearts. In our previous work, we have endeavored to increase knowledge about how life stories facilitate well-being,[41,45,46] and we review relevant studies in Chapter 6 as a part of contextualizing the present life story analyses. As mentioned above, we have explored how life stories illuminate mental illnesses. Such clinically inspired research often emphasizes deficiencies in narrative identity (e.g., lack of coherence) based on the assumption that maladaptive storytelling contributes to mental illness and poorer well-being. The present book contrasts this perspective. Here, we zoom in on the content of the stories, taking our participants' interpretations of costs and helpful events at face value, to learn about their perspective. To anchor the book in clinical practice, we have asked friends and colleagues with extensive clinical experience to consider the practical utility of the ideas advocated in the book. We believe that the book can add new perspectives to the science of mental illness by allowing afflicted individuals to emerge as protagonists who strive to find meaning in their lives and thrive while struggling with their own minds.

As a final note of introduction, we would like to share our own experiences with psychopathology. Some of us have personal and painful experience with mental illness (see Appendix 1). Therefore, like many other people around the world, we have psychopathology as a part of our lives, and we want to make sense of it.

Outline of the Book

It is almost time to get started and here we give a brief overview of the chapters. This overview serves the purpose of presenting the structure of the book and guide selective reading of chapters. We hope the book will reach not only a professional audience, including researchers and healthcare professionals, but also individuals with a more personal interest – readers who have mental illness in their own or close others' lives. Hence, we wrote the book with these different audiences in mind, realizing that the background of the reader matters to the relevance of the chapters. At the end of each chapter, we therefore provide a summary of the main content to assist readers who prefer to skip detailed reading but desire a quick overview. For readers who wish to delve more deeply into the research, we provide references at the end of the book as well as more extensive method descriptions in Appendices 4–6. Throughout the book, but mostly in Chapters 9–12, we present extended quotes from the life stories of our participants and emphasize these in italics.

In Chapter 2, we contextualize the book with reference to the science of mental illness. The chapter opens with considerations on the disease model of mental illness and a description of the diagnostic system, which comprise the established taxonomy in the area. Here, we give more details on the symptoms of the four disturbances our participants suffer from, including bipolar disorder, schizophrenia, major depressive disorder, and borderline personality disorder. As a contrast to this approach, we highlight support for transdiagnostic approaches to psychiatric disorders. We argue that although the diagnostic system represents these as distinct disorders, meaningful insights may surface when analyzing life stories across disorders. By exploring life stories from individuals with different mental illnesses, we can discover both commonalities and contrasts in the personal costs and well-being sources that become a part of their narrative identities and shape their lives.

In Chapter 3, we turn to diathesis-stress models, which is the main framework guiding research on psychopathology. Within this framework, we describe examples of theories that seek to explain schizophrenia, bipolar disorder, major depressive disorder, and borderline personality disorder. We show that despite their differences, the theories are similar in their foci on understanding causal mechanisms and utilizing knowledge of causal mechanisms to develop treatment. Subsequently, we review research on consequences of mental disorders. Based on these two lines of research, we argue that mainstream research in mental illness needs to be extended with research on subjectively experienced consequences. Furthermore, if we acknowledge that disorders give rise to multitudes of costs to identity, this begs the question of how individuals living with psychiatric disorder can experience well-being and personal recovery?

Expanding on these issues, we highlight insights from the literature on recovery in Chapter 4. We outline different approaches and then zoom in on personal recovery, including positive identity, hope, purpose and meaning, social connection, and taking responsibility for managing one's mental illness. As such, personal recovery is closely related to well-being. We argue that our analyses illuminate narrative identity processes involved in personal recovery, including costs individuals with psychopathology need to recover from and experiences narrated as facilitating well-being. Note that we employ a variety of terms to capture a broad conceptualization of well-being, including happiness, thriving, and a good life.

In Chapters 5 and 6, we take readers into the scientific study of life stories and describe the central concepts in this area (we use the terms story and narrative interchangeably). We explain how narratives are a basic mode of understanding and how individuals craft life stories to create identity. To introduce readers to the deeply social nature of narrative identity, we review ideas suggesting that relationships and culture impact how people story their identities. We present novel studies suggesting that individuals do not just construct stories about their own lives; they create narratives with other people as the main characters. These vicarious life stories embody the storyteller's version of close others' lives and intertwine with personal life stories. Research on vicarious life stories is especially relevant for this book, because it suggests that others' stories may inspire readers to reflect on, and possibly modify, their own life narratives. In Chapter 6, we discuss diverse perspectives on relationships between narrative, mental illness, psychotherapy, and well-being showing how the present book is inspired by and broadens this research. We close the chapter with a selective review of previous studies relevant to our main questions.

Chapter 7 is a method chapter and here we summarize information about our participants and the methods used to elicit life stories in the different studies. In addition, we explain the analyses we employed to extract themes from the life stories and briefly discuss limitations of the approach that should be borne in mind when reading Chapters 8–12. In the chapter, we give an overview and provide more details for readers interested in the mechanics of research in Appendices 4–6.

Outline of the Book

Chapters 8–12 are the core of the book and here we present the results of our analyses. In Chapter 8, we provide an overview of the consequences of mental illness and well-being sources individuals story into their identities. We display tables with an overview of the number of participants showing evidence of each theme, including information about frequencies for individuals with schizophrenia, major depressive disorder, bipolar disorder, and borderline personality disorder. In Chapters 9–12, we dive deeper into the diverse meanings and identity conclusions expressed by our participants when narrating the costs of mental illness and well-being experiences. We organize these analyses into four superordinate themes: relationships (Chapter 9), self (Chapter 10), functional level (Chapter 11), and treatment (Chapter 12). In each chapter, we first describe subthemes and associated identity conclusions emerging from our analyses on personal consequences. We contrast these with subthemes and identity implications surfacing from analyses of thriving experiences. We develop models of common storylines for subjective impact of psychopathology and well-being, step by step in the four chapters. Illustrating the subthemes, we include a broad selection of extensive examples from participants, increasing the transparency of the analyses. We hope that the life story quotes will serve as vicarious life narratives to readers and inspire reflections on their own lives.

In the final three Chapters (13–15), we summarize the findings, integrate them with existing literature, and consider practical implications. In Chapter 13, we discuss how insights from our analyses supplement existing research in mental illness and personal recovery. Based on a synthesis of our analyses and literature reviewed in earlier chapters, we develop a framework for understanding psychopathology from a narrative identity perspective in Chapter 14. As a part of this, we discuss narrative identity as a vulnerability to mental illness, how narrative identity is challenged by psychopathology, and how it is crucial to personal recovery. Finally, in Chapter 15, we use this framework to suggest that healthcare professionals and individuals living with psychopathology employ our narrative identity approach to aid exploration of personal consequences of mental disorder and possibilities for thriving. To render the approach easily accessible, we outline a structured guide for narrative repair. The guide targets the narrative identity problems that we identified in our analyses as arising from mental illness. It aims to facilitate coping with fear of the ill self and grief for lost selves and dreams, and to resist negative self-views. It further structures narrative work to revive and identify valued aspects of the self, to construct hopeful, yet realistic futures, and to anchor these selves and futures in daily life. To illustrate how the guide can be employed, we have included a case story in Appendix 8. We hope the guide will advance interventions targeting the identity challenges facing many individuals with mental disorder, thereby assisting personal recovery.

CHAPTER 2

The Science of Mental Illness

When mental illness hits, it hits hard. One of our participants with schizophrenia had been in treatment for suicidal ideation for some time when his therapist suspected that something more was at stake:

> *Then they started asking: "do you hear voices?," and so on, and I couldn't answer, I just started crying. I was completely . . . they just could not ask that. I had this thought: How the hell did they know . . . . I remember they asked me to complete this questionnaire and the questions were very . . . when you have never dared telling someone that you see things and hear things and then out of the blue a series of questions. I just remember I got more and more confused, and suddenly my parents were there. And some time must have passed, and I don't remember that time. I just remember total chaos and why do they suddenly ask these questions, who told them, who . . . nobody knew, so it was a sense of total chaos and suddenly my parents were there, and we were going to the psychiatric hospital, which I was terrified of. I didn't want to . . . and we are having this conversation concerning hospitalization, and all of a sudden my parents emerge from one of the therapy rooms . . . they had just been to see someone, and I couldn't understand it and I felt like ambushed or something, and my parents cried. . .*

The quote vividly illustrates the turmoil, chaos, and crisis that individuals and their close others may experience when mental illness erupts. The scientific approach to psychopathology seeks to create order in this personal chaos. In the present chapter, we present the taxonomies and research applied to comprehend psychiatric disturbance. The chapter will illuminate the specific disorders our participants suffer from while also introducing the transdiagnostic perspective, which provides the foundation for analyzing how individuals narrate personal costs and sources of well-being across disorders.

Making Order in Disorder: Taxonomies of Mental Illness

Taxonomies of mental illness are grounded in the disease model and here we locate our approach with respect to this influential framework.

Healthcare professionals and scientists have traditionally understood mental illness utilizing a disease model imported from medicine. Despite criticism, the model still pervasively influences the science of mental illness. A detailed discussion of the pros and cons is beyond the scope of the present book; interested readers may consult other sources.[47–49] The model has been criticized for neglecting the socio-cultural aspects of mental disorder while emphasizing an individualized view. Further, evidence for specific disease mechanisms is less than clear-cut or lacking for some psychiatric disorders,[5] and the model fits personality disorders poorly. As we will discuss in more depth later in the chapter, the idea of separate delimited disorders has also been challenged.[50] Still, the disease model also shaped our understanding, including the formulation of our two main questions and the analyses of the life stories. Following the model, we view mental illness as a delimited entity with identifiable consequences for individuals. Our starting point is that some segments of individuals' experiences qualify as symptoms of mental illness (e.g., hallucinations, diminished pleasure), other parts of their experiences we view as consequences of the illness (e.g., self-stigmatization, loss of relationships), and still others we see as sources of well-being (e.g., mastery in academic pursuits, leisure activities). In other words, we adopt the parsing of individuals' experiences into "illness" and "not illness" implicit in the disease model. However, we strive toward a more contextualized view of psychopathology by providing a narrative identity perspective.

According to the disease model, there are different types of mental disorders, each with an underlying malfunction expressed in specific symptoms. To map out the different types of psychopathology, expert panels have developed comprehensive and detailed taxonomies. The two most prominent systems are the Diagnostic and Statistical Manual of Mental Disorders[51] (DSM) initiated by the American Psychiatric Association[51] and the International Classification of Disease (ICD) advanced by the World Health Organization.[52] The two classification systems have evolved over time and emerged in different versions. Currently, the DSM-5 is in operation and the two organizations strove to harmonize the upcoming ICD-11 and the DSM-5. Hence, the categories of psychopathology captured in these most updated versions of the ICD and DSM are similar for most disorders. We focus on the DSM-5 in describing mental illness because researchers often utilize this system, and it comprises a treasury of valuable insights about psychiatric disturbances.

The DSM-5 represents scientific and clinical knowledge about mental disorder, defined as: "A syndrome characterized by clinically significant disturbance in an individual's cognition, emotion regulation, or behavior that reflects a dysfunction in the psychological, biological, or developmental processes underlying mental functioning. Mental disorders are usually associated with significant distress or disability in social, occupational, or other important activities" (p. 20).[51] The disturbances in cognition, emotion regulation, and behavior emerge as symptoms of psychiatric disorder and the DSM-5 includes sets of symptoms for each specific mental illness as well as additional criteria to decide whether individuals qualify for the diagnosis in question.

The DSM-5 manifests "a historically determined cognitive schema imposed on clinical and scientific information to increase its comprehensibility and utility" (p. 10).[51] In other words, the DSM-5 makes no absolute truth claims, and it acknowledges that the categories reflect the present state of research as well as consideration of how the DSM will best support practice. As such, the DSM-5 is one way to get a handle on the complex phenomenon of psychopathology and future research may reveal that the present categories are not the optimal conceptualization of psychopathology. Despite this acknowledged limitation, the DSM (and the ICD) system massively influences research on mental illness. Following the taxonomies of the diagnostic systems, most research is disorder specific, illuminating characteristics of a specified mental illness, such as major depressive disorder or schizophrenia. Thus, diagnostic systems implicitly guide researchers to examine delimited types of psychopathology. This disorder-specific approach in research facilitates communication of findings because researchers can utilize diagnostic categories to compare results, which scaffold knowledge build-up across studies. Such research also yields public health information, like the prevalence of a given mental disorder that may guide policymaking and insurance coverage.[53] We discuss problems with the disorder-specific approach later in this chapter.

In the healthcare system, the DSM-5 (or the ICD system) is widely utilized to assess individuals suffering from psychopathology. Based on the criteria outlined in the manual, clinicians interview individuals about symptoms and, combined with careful observation of relevant behaviors, they diagnose individuals as suffering from one or more mental illnesses. Such diagnoses are invaluable in offering the best possible treatment for the individual and may be a prerequisite for treatment. Furthermore, afflicted individuals may experience a diagnosis as helpful, since it conveys that they are not alone but plagued by a well-known malady for which treatment exists.[53]

The Diagnoses of Our Participants

When we recruited participants, we invited them into studies based on their status as suffering from a specified mental disorder. While our participants were diagnosed under the ICD system, we base the description in this section on the DSM-5,[51] because it represents the most updated research and understandings of these disorders.

Many of our participants were diagnosed with schizophrenia, which is a severe and debilitating mental illness. Individuals with schizophrenia may experience hallucinations, delusions, lack of motivation, flattened emotional experience, disorganized thinking, and grossly disorganized or catatonic behavior (see Table 2.1 for an overview of diagnostic criteria). As is clear from the opening quote of this chapter, hallucinations, such as hearing and seeing things that others do not perceive, may be a frightening sign of mental illness. However, clinicians only assign the diagnosis of schizophrenia if the symptoms interfere with functioning. That is, if the symptoms hinder engagement in work and education, social relationships, and daily living (e.g., household chores and personal hygiene). According to the DSM-5, the course of the illness varies, but often individuals with schizophrenia continue to require support as the illness waxes and wanes, with many remaining chronically ill. As will become clear in Chapter 4, this view may be too pessimistic.

Individuals with bipolar disorder form another subset of our participants. Bipolar disorder, or manic-depressive illness as it was termed in earlier versions of the DSM, is characterized by episodes of mania (type 1) or by episodes of major depressive disorder and hypomania (type 2). Mania and hypomania differ in their functional impairment and duration, but both feature symptoms such as elated mood and grandiose self-views (see Table 2.1 for overview of diagnostic criteria). One of our participants described an episode of mania:

> *The last time I came to see my doctor, he wanted to talk to me. He thought I had a depression and gave me anti-depressants. I became severely manic and for a long time I was convinced that I was a messenger from God, that I could fly, and that I could control destiny by casting dice. I saw shadows and demons everywhere.*

As a psychological opposite to mania, episodes of major depressive disorder comprise several symptoms such as diminished pleasure, immense sadness, self-blame, and disturbed sleep. A diagnosis of bipolar disorder also includes consideration of impairments in functional level and distress about

Table 2.1 *DSM-5 diagnostic criteria for schizophrenia, manic episode, hypomanic episode, major depressive disorder, and borderline personality disorder*

	Schizophrenia	Manic/hypomanic episode	Major depressive disorder	Borderline personality disorder
Symptoms	Two or more of the following symptoms, at least one of these must be 1, 2, or 3: 1. Delusions. 2. Hallucinations. 3. Disorganized speech. 4. Grossly disorganized or catatonic behavior. 5. Negative symptoms.	A distinct period of abnormally and persistently elevated, expansive, or irritable mood and abnormally and persistently increased goal-directed activity or energy. During the period, at least three of the following symptoms (four if the mood is only irritable): 1. Inflated self-esteem or grandiosity. 2. Decreased need for sleep. 3. More talkative than usual or pressure to keep talking. 4. Flight of ideas or subjective experience that thoughts are racing. 5. Distractibility. 6. Increase in goal-directed activity or psychomotor agitation. 7. Excessive involvement in activities that have a high potential for painful consequences.	Five or more of the following symptoms, at least one of these is 1 or 2: 1. Depressed mood. 2. Diminished interest or pleasure. 3. Significant weight loss or weight gain or in/decrease in appetite. 4. Insomnia or hypersomnia. 5. Psychomotor agitation or retardation. 6. Fatigue or loss of energy. 7. Feelings of worthlessness or inappropriate guilt. 8. Diminished ability to think or concentrate, or indecisiveness. 9. Recurrent thoughts of death, suicidal ideation, or suicide attempt or plan.	Fulfills general criteria for personality disorder. In addition, five or more of the following symptoms: 1. Frantic effort to avoid real or imagined abandonment. 2. Pattern of unstable and intense interpersonal relationships, alternating between extremes of idealization and devaluation. 3. Identity disturbance: Persistent and markedly unstable self-image. 4. Impulsivity in at least two areas that are potentially self-damaging. 5. Recurrent suicidal behavior, gestures, or threats, or self-mutilating behavior. 6. Affective instability due to marked reactivity of mood. 7. Chronic feelings of emptiness. 8. Difficulty controlling anger or inappropriate intense anger. 9. Transient, stress-related paranoid ideation or severe dissociative symptoms.

Table 2.1 (cont.)

	Schizophrenia	Manic/hypomanic episode	Major depressive disorder	Borderline personality disorder
Functional impairment	Level of functioning markedly below the level achieved prior to onset in one or more major areas, such as work, interpersonal relations, or self-care.	Manic episode: Marked impairment in social or occupational functioning or hospitalization necessary to prevent harm to self or others. Hypomanic episode: Clear change in functioning; not severe enough to cause marked impairment in social or occupational functioning or to necessitate hospitalization.	Symptoms cause clinically significant distress or impairment in social, occupational, or other important areas of functioning.	Enduring pattern leads to clinically significant distress or impairment in social, occupational, or other important areas of functioning.
Duration	Continuous attenuated symptoms that persists for at least six months and this period must include at least one month with full symptom criteria fulfilled.	Manic episode: At least one week, nearly every day for most of the day. Hypomanic episode: At least four consecutive days, nearly every day for most of the day.	At least for a two-week period, several of the symptoms should occur nearly every day.	Pervasive pattern, beginning by early adulthood.

Note that exclusion criteria are not displayed.

symptoms. Like schizophrenia, bipolar disorder is considered severely disabling as individuals may experience multiple recurrent episodes.

Major depressive disorder is one of the most common mental disorders and can cause substantially lowered functional level. When individuals display symptoms of a depressive episode for at least two weeks, but has no history of manic or hypomanic episodes, they may suffer from major depressive disorder. One of our participants described an episode of depression:

> *I became more and more introverted and didn't go out to see people and cancelled all the time . . . . I almost didn't have the energy to go to the toilet. I was in my own little bubble and couldn't be bothered with the world. Crawled into my own little lair in bed and I would just let the world slide.*

While an episode of major depressive disorder typically lifts, many individuals are victimized by recurrences or in some instances a more chronic course.

The last group of our participants were diagnosed with borderline personality disorder. According to the DSM-5, personality disorders represent "an enduring pattern of inner experience and behavior that deviates markedly from the expectations of the individual's culture" (p. 646)[51] with deviances apparent in cognition, affect, social relations, and/or impulse control. Individuals under consideration for a diagnosis of personality disorder must display a stable and inflexible problem pattern in these areas beginning in early adulthood and impacting functional level. Depending on the pattern of symptoms, clinicians may diagnose the individual with a specific type of personality disorder. When preparing the DSM-5, scientists disagreed on the best way to diagnose personality disorders and consequently the manual includes two different approaches (see Appendix 2 for the alternative approach). Here, we present the diagnostic view that stayed close to earlier versions of the DSM, where the symptoms for borderline personality disorder encompass a markedly unstable sense of self, accompanied by instability in close relationships. Other central features include impulsive behavior, emotional instability, and self-harm. One of our participants with borderline personality disorder described a chapter with massive self-harm: "*More self-harm. It was the worst year with self-harm . . . . I just remember that it was really, really awful . . . .. Mostly emptiness. Like really, really deep emptiness. It was like I was overloaded. Felt so much that it just became nothing.*" As stated in the DSM-5, many individuals with borderline personality disorder improve over time, although the period of young adulthood is characterized by intense instability.

To recap, schizophrenia, bipolar disorder, major depressive disorder, and borderline personality disorder represent four different types of psychopathology in the DSM-5 (and the ICD system). Each disorder emerges as a pattern of symptoms and individuals who display certain symptoms for a given amount of time qualify for a diagnosis if they also evidence functional impairment or distress over their symptoms.

Limits to the Diagnostic Systems

Despite the many advantages of the DSM-5 (and the ICD system), which represents mental disorders as distinct categories, researchers and clinicians increasingly acknowledge that insights about commonalities across disorders may enhance understandings of psychopathology. A transdiagnostic perspective on mental illness involves looking across disorders to examine shared features.[50,54] A variety of observations pointing to problems with the categorical understanding of mental illness support this view. Below, we list some of these problems to bolster the transdiagnostic perspective, which grounded our decision to analyze life stories across disorders in the present book. However, it is important to keep in mind that the limits of the diagnostic systems should be viewed in context with their many advantages. We perceive the transdiagnostic perspective as enriching, not replacing, categorical understandings of mental illness.

One clue that mental illness may not reflect distinct syndromes is that the DSM diagnoses have changed dramatically over the years. As expertly laid out by Richard McNally in his book *What Is Mental Illness?*,[4] the number of diagnoses in the DSM has increased markedly from the first to the latest version. Some disorders, like homosexuality, have thankfully slipped away and other disorders, like post-traumatic stress disorder, have emerged. The fluidity of diagnostic categories may arise for a number of reasons, but one possible explanation is that the complex patterns of symptoms displayed by suffering individuals do not reflect neatly separated categories of psychopathology.

As McNally points out, the widespread use of diagnoses "not otherwise specified" (NOS diagnoses) also suggests that disorders are not clearly delimited. The present DSM-5 as well as earlier versions include the possibility of diagnosing a general disorder, such as unspecified personality disorder or unspecified depressive disorder. Clinicians utilize these broader diagnoses when the pattern of symptoms does not fit tidily into one of the delineated categories of mental disorder. When the NOS or unspecified diagnoses are common, it suggests that psychopathology takes on shapes not easily accommodated into circumscribed syndromes.

Another sign that the categories of psychopathology represented in the DSM-5 may not reflect clear-cut syndromes is that some disorders appear to be blended. For example, schizoaffective disorder is characterized by symptoms of schizophrenia along with an episode of mania and/or major depressive disorder. The DSM-5 openly acknowledges problems with the diagnosis and explicitly states that schizoaffective disorder may not represent a separate diagnostic category. This problem may extend to other disorders.

Notwithstanding overlap in classifications due to some shared symptoms, essential sets of symptoms could still characterize each mental disorder. However, this is not the case in the present formulation of the DSM-5. Individuals with a given psychiatric disorder may vary widely in their presentation. For example, to be diagnosed with borderline personality disorder, individuals should display five or more out of nine possible symptoms (see Table 2.1). One individual may present with the first five symptoms and another individual may present with the last five symptoms, leaving one shared symptom between the two. Thus, despite little overlap in symptoms, they could be diagnosed with the same disorder. In fact, there are 256 different symptom presentations that fit the diagnosis of borderline personality disorder and the picture is similar for other diagnoses. Indeed, the DSM-5 generally acknowledges that groups of individuals with identical diagnoses can be highly heterogeneous.

The above points hammer home the message that individuals may display patterns of symptoms indicating fuzzy rather than well-defined categories of psychopathology. The fuzziness may also explain why diagnostic agreement between clinicians is a challenge. When two clinicians diagnose the same person using the most recent version of the DSM, which represents state-of-the-art knowledge on mental illness, inconsistencies frequently appear. A large field trial conducted by Darrel Regier and colleagues showed that when the diagnoses of two clinicians were compared, they often disagreed.[55] While agreement between clinicians was good (although never perfect) for some disorders, for other disorders such as major depressive disorder, agreement was relatively low. The discrepancies emerged even though clinicians were encouraged to assign multiple diagnoses. In other words, the result did not reflect that clinicians were forced to decide between several relevant diagnoses for individuals with ambiguous symptom presentation. Clinicians may struggle to provide consistent diagnoses because many individuals do not present with discrete sets of symptoms. Consequently, the view that mental disorders reflect distinct and demarcated categories needs to be supplemented with other perspectives.

The Transdiagnostic View of Mental Illness

Findings from research on comorbidity has paved the way for the transdiagnostic perspective on psychopathology.[50,53] Comorbidity refers to suffering from multiple illnesses. That is, an individual may be afflicted by both schizophrenia and major depressive disorder at the same time. Although less often considered, some researchers study sequential comorbidity, as when an individual suffers from major depressive disorder in young adulthood and later develops schizophrenia. Both types of comorbidity are relevant for the transdiagnostic view of mental illness.

In a now classic study, Ronald Kessler and colleagues examined prevalence of psychiatric disorders in a large group of American adults.[56] Each participant was carefully interviewed and assigned diagnoses according to an older version of the DSM and analyses showed that comorbidity was widespread. Presently, it is commonly accepted knowledge that approximately 50 percent of individuals with a mental illness have a comorbid disorder and severely afflicted individuals can suffer from multiple comorbidities. Intuitively, certain comorbidities would seem orderly, like developing major depressive disorder in response to the severe functional impairments some individuals with schizophrenia live with. However, a group of researchers led by Oleguer Plana-Ripoll conducted an impressive study showing that sequential comorbidity occurs across all disorders and in various temporal patterns.[54] The researchers analyzed psychiatric diagnoses recorded in Danish public registers spanning 16 years and including data from almost six million individuals. They then examined relations between diagnoses and found increased risk of comorbidity across all disorders. Comorbidity was also pairwise bidirectional. That is, receiving a diagnosis of major depressive disorder was related to increased risk of later schizophrenia and an initial diagnosis of schizophrenia was linked to a higher probability of subsequent major depressive disorder. Scientists suggest that the high comorbidity reflects common factors involved in different types of mental disorders, although other explanations are also possible. In general, studies of comorbidity have been major building blocks in transdiagnostic understandings of mental illness.

Research by Avshalom Caspi and colleagues serves as an example of the studies amassing to show that a pure categorical approach to mental illness is too simplified.[50] In their ambitious study, the authors followed a large group of adults over 20 years, from adolescence to middle age. The researchers thoroughly assessed participants on mental disorders several times over the course of the study. They then examined whether a common dimension of psychopathology, the *p-factor*, could explain presence of mental illnesses. In other words, did individuals express waxing and waning of underlying distinct syndromes with their associated symptoms or a more general tendency to suffer from various forms of psychopathology? The authors concluded that the results were most consistent with "one general underlying dimension that summarized individuals' propensity to develop any and all forms of common psychopathologies" (p. 131). The authors further suggested that this core dimension reflected tendencies toward disordered thought processes characterizing many mental illnesses and targeted in diverse psychotherapies.

Other researchers agree that we can gain much from understanding common dimensions of psychopathology. In their book on transdiagnostic factors, Harvey and colleagues argue that disordered cognitive processes maintain a broad array of mental illnesses.[53] The authors ground their analyses in the central idea that while the *content* of cognitive processes may diverge across disorders, certain cognitive *processes* may cut across diagnoses. To provide support for this idea, they carefully reviewed studies of a range of cognitive processes over diverse disorders. They found convergent evidence that disturbances in cognitive processes, such as selective memory and attention, feature in different disorders. As a case in point, recurrent thoughts, such as worry and rumination, were found to be elevated in social phobia, obsessive compulsive disorder, post-traumatic stress disorder, generalized anxiety disorder, pain disorder, eating disorder, sleep disorder, unipolar depression, and psychotic disorder. Based on their review, the authors propose that studying common factors across disorders may provide fertile ground for exchange of knowledge in an area of scientific inquiry otherwise dominated by disorder-specific research.

The Approach to Mental Illness Adopted in the Present Book

Even though the participants were enrolled in our studies based on a diagnosis of either schizophrenia, bipolar disorder, major depressive disorder, or borderline personality disorder, many probably suffered from comorbid disorders. In two of our studies, participants were checked for comorbidity (see Chapter 7). However, the porous boundaries between disorders were also evident in the life stories of our participants. They often described diverse forms of mental disorders erupting over their life course. For example, one participant whom we invited into our study because she was diagnosed with bipolar disorder described suffering from an eating disorder as a teenager and receiving an additional diagnosis of attention deficit and hyperactivity disorder (also known as ADHD) in her late 30s. Across the life stories of our participants, we encountered a range of diagnoses, including eating disorders, anxiety disorders, obsessive-compulsive disorder, other types of personality disorders, and ADHD.

Given that our participants suffer from many different disorders, both concurrently and over their life span, we cannot separate the subjective consequences of major depressive disorder from the subjective consequences of schizophrenia. The life stories simply do not allow such fine-grained analyses. While unique consequences may flow from a given mental illness, the starting point of our analyses is to discover personal costs and sources of well-being as they are narrated into identity across different disorders. As such, we adopt a transdiagnostic approach to mental illness following the succinct statement by Avshalom Caspi and colleagues: "At a minimum, researchers should no longer assume a specific relation between the disorder they study and a biomarker/cause/consequence/treatment without empirical verification. Rather, our findings suggest the default assumption must be that biomarkers/causes/consequences/treatment relate first to p [p = general dimension of psychopathology]" (p. 18).[50]

Transdiagnostic approaches to mental illness are currently expanding their scholarly terrain. However, as pointed out by many researchers, including the ones cited above, transdiagnostic approaches to mental illness do not preclude disorder specific understandings and treatments. Nor do transdiagnostic researchers burn the DSM-5 on the bonfire of revolution. Rather, transdiagnostic approaches direct our attention toward possible shared factors across disorders at the level of etiology, symptoms, maintaining processes, consequences, and treatment. However, even when there are similarities and common factors across disorders, they do differ. For example, Joel Paris and colleagues analyzed similarities and differences between bipolar disorder and borderline personality disorder that are commonly considered related.[57] Despite many similarities, they concluded that the evidence was most consistent with viewing the two disorders as distinct. Thus, even when two disorders share characteristics, they also differ in meaningful ways. Clearly, disorders less closely related than borderline personality disorder and bipolar disorder vary even more. The implication is that our answers to the two questions concerning a narrative identity perspective on the subjective consequences of mental illness and sources of well-being may not generalize to other mental illnesses.

We approach the questions of how individuals story the personal impact of psychiatric disturbance and pathways to happiness from a transdiagnostic perspective. However, we keep an open mind toward possible distinct patterns within disorders and present an overview of analyses both across disorders and separated by disorder. This seemed like the most fruitful strategy, as the book is a first step toward a life story perspective on the impact of mental illness and thriving despite it.

Summary

- Clinicians diagnose mental illness using the DSM or ICD system.
- The DSM-5 (and the ICD system) represent mental disorders as distinct categories (e.g., schizophrenia and bipolar disorder), where underlying malfunctions cause specific symptoms.
- Scientists have questioned the use of rigid diagnostic categories, based on observations suggesting that boundaries between disorders are not clearly delimited.
- These analyses have led to the idea that transdiagnostic approaches may enrich categorical understandings of mental illness.
- Transdiagnostic views of mental illness examine common processes involved in a range of mental disorders and find support in studies showing extensive comorbidity.
- The participants in our studies likely also suffered from other psychiatric disturbances.
- In the present book, we therefore adopt a transdiagnostic approach and analyze personal costs and sources of well-being as represented in the narrative identities of individuals with schizophrenia, bipolar disorder, major depressive disorder, or borderline personality disorder.

CHAPTER 3

Vulnerability, Stress, and Burden in Mental Illness

Traditionally, much research into mental illness has concentrated on explaining *why* individuals develop a disorder, that is, the etiology of the disorder. Why do some individuals hear voices continuously telling them that other people are out to get them and embed these hallucinations in complex systems of persecutory delusions? And why would someone spiral downward into sadness, self-blame, and overwhelming fatigue? In the present chapter, we briefly review examples of theories explaining each of the four disorders our participants suffer from. We show that this literature mainly illuminates causes of psychopathology to develop treatments targeting these causes. Throughout the chapter, we also note important ideas that go beyond the "understand-etiology-to-develop-treatment" thinking. Finally, we consider central insights from research on the negative impact of mental illness. The chapter serves to clarify the scientific contributions of our life story analyses, which are to go beyond models centering on causal processes and treatments targeting these processes to develop a fuller comprehension of the costs of mental disorder and the sources of well-being that individuals story into their identities.

Diathesis-Stress Models

To date, the dominant framework to explain the personal tragedy of mental illness has been diathesis-stress models, excellently reviewed by Rick Ingram and David Luxton.[58] According to such models, individuals develop a psychiatric disorder from a combination of diathesis, or vulnerability, and stress. Diathesis-stress theories for specific mental disorders, such as major depressive disorder or borderline personality disorder, vary in how they conceptualize relationships between stress and diathesis as well as the types of stress and vulnerability emphasized. We provide concrete examples of these theories in the next sections.

Stress is broadly defined as life events that tax or overwhelm the individual's resources. Such stressors may come in the form of highly traumatic events or as an accumulation of many less severe events. Individuals differ in what constitutes stress, such that an event experienced by one person as overwhelming and traumatic may not be experienced the same way by another individual. Stress is painfully evident in the life stories of our participants in far too many life story chapters, depicting neglect, sexual abuse, bullying, rape, homelessness, deaths, and violence. Listen to a participant with borderline personality disorder who was placed in foster care when she was 13 years old: "*My dad started drinking, that was his hobby. Then he became violent as a result . . .. I came home from school and my dad was beating my mom. I felt sorry for her and my dad didn't care who he beat, so I protected my mom.*" Or listen to another participant with major depressive disorder, who lived with her dad from she was 12 years old, because her mom was unable to care for her due to alcohol abuse: "*[M]y dad is without a job in that period and then he gets a job in Germany. He goes to Germany and I take care of everything myself. He leaves me some money when he departs and then he comes home every five weeks or so. I am left to myself.*"

However, not all individuals exposed to negative life events develop a mental disorder. Researchers have suggested that some individuals are especially vulnerable to mental disorders. Vulnerability is conceptualized as both biological and psychological. In biological terms, individuals may be susceptible because of genetic makeup and/or altered brain architecture. From a psychological perspective, individuals may be prone to develop mental disorders based on maladaptive patterns of behaviors, thoughts, and emotions. Diathesis-stress models often integrate biological and psychological vulnerability to explain the emergence of psychopathology.

Despite the recent emphasis on transdiagnostic approaches to mental illness and high comorbidity between disorders, most diathesis-stress models focus on explaining specific disorders. Based on detailed theories of the causal and maintaining factors involved in each mental disorder, healthcare professionals develop treatment methods to target the problematic psychological and biological processes.

Below, we outline examples of diathesis-stress theories of the four disorders our participants suffer from. There are many more theories of mental disorders than we can present here, so we have selected commonly accepted theories that illustrate both similarities and differences in diathesis-stress conceptions of mental disorders. The narrow selection is not intended to emphasize some theories as more or less important, but to keep the review centered on exemplifying the underlying logic of diathesis-stress models and their blind spots. Note that we only give the bare bones of each approach and do not delve into the complexities of specific genes, brain processes, and psychological concepts. Nor will we systematically review evidence for and against each model and the treatments nested within the models. Such details are not necessary for our main purpose, which is to demonstrate that most theories highlight diathesis and stress as causes of mental illness and are silent on identity-salient consequences of psychopathology and sources of well-being. We recommend that interested readers consult the literature we cite for each theory.

Diathesis and Stress in Schizophrenia

One of our participants shared a vivid memory of witnessing a close friend in a bloody traffic accident when he was 16 years old. The friend is brought to the hospital where he is pronounced brain-dead after two weeks in a respirator: *"At the funeral it was absolutely horrible. Looking at the coffin being lowered into the grave and as I was about to put a rose into it, I broke down completely. Totally."* He later connects the event with the development of his schizophrenia: *"Slowly the thought grew that my brain could take harm. I can see now that it came creeping and developed into my illness, like an enormous delusion that everything can affect my brain . . .. I have left many apartments because I thought poison was seeping out of the walls and the bookcases, destroying my brain."* The example illustrates the solid empirical observation that stress can trigger or exacerbate psychotic episodes, a central assumption in the neural diathesis-stress model proposed by Elaine Walker and colleagues.[6,16,59] In their theory, they seek to explain the biological processes involved and focus on the hypothalamic-pituitary-adrenal (HPA) axis. The HPA axis is widely acknowledged as the primary biological stress system. It comprises a chain reaction of hormone release in certain brain areas (the hypothalamus, the pituitary, and the adrenal cortex) with widespread consequences for brain functioning. According to Walker and colleagues, the HPA axis may trigger psychosis through its effects on the neurotransmitter dopamine, which other lines of research have implicated in psychosis.

Theories are evaluated by their explanatory power, that is, whether they account for common findings in the area. The neural diathesis-stress model offers explanations of why psychosis often erupts in adolescence and young adulthood. During the teenage years, the HPA axis increases activity and teenagers become more sensitive to stress. In those individuals genetically predisposed to psychotic disorders, the higher biological stress activity may cause expression of genes coding for psychosis. Consequently, psychotic disorders are more likely to emerge during adolescence and young adulthood in the context of stressful events. Furthermore, Walker and colleagues suggest that known etiological factors, such as cannabis use, may exert their influence on psychosis through the HPA axis.

The neural diathesis-stress model advances understanding of causal factors in psychosis and potential for treatment. It explains schizophrenia as emerging based on interactions between genetic vulnerability, altered brain functioning, and psychosocial stressors that spark psychotic episodes. Consequently, the model conceptualizes effective treatment as targeting disrupted brain function through medication engineered to restore chemical balance in the brain. For example, Walker and colleagues suggest that down-regulation of the overactive HPA axis in psychosis may be the mechanism of effective medical intervention.

Diathesis and Stress in Bipolar Disorder

Traditionally, biological explanations have dominated conceptualizations of bipolar disorder with less room for other processes.[60] Two observations have undergirded the focus on biological factors. First, like schizophrenia, bipolar disorder is highly heritable. It tends to run in families with the implication that it is genetically transmitted. Second, the drug lithium is effective in preventing relapse in individuals with bipolar disorder, suggesting that biochemical imbalances are key causal factors.[61] More recently, however, researchers have begun to acknowledge that psychosocial factors and stress may also play a role. Notably, studies have shown that both positive and negative life events may onset episodes of mania and depression. Ellen Frank and colleagues have suggested that individuals prone to develop bipolar disorder are highly sensitive to changes in daily rhythms, including sleep–wake patterns.[62] When individuals lack stability in their daily routines or when life events disrupt daily rhythms, individuals may spin into episodes of mania or depression. A quote from one of our participants illustrates this idea:

> *We went on tour with the show and started making a little money. It was a hard time. I drank a lot and slept very little. Life was about promotion, appearing the right way and mingling with the right people. After half a year, I started feeling so bad, especially when I was performing. When we had a gig, I was picked up in the show bus. I couldn't dress myself or eat. I went onto the stage and did my thing and afterwards I sat staring into the air, drinking heavily.*

Based on this theory, healthcare professionals can promote healing by supplementing medical treatment with therapy guiding individuals with bipolar disorder to realize the importance of stable daily routines. Therapists working with interpersonal and social rhythm therapy assist individuals in mapping out their habits (e.g., wake-up times, meal times, work times, bed times), detecting how instability in routines may trigger mood episodes, and guiding individuals to plan their lives to minimize the risk of new episodes. This involves stabilizing sleep–wake times and reducing activities that disrupt daily routines. Most parts of interpersonal and social rhythm therapy follow a diathesis-stress framework of bipolar disorder by targeting the reduction of life events that may ignite episodes. However, interpersonal and social rhythm therapy goes beyond the diathesis-stress model in also facilitating mourning for the lost healthy self. This aspect of treatment acknowledges that individuals with bipolar disorder grieve for lost opportunities, for the person they could have become had bipolar disorder not been a part of their life. The therapist assists the individual in mourning the lost self while offering encouragement to seek out new goals and opportunities.

Diathesis and Stress in Major Depressive Disorder

In his late teens, one of our participants experienced a major romantic disappointment and loss of self-esteem:

> *She said: "You don't turn me on." As a guy, I thought OK, now I'll do everything I can to get her. I am not giving up .... She called, but she wasn't romantically interested in me. I couldn't accept it. It wasn't like I wrote or called all the time, because I knew you shouldn't do that. But I was waiting all the time. I remember once we went on a date, then even before the date, I walked the route I thought we would take, planned what we would be doing, just to check that everything was perfect .... I thought about her all the time. All the time. And that stuff killed me. Afterwards I didn't want to make music anymore. It disappeared. I had no ... in reality, I was depressed and started on medication.*

Loss is an important concept in Aaron Beck's conceptualization of major depressive disorder. His initial theory focused on disturbed cognitive processes involved in eliciting sadness, hopelessness, and lack of motivation.[63] Over the last few decades, he has further developed his influential theory and it now incorporates several layers of analyses extending from psychological concepts, to neurotransmitters and immune responses, to functions of major depressive disorder from an evolutionary perspective.

According to Beck and his colleague Keith Bredemeier,[64] genetic predispositions interact with early traumatic experiences to render individuals vulnerable to major depressive disorder. The vulnerability is anchored in increased reactivity of the brain's main stress system, the HPA axis, and is manifested in tendencies toward biased cognitive processes. These vulnerabilities are involved in developing depressive beliefs including negative beliefs about the self, the world, and the future. When individuals encounter losses that deplete vital resources (e.g., relationships), these negative beliefs hijack cognitive processes such as interpretation and memory. Given an inner world suffused with pessimistic thoughts and unhappy memories, individuals gradually lose hope and become dominated by sadness and guilt.

Following the logic inherent in diathesis-stress models, the theory conceptualizes treatment as intervening at the psychological and/or biological level of vulnerability. At the biological level, an imbalance in neurotransmitters contributes to major depressive episodes and antidepressant medicine is effective because it restores the balance. Psychotherapeutic approaches flowing from this model emphasize becoming aware of negative beliefs and correcting them to counter biases in memory and interpretation.

Diathesis and Stress in Borderline Personality Disorder

According to Anthony Bateman, Peter Fonagy, and colleagues, the root of borderline personality disorder is maladaptive early relationships between caregivers and their offspring.[7,65,66] When caregivers respond sensitively to the needs of their children, provide safety in stressful situations, and support playful exploration of the environment, the child develops secure attachment to the caregiver. At the same time, the interaction scaffolds the growth of mentalization, the capacity to understand mental states (e.g., thoughts, intentions, and emotions) within oneself and in other people and how such mental states relate to behavior. However, caregivers who have experienced traumas in their own lives may struggle to engage with the child, leading to a disrupted attachment bond. A quote from a childhood chapter of a participant who returned to the problematic relationship with her parents several times during her life story illustrates this idea: *"But there was very little contact with my parents. I had to fight to get my parents' attention. I think I was very lonely, very alone . . . it is low self-worth, that you feel you are not good enough, that you have to fight to get attention or be recognized."* When the relationship is strained and the child is temperamentally vulnerable, they may not acquire adaptive mentalization, setting the scene for vulnerability to psychopathology. Individuals with borderline personality disorder may display deficits in mentalization, especially during times of high stress in intimate relationships, which may over time erode their self-understanding and spur chaotic relationships.

Accordingly, Bateman, Fonagy, and colleagues have proposed mentalization-based therapy.[67] This approach provides guidelines for how therapists can support mentalization during sessions with the rationale that in-session mentalization will slowly build adaptive use of this complex process over time leading to reductions in central problem areas. As such, mentalization is both the tool and a central outcome in therapy.

The Limits of Diathesis-Stress Theories

Diathesis-stress theories share the aim of understanding the dysfunctional psychological and biological processes causing and maintaining the disorder in order to target these processes in treatment. Such theories represent key pieces in the puzzle of mental illness. In our life story analyses, we zoom in on other pieces: How individuals create their narrative identities to reflect the consequences of their disorders and find paths to well-being. We elucidate life and identity *after* mental illness; diathesis-stress theories center on causal processes in play *before* the illness. We highlight *subjective meaning*; diathesis-stress theories strive for *objective explanation*.

Despite the similarity in underlying logic, diathesis-stress theories also diverge. The foci may be on psychological processes or on neurotransmitters, on how stressors disrupt daily rhythms or on the ability to understand the mind; how factors as diverse as cannabis, disrupted attachment, and negative cognitive patterns play a role in psychopathology. How does this diversity mesh with the transdiagnostic conceptualization of mental disorders presented in Chapter 2? Can such dissimilar frameworks for understanding specific mental disorders capture the high comorbidity and overlap between disorders?

As acknowledged earlier, most research in psychopathology is disorder specific. It aims to illuminate either bipolar disorder, schizophrenia, or some other disorder. Nevertheless, proponents of the theories delineated above acknowledge that the vulnerability and stress processes built into their theories may hold explanatory power for other disorders. For example, Bateman and Fonagy explicitly state that mentalization deficits are probably involved in many forms of psychopathology.[7] In a similar vein, Walker and colleagues suggest that increased activation of the HPA axis may characterize both schizophrenia and major depressive disorder.[6]

Studies of genetic vulnerability also suggest that the many different genes involved in the genesis of psychopathology may not be disorder specific. For example, a group of researchers led by Katherine Musliner found overlap in the genes involved in major depressive disorder, bipolar disorder, and schizophrenia.[68] Further extending these insights, Avshalom Caspi and Terrie Moffitt suggested that psychopathology processes common to many disorders share genetic etiology and that psychological trauma may be another common vulnerability factor.[69] In short, the disorder-specific diathesis-stress theories of psychopathology encompass potential transdiagnostic factors. In Chapter 14, we build on this insight when we discuss how narrative identity can constitute a vulnerability to mental illness. However, even when diathesis-stress models turn transdiagnostic, they emphasize vulnerability and stress rather than personal impact and possibilities for thriving as constructed through narrative identity, which is the center of gravity in our analyses.

There are of course exceptions to this general picture of diathesis-stress research in psychopathology. As outlined above, interpersonal and social rhythm therapy for bipolar disorder includes a focus on mourning the lost self, similar to our emphasis on personal costs incorporated into life stories, and exploring possibilities for new goals and roles, related to our question concerning sources of well-being. Another example is acceptance and commitment therapy advanced by Steven Hayes and colleagues, one among several "third wave" cognitive therapies with the core idea that acceptance is a crucial aspect of healing.[70] The literature on acceptance and commitment therapy is complex and here we highlight only the assumption that psychopathology hinders individuals' pursuit of valued goals. Consequently, a central tenet of therapy is to guide individuals in clarifying their values and supporting actions consistent with these values. This approach clearly aligns with the target of the present book, which is to expand conceptualizations of mental illness to include a narrative identity perspective on the personal costs of mental illness and pathways to a valuable life.

For our purposes, the major take-home message is that much research and theorizing about mental disorders has been dedicated to comprehending etiology and advancing corresponding treatments. Such diathesis-stress frameworks are invaluable in aiding individuals with mental disorders. Relieving symptoms is a major accomplishment when it helps restore meaning, peace of mind, and supportive relationships. Treatments that heal underlying vulnerabilities further contribute by preventing relapse. However, in some cases, focusing on etiology and eliminating causal

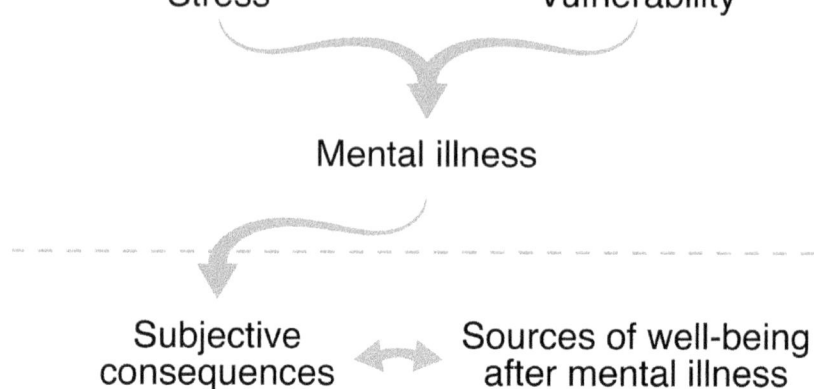

Figure 3.1 How the life story analyses complement diathesis-stress models

factors may not be enough to restore well-being. We argue that illuminating the personal costs of mental illness and sources of well-being as individuals narrate these into their identities may at times be necessary to support individuals with mental illness in their pursuit of thriving. The emphasis on identity and thriving is shared by researchers in recovery, a concept we introduce in the chapter.

We depict a simplified version of diathesis-stress theories in Figure 3.1 along with the questions we seek to illuminate in the life story analyses: What are the subjective consequences of mental illness and sources of well-being? In other words, the model illustrates how our life story analyses complement the well-established diathesis-stress framework. We put flesh on the bones of this model in Chapters 9–12, where we elaborate on the diverse array of personal impacts and well-being experiences voiced by our participants as they share their narrative identities.

The Burden of Mental Disorder

While diathesis-stress models spotlight causal mechanisms of psychopathology, notable exceptions to this focus are studies illuminating the consequences of mental illness. Such studies typically aim to examine how mental illness affects a given outcome, such as employment rate or stigmatization. Researchers pre-define the relevant outcome and, as such, the field is less concerned with the personal perspectives of individuals with mental illness. It leaves unanswered the question of what consequences individuals with mental disorders identify as important for their identities. Furthermore, this research typically does not examine the *meaning* of these outcomes. That is, what does unemployment or dropping out of school signify for the individual? The life story analyses presented in Chapters 8–12 take individuals' subjective experience and meaning as the starting points for illuminating the impact of psychopathology. This open-ended approach allows detection of a broader range of costs than research with outcomes defined a priori. In addition, we explore the identity implications individuals ascribe to these consequences (e.g., "I am a failure").

Despite these differences in approach, it is worth delving into research on the burden of psychopathology in order to contextualize our life story analyses. Ronald Kessler has provided a systematic overview of studies examining the costs of major depressive disorder and since the reviewed studies also addressed other types of mental illness, his contribution is especially useful here.[17,19] He suggested that mental illness may interfere with age-graded transitions such as education, work, and marriage. Confirming this idea, mental illness predicts failure to complete further education, lower likelihood of marriage, and higher rates of unemployment. Furthermore, mental illness may interfere with role performance across domains and studies show that major depressive disorder is related to lower marital satisfaction and negative interactions with children as well as indicators of poorer role functioning at work (e.g., reduced income). Finally, mental illness also predicts deteriorating physical health and is associated with increased risk of a range of illnesses, such as cancer and cardiovascular disease that together with higher risk of suicide explain why individuals with mental illness are at risk of early death. In short, the review paints a bleak picture of the costs of mental illness.

Focusing specifically on the burden of schizophrenia, Aurélie Millier and colleagues reviewed studies examining an even broader array of negative consequences.[71] In addition to the negative impacts of psychopathology identified by Kessler, they concluded that schizophrenia is associated with lower quality of life, which incorporates happiness, functional ability, and material resources. Furthermore, schizophrenia was accompanied by problematic side effects from medical treatment (e.g., sexual dysfunction and weight gain), higher likelihood of homelessness, and stigmatization.

Stigmatization is an important concept to which we return in later chapters. According to Patrick Corrigan, it includes a range of phenomena from laws that discriminate against individuals with mental illness to rejection by other individuals based on inaccurate stereotypes of individuals with mental illness as dangerous, weak, and out of control.[20] Stigmatization may turn inward if individuals accept these negative prejudices and apply them to themselves. Individuals with mental illness may consequently perceive themselves as less valuable and weak. Such self-stigmatization has downstream consequences in prohibiting individuals from seeking out opportunities that would otherwise be within their abilities, including independent living and employment. Clearly, the consequences of psychopathology form an intricate web of interconnected negative events that deplete individuals' resources.

Building on research examining the burden of psychopathology, researchers have called for treatments targeting the negative outcomes of psychiatric disturbance. This expands interventions inspired by diathesis-stress theories that emphasize causal mechanisms with approaches that aim to enhance functional level and well-being. For example, Erin Michalak and colleagues argued convincingly that evaluations of bipolar disorder treatment should encompass quality of life.[21] Other strands of research examine interventions directly targeting negative outcomes of psychopathology, such as work ability and self-stigmatization. For example, Paul Lysaker and colleagues found that cognitive behavioral therapy was effective in increasing work hours and work performance in individuals with schizophrenia.[72] This and other similar research go beyond the logic inherent in diathesis-stress theories as it addresses the negative impact of psychopathology, rather than the underlying causal processes giving rise to it. It underscores the idea that healthcare professionals could prioritize interventions targeting well-being and functional level.

The Contribution of the Present Book

The analyses of the life stories in Chapters 8–12 will target subjective costs of mental illness and sources of well-being. As such, the analyses tackle issues not often captured in traditional diathesis-stress theories. The life story analyses supplement other efforts to target personal consequences and well-being, such as interpersonal and social rhythm therapy[62] as well as acceptance and commitment therapy,[70] but we explicitly embrace a narrative perspective to expand knowledge on the meaning-making processes underpinning the impact of mental illness on identity and involved in creating a good life.

Our life story analyses go beyond existing research on the outcomes of mental illness by zooming in on the subjective perspective of individuals with psychiatric disturbance. What is the personal meaning of the somewhat dry and abstract statistics of lower educational attainment and medicine side effects? What experiences are narrated as fostering well-being despite the cascades of negative events? When we analyze the stories generously shared by our participants, we complement insights derived from scientific experts with the lived experience of mental illness.

A central premise of the book, which we elaborate on in Chapters 5–6, is that narrative comprises a central mode of understanding and this insight could benefit therapeutic approaches. Storytelling elicits rich, experience-near accounts of the impact of disorders and sources of well-being, providing low-hanging fruit for healthcare professionals working to support clients in pursuing value and meaning in life. Likely, many experienced psychotherapists already employ this perspective in their efforts to aid individuals with mental illness. Grounded in our life story analyses, which elucidate identity challenges confronting individuals living with psychopathology and identity resources for gaining well-being, we suggest practical guidance for targeting these challenges and resources in Chapter 15 (and offer an illustrative case story in Appendix 8). We hope the guide will inspire healthcare professionals to engage in narrative work with identity problems to scaffold personal recovery.

Summary

- Scientists have traditionally conceptualized mental illness as emerging from the interplay between vulnerability and stress.
- For schizophrenia, bipolar disorder, major depressive disorder, and borderline personality disorder, researchers have proposed theories outlining diverse vulnerability and stress factors leading to the specific disorder.
- Despite difference in processes and disorders, the theories share the underlying logic that processes causing and maintaining disorders are the target of treatment.
- As such, diathesis-stress theories are silent about the main questions driving the life story analyses in the present book: What do individuals see as the personal costs of mental disorder and as sources of well-being when they make meaning of their lives and create narrative identity?

- Some therapeutic approaches, including interpersonal and social rhythm therapy as well as acceptance and commitment therapy, align with our perspective in addressing the subjective costs of mental illness and obstacles to living a valuable life, but do not emphasize narrative identity processes.
- Research on the consequences of mental illness indicates a variety of negative outcomes, including lower educational attainment, problematic interpersonal relationships, lower quality of life, stigmatization, higher unemployment rates, problematic side effects of medicine, as well as poorer physical health and risk of early death.
- The life story analyses presented in Chapters 8–12 supplement this literature by providing an overview and in-depth analyses of identity-salient consequences of psychiatric disturbance from the personal perspective of individuals suffering from mental illness, as well as potential pathways to enhanced well-being.

CHAPTER 4

Recovery and Mental Illness

The science reviewed in Chapter 3 tells a bleak story of mental illness. Individuals who suffer from psychiatric disorders are haunted by stress, dysfunctional brain processes, insecure attachment, loss of resources, and/or genes that set them up for vulnerability. After mental illness erupts, the story takes a downward turn, including a high risk of relapse, educational underachievement, unemployment, stigmatization, and somatic illness. Statistics such as these kill hope in both healthcare professionals and individuals living with mental illness. However, listen to one of our participants with schizophrenia:

> *As I said, one of my big hobbies is bird watching, and that kind of took over and takes up a big part of my life also today, where I am very active on that front. I am in several committees concerned with ornithology . . . . I was a part of starting up this organization, where we raise funding to support bird populations . . . . So you could say that bird watching means a lot to me socially, because that is where I have a big part of my network and then of course because the hobby in itself gives me something. It gives me peace and it lowers my stress. In that context, I forget that I am ill. Not because I am very marked by illness in my day-to-day life, but, you know, occasionally it has been necessary for me to be hospitalized.*

The quote illustrates that the toxic story emerging from Chapter 3 is just one side of the coin. Massive research documents that recovery from severe mental illness is possible and even likely.

Perspectives on Recovery

The field of recovery houses many passionate voices about what it means to get well. A sprawling array of dichotomies have been introduced to capture the different meanings, including recovery *from* versus recovery *in*, subjective versus objective recovery, personal versus clinical recovery, recovery as process versus outcome, and consumer versus scientific models of recovery.[5,73-75] The many dichotomies capture diverse aspects of recovery, but experts often accentuate one major divide. One meaning of recovery (recovery from, objective recovery, clinical recovery, recovery as outcome, scientific model of recovery) refers to getting well through reduction of symptoms and functional impairment, which are diagnostic criteria of mental illness. The other approach to recovery (recovery in, subjective recovery, personal recovery, recovery as process, consumer model of recovery) puts primacy on subjective feelings of well-being. Importantly, within the latter recovery framework, individuals can live a good life despite recurrence and continuing symptoms. This conceptualization underscores that recovery is distinct from remission, which refers to symptoms below diagnostic threshold or complete absence of symptoms. We elaborate on the two approaches to recovery below, utilizing the terminology *personal recovery* and *clinical recovery* adopted by Mike Slade in his influential work.[5] Note, however, that we do so without claiming that this conceptualization is superior to or equivalent to other recovery approaches.

Most research in recovery has taken its starting point in severe mental disorders, often psychotic disorders and schizophrenia.[3,74] There are good reasons for this focus. Historically, the prognosis for individuals diagnosed with schizophrenia was considered poor. Deterioration over time was the norm and mental healthcare professionals perceived exceptions from this pattern as indicating that the initial diagnosis was misplaced. This view was challenged when individuals began to come forward telling their own stories of recovering from schizophrenia. Supporting these personal accounts, scientific studies with a similar message started to surface. This research showed that many individuals with expert-established diagnoses of schizophrenia evidenced substantial improvement when followed over decades. Scientists have reached similar conclusions for other severe mental illnesses, such as borderline personality disorder.[76]

Even though the recovery paradigm emerged mostly from research on schizophrenia spectrum disorders, the concept of personal recovery applies to severe mental illness in general. As such, it may provide useful insights into other forms of psychopathology with high risk of a recurrent/chronic course and extensive functional impairment, including the other three disorders our participants suffer from (bipolar disorder, borderline personality disorder, and major depressive disorder). That is, individuals with other psychiatric disorders, where current research seems to offer steep odds for thriving, may subjectively experience recovery from their illness. Several researchers have advocated for a recovery perspective on these other disorders and highlighted that promoting well-being may be fruitful, even in spite of continuing symptoms and functional impairment. For example, Greg Murray and colleagues presented a recovery perspective on bipolar disorder.[77] Echoing this call, Fiona Ng and her collaborators explored personal recovery in borderline personality disorder.[78] Finally, current conceptualizations of major depressive disorder could harvest insights from recovery approaches. Augustus Rush and colleagues have pointed out that a substantial subset of individuals with major depressive disorder show little benefit from traditional treatment approaches aiming toward sustained symptom remission.[79] They suggest that when several treatment attempts have been unsuccessful, healthcare professionals should shift their efforts to symptom management and personal recovery. We note that addressing personal recovery as a last option seems overly conservative and suggest that personal recovery could be targeted in parallel with the more traditional treatment focus on symptom remission.

Based on these calls for a recovery perspective across disorders and following the pointers from transdiagnostic perspectives on mental illness, we apply recovery research to ground our life story analyses of individuals with schizophrenia, bipolar disorder, borderline personality disorder, and major depressive disorder. Still, the research we review below is mostly based on individuals with schizophrenia spectrum disorders and it seems pertinent to alert readers that the insights may not apply equally well to those diagnosed with other disorders. When we analyze the life stories in Chapter 8, we note diagnostic differences in sources of well-being and personal costs.

Clinical Recovery

While consumer movements arguably ignited the massive interest in recovery, scientific studies helped convince healthcare professionals that getting well is a very real and likely outcome for individuals with severe psychopathology. By now, the scientific community estimates that up to 50 percent of individuals achieve clinical recovery from schizophrenia.[73,74,80] Although studies measure clinical recovery in different ways, there is some agreement. Often recovery includes remission from symptoms for an extended period (e.g., two years). Sometimes, researchers supplement the symptom criteria with indicators of low illness activity, such as no hospital admissions. In addition, recovery comprises objectively measured good functional level, for example living independently, maintaining social relationships, and being involved in employment or education. As an illustrative example, the International Study of Schizophrenia followed individuals originally diagnosed with schizophrenia for 15 and 25 years and assessed clinical recovery by a combination of several criteria, including no overt psychotic symptoms, resumed functional level, employment, and not being perceived as mentally ill by family members.[81] Reviewing this and other studies of clinical recovery, Bethany Leonhardt and colleagues concluded: "While the idea of recovery is far from integrated within mainstream psychiatry, as illustrated by its absence in the DSM-5, abundant evidence exists showing recovery is possible and in fact a likely outcome for those with SMI [serious mental illness]" (p. 1124).[80]

Although recovery may not feature in the DSM-5, the concept of clinical recovery arises directly from diagnostic criteria of mental illness. As elaborated on in Chapter 2, the two major diagnostic systems, the DSM and the ICD, operate with diagnostic categories that encompass a predefined number of symptoms for an established length of time coupled with reduced functional level.[51,52] In other words, the core indicators of mental illness are symptoms and functional impairment and getting well means returning to a state where these are no longer present. Many authors have pointed out problems with this understanding.[2,73,74] Feeling well does not necessarily flow from getting rid of symptoms and showing average levels of functioning. Indeed, a range of evidence suggests that well-being and symptom reduction do not go hand in hand. For example, Carmen Valiente and colleagues reviewed psychological interventions in schizophrenia with respect to their effects on well-being and concluded: "These findings suggest that symptom or functional improvement does not necessarily lead to an improvement in well-being" (p. 16).[82] Why would that be? If the illness with its symptoms and functional impairment is the problem and treatments effectively address this, why do individuals not feel well as a result? Proponents of personal recovery provide an answer to that question. Symptoms and diminished functional level are not the only obstacles to well-being and perhaps not even the most important ones.

The Personal Recovery Movement

Individuals who suffer from mental disorder have pushed for a different meaning of recovery. The recovery movement was initiated by firebrands who came forward to share their recovery experiences, and this approach houses a regular grassroots movement that has massively influenced healthcare systems, research on recovery, and policymaking. As reviewed by

Mike Slade, the USA, England, Scotland, New Zealand, and Australia are among the countries that have adopted personal recovery as a primary aim in mental healthcare service.[5] Our own country, Denmark, has in recent years followed in the footsteps of this international trend and policy papers on mental health care include personal recovery as a central outcome.[83] An important point in the personal recovery movement is that individuals with psychopathology are better referred to as consumers, service users, or experts-by-experience, because these terms are less stigmatizing. However, for consistency, we continue to employ "individuals with mental illness" or related terms such as "psychiatric disorder," while intermittently reminding readers of these alternative terms and their associated meanings.

It is invigorating that experts-by-experience seized the power to define what it means to get well, while it is sobering that science and clinical expertise lagged behind. By now, personal recovery perspectives have gained ground and although healthcare systems and scientific paradigms change slowly, the field seems to welcome the change. One central tenet of the recovery movement is protesting against the traditionally paternalistic approach to treatment, where the healthcare professional is the expert who tells the individual with mental illness what to do in order to get better.[5] While well intentioned, a toxic side effect of this approach is eroding individuals' sense of responsibility and choice, which is crucial to personal recovery. Instead, the personal recovery movement embraces a partnership model of treatment. In this model, individuals with psychopathology are responsible for making decisions about treatment, assisted by healthcare professionals who have expertise in evidence-based interventions targeting a range of outcomes, from symptoms to well-being to goal achievement. Importantly, the responsibility of service users can vary according to stage of illness. Individuals in severe crisis are not pushed to shoulder decisions on major life goals. A detailed account of this conceptualization of treatment is beyond the scope of the present book and interested readers can consult other sources.[5] We return to how insights from our life story analyses may inform psychiatric care in Chapters 12 and 15.

Where much research in psychopathology has traditionally been built on the logic of diathesis-stress models, many experts in personal recovery view mental illness through another lens.[5,73] Rather than targeting underlying maladaptive processes that give rise to symptoms, they understand mental illness as a disability that can be circumvented with appropriate environmental adaptions. Or they conceptualize mental illness in terms of chronic illness management where symptom control rather than cure is the focal treatment point. Many healthcare professionals working with individuals suffering from severe mental illness also adopt these views. Along similar lines, Mary Zanarini and colleagues proposed that individuals with borderline personality disorder may benefit from rehabilitation when functional levels do not follow symptom improvement.[76]

Clearly, stakeholders ground their views in different models of mental illness. Approaching mental illness as a disability or as a chronic illness is not necessarily truer than viewing mental illness as resulting from pathological processes that treatment may restore to normality. In fact, Mike Slade has argued that since approximately 50 percent of individuals with severe mental illness display clinical recovery, mental illness is not necessarily chronic and hence neither the disability model nor the chronic illness model provides a good fit.[5] Still, inspiration from chronic illness and disability models may yield insights about recovering from mental illness that would remain hidden under other conceptualizations of psychopathology.

Core Aspects of Personal Recovery

Researchers examining clinical recovery strive to develop standard tools to assess absence of symptoms and functional improvement. In contrast, experts in personal recovery argue that it is unique to the individual, implying that it cannot be captured by standardized measurement. William Anthony, who wrote one of the most widely used definitions of personal recovery, spotlighted this idea: "[A] deeply personal, unique process of changing one's attitudes, values, feelings, goals, skills, and/or roles. It is a way of living a satisfying, hopeful, and contributing life even with the limitations caused by illness" (p. 15).[84] Clearly, personal recovery and clinical recovery are different kinds.

When scholars examine personal recovery, they rely on accounts of recovered individuals. For example, Priscilla Ridgway analyzed four published narratives of first-person experiences with recovery from severe mental illness.[33] She discovered that certain themes emerged as central to recovery. Unearthing hope that well-being was even a possibility surfaced as one core issue in the accounts. Other themes included developing explanations to understand the experience of mental disorder, taking an active role in coping and engaging with life again, finding sources of meaning and purpose, and moving toward new and more positive identities not dominated by mental illness. Ridgway's participants also highlighted overcoming isolation and reconnecting with the social world.

One limitation of studies such as the one conducted by Ridgway is that they include only a few individuals who may be highly selected outliers.

Consequently, this raises doubts about whether these themes are common among individuals recovering from mental illness or merely among a privileged subgroup that excel in verbalizing their experiences, publish their accounts, and volunteer for interview studies. Taking this criticism further, some may argue that personal recovery is so uniquely personal that insights from one study can never be extended to other individuals. However, subsequent research has compiled studies of individuals in recovery and distilled common themes.[3,85,86] The basis for this approach seems to be that although personal recovery may be unique for each individual, commonalities surface. This aligns with the perspective of life story research. Although life stories are unique, they share similarities.

In a review of studies, Retta Andresen and colleagues extracted themes of attaining hope, reestablishing identity, finding meaning in life, and assuming responsibility for recovery.[3] Furthermore, they suggested that personal recovery is a staged process that begins with moratorium, which comprises denial, confusion, and hopelessness. This is followed by awareness that recovery is possible and some small measure of hope, preparation to recover, and rebuilding a positive identity. The final stage involves a sense of having grown from the experience. Echoing these themes, Mike Slade suggested that personal recovery involves working with four tasks, including developing a positive identity, not defined by mental illness; making the experience of mental illness comprehensible and understanding its personal impact; assuming responsibility for managing the disorder and learning self-management skills; and, finally, engaging in valued social roles.[5] Along similar lines, CHIME, an influential conceptual framework proposed by Mary Leamy and colleagues, comprises five categories of recovery processes, labeled Connectedness, Hope, Identity, Meaning, and Empowerment.[86] Each of these nest more specific factors – for example, Identity concerns self-esteem, acceptance, and overcoming self-stigma.

Despite some variation in core aspects, many similarities appear. These include but are not limited to: hope, meaning, purpose, positive identity, personal responsibility, and social connectedness. From the emerging agreement on these central aspects identified in qualitative studies, researchers have now developed scales as standard measures of personal recovery.[87,88] Underlying the insights from research into these themes is a shared understanding that personal recovery is about recovering from the *impact* of mental illness – not mental illness in itself. Several authors make this point explicitly. For example, Larry Davidson and David Roe state: "Recovery refers instead to overcoming the effects of being a mental patient" (p. 462).[73] Thus, while clinical recovery can be framed as recovering from mental illness defined by symptom remission and restored functional level, personal recovery may be conceptualized as recovering from the consequences of mental illness. The affinity to the first question that we seek to answer in this book is clear – what are the personal costs of mental illness narrated into identity that stand in the way of thriving?

Following Mike Slade, we suggest that gaining insight into the identity costs of mental illness is an important step in personal recovery[5] and this is a key contribution of our life story analyses. To recover from the effects of psychopathology, individuals need to understand what those effects are. Taking a life story perspective provides a broad picture. Life stories encompass the past leading up to mental illness and years living with illness, therefore illuminating how individuals interpret changes resulting from psychiatric disorder and their relevance for identity. A quote from one of our participants with schizophrenia illustrates this point:

> *Where I am now, like, I am trying to sort out ... so because I have had a good long stable period, like the past half year I have felt really well, then you start dreaming. It is really cool with some hope and also support from family and friends. It is really, really important. Because it has been a major reduction, like compared to what I dreamed about when I was 15 and to where I am today, like coming to terms with the fact that life did not look as you thought it would. At the same time, you have to say that compared to what I was told when I was diagnosed, it was like, now you get this diagnosis and then you have to take medication for the rest of your life and that is what you have to live with. Then you can get disability benefits when you are 18 and that is your life. I have to say, then it looks a lot better. At the same time, you don't grow up dreaming about spending a large chunk of your life in treatment, you don't.*

Life stories go way beyond the immediate consequences of mental illness and capture how it impacts identity. What happened in the years and decades following illness? How did it shape who I am? Consequently, analyzing life stories yields a temporally extended identity perspective on the costs of mental illness, which expands our understanding of obstacles to the core aspects of personal recovery.

Personal Recovery and Well-Being

The core of personal recovery encompasses concepts that other researchers would qualify as well-being, including hope, meaning, purpose, personal responsibility, and social connectedness.[89] Some personal recovery researchers explicitly make a connection between personal recovery and the scientific concept of well-being. For example, Retta Andresen and colleagues stated that: "Elements of the final stage of recovery closely mirror the dimensions of psychological wellbeing (PWB), defined as personal growth, self-acceptance, autonomy, positive relationships, environmental mastery, and purpose in life" (p. 591).[3] In other words, personal recovery involves achieving well-being following or while living with severe psychopathology. Consequently, we view well-being as central to personal recovery and below we review research relevant to understanding well-being in the context of mental illness.

The scientific pursuit of knowledge about well-being has emerged from two camps. One branch research *subjective well-being*. Ed Diener, who was a prominent researcher in the field, conceptualized subjective well-being as the presence of positive emotions, the absence of negative emotions, and high satisfaction with life.[90] Other scientists label this concept hedonic well-being as its essence is pleasure (positive emotions) and pain (negative emotions). The alternative approach to well-being centers on eudamonic or *psychological well-being*.[91] Carol Ryff, another key figure, has argued that the good life is composed of more than the presence of positive emotions and the absence of negative emotions.[92] To live a good life, individuals need a sense of meaning and purpose. They need autonomy to live in congruence with their values, to master their environment, and to feel connected to others. And they need to accept who they are and grow by expressing their talents and skills. The proponents of subjective and psychological well-being have had heated disputes about the center of gravity in well-being.[93] However, many scholars, including us, take the broad view of well-being. It includes both subjective and psychological well-being.[91,94] As such a variety of terms capture this broad view of well-being, including thriving, meaning, value, happiness, and a good life, and we employ these throughout the book.

The second question that we seek to answer in the book concerns what narrative identity can reveal about sources of well-being for individuals living with mental illness. Clearly, elucidating such sources meshes with the aim of personal recovery research. Readers may wonder whether a focus on well-being should not take a back seat to treating symptoms and supporting functioning. Or, whether gains in well-being will simply follow naturally when symptoms are treated successfully. However, it is widely accepted that while improvements in symptoms and functional level may be related to increased well-being, these concepts are not reducible to each other. They are different dimensions. The World Health Organization definition also expressed the idea that *health* is more than the absence of illness, it is "[a] state of complete physical, mental and social well-being and not merely the absence of disease or infirmity."[95] While symptoms and functional impairments may be obstacles to well-being in some cases, such as when negative symptoms in schizophrenia hinder social activities, the relationship between symptoms, functional level, and well-being is not straightforward. Importantly, individuals living with mental illness rank achieving well-being as a highly desirable outcome.[96,97] In short, well-being is best considered a primary outcome in its own right. It is not merely a reflection of symptoms and functional improvement and it is important to individuals who know what they are talking about, experts-by-experience.

A final objection that critics could raise to studying and promoting well-being in individuals with mental disorders may be that it is simply unrealistic. After all, they have a severe chronic illness, which constitutes an objective life circumstance that compromises well-being. Consequently, individuals with mental illness can never hope to gain well-being, and targeting improved well-being in healthcare instills false hope and sets individuals up for failure. Against this view, research on well-being uniformly disproves the notion that well-being directly mirrors objective life circumstances. Major reviews in the area have concluded that although life circumstances influence well-being, psychosocial factors play a larger role.[90,91] Accordingly, mental illness is not necessarily a permanent obstacle to well-being. Although ripple effects of psychopathology such as stigmatization, social isolation, reduced self-esteem, and traditional paternalistic approaches to healthcare may contribute to lower well-being, lack of thriving is not a given for individuals with psychopathology. Consequently, shining light on how individuals living with mental disorder story experiences that foster well-being is a realistic and much needed endeavor.

The Contribution of the Present Book

In the present book, we stand on the shoulders of research in personal recovery. We view our life story analyses as yielding important insights about central steps in personal recovery as we focus on illuminating the identity costs individuals need to cope with and identity sources of well-being. When we analyze the life stories in Chapters 8–12, our themes echo some of the processes unearthed by personal recovery research and we show how narrative identity underpins these processes.

At the same time, the life story analyses extend research in personal recovery by taking a broader perspective and by not spotlighting individuals recruited due to their status as recovered. Rather, our participants span a wide range of disorders and are at different places with respect to recovery. Consequently, the life story analyses zoom out from personal recovery and answer questions about identity-salient consequences of mental illness and sources of well-being. While these may be aspects of personal recovery, they are phenomena in their own right too and a richer appreciation of their nature will expand theories of mental illness and personal recovery.

Importantly, taking a life story perspective to analyze subjective costs of mental illness and events fostering well-being is not just a methodological choice. We do not conceive of life stories as just one possible way to gain insights into these questions. Rather, we take the stronger stand that these phenomena are narrative in nature. That is, individuals understand the consequences of mental illness on their identities by forming stories. Individuals construct themselves as someone who can live a good life by weaving well-being experiences into their life stories. The strong view that these phenomena are narrative in nature aligns with observations put forward by other researchers.[98] For example, David Roe and Larry Davidson argued that life stories are keys to grasping recovery: "Processes of re-authoring one's life story are actually integral components of the recovery process itself" (p. 89).[99] We delve into the narrative identity processes involved in personal recovery when we draw out themes across well-being experiences. In the next chapters, we unpack how individuals construct life stories and why these stories sit at the nexus of meaning, identity, and well-being.

Summary

- Robust research documents that recovery from severe mental illness is relatively common.
- Different concepts of recovery have been proposed with some concepts highlighting reduced symptoms and functional improvement (clinical recovery) while other concepts accentuate subjective experience of getting well (personal recovery).
- Recovery research has primarily focused on schizophrenia but approaches to other mental illnesses may benefit from a recovery perspective.
- The scientific community estimates that up to 50 percent of individuals with schizophrenia reach clinical recovery.

- Personal recovery comprises the core aspects of embracing hope and a positive identity, gaining meaning and purpose, taking responsibility for managing the mental illness and one's life, and engaging with the social world.
- Personal recovery encompasses healing from the negative impact of mental illness, whereas clinical recovery encompasses healing from the mental illness itself.
- Our analyses illuminate narrative identity processes involved in personal recovery, including how individuals story costs of psychopathology and well-being sources.

CHAPTER 5

Narrative Identity

To discuss the nature of narrative, we start this chapter with an extended quote from a life story shared by one of our participants with schizophrenia. She was first hospitalized when she was 16 years old and struggling to complete high school. Listen to how psychosis ravaged her life:

> I was really ill. I was hospitalized many times and was hospitalized most of the 90s and in the end, I had to give up completing my program in sociology and accept disability benefits, which they said I should. At the time I was 28, so I thought it was a bit early. They also said in the psychiatric system that I should give up my study program and I had to stop taking exams, but I didn't want to drop out of university.

Subsequently, she depicts years with changes in medication and suffering from several medical conditions. By the end of her life story, she revisits the theme of education and says:

> [S]ince then I have slowly recovered and recovered so much that I had the courage to start my studies again. I didn't know exactly how to do it, but I knew I couldn't do it alone, like without any study companions, without anyone ... so ... so I helped start up this study group at [name of day center for individuals with mental illness] and had courses there and have had it for ... well, every semester in 10 years. This is the first semester I don't have courses there and it's only because I am writing my master's thesis .... I started on the two-year master program in 2005 and should have completed it long ago. But at the same time, it had to be a recovery, a getting well process, and then some life events happened, like my father got cancer and died and the last couple of years it has been my mentally ill sister, who has made it all chaotic. So, there have been semesters where I couldn't take any courses, and semesters where I could only take one course. The end of the story is that a couple of years ago I was offered some counseling sessions with a psychologist in the outpatient psychiatric unit, and since then here [reference to current treatment unit], and over this course of treatment I ended up last summer without symptoms for the first time since I was 14 .... It is 35–36 years that I have been ill, so it is amazing to be free of symptoms. That has opened the

> *possibility that I can get my degree and can look forward to a hopefully long and active work life, which I really look forward to and is like what I always wanted ... like an ordinary life with work and family and stuff and now we'll see how much of that I can achieve. But the requirement for my work life is that there can be no retirement. I will do something where I don't get retired, because I have been retired from age 28 until 48, 49, 50 ..... It is a requirement that I will not be retired, ever again! They should simply take the wheelchair when I collapse and then load me into a container and then that's the end. It would be fine with me if it could be that way.*

Below, we elaborate on key attributes of narratives exemplifying with this story of pain, courage, and hope. We then detail how individuals craft life stories to gain identity and meaning. Further, we locate life stories in the sociocultural contexts that shape how stories evolve. In the next chapter, we address the relationship between narrative and mental illness. In Chapters 14 and 15, we return to many of these ideas when we build our framework for understanding mental illness from a narrative identity perspective and propose a guide to repair the identity damage done by psychopathology and promote personal recovery.

What Is Narrative?

Jerome Bruner and Donald Polkinghorne were early proponents arguing for the importance of narrative as a mode of thought and they have remained prominent figures in the field of narrative psychology. The above story from our participant illustrates the fundamental features of narrative identified by these and other leading scholars.[9,10] Using this example, we elaborate on the nature of narrative as it is understood across a range of contexts. An understanding of narrative is central because we touch upon various types of narratives in the remaining chapters, both culturally shared stories (books and movies), stories individuals hear from close others (vicarious stories), and stories they form based on their own experiences (personal stories). We illustrate the key features of these various types of narrative using the life story segment as an example, but we save the identity functions salient to personal life stories for a later section.

First, the life story segment from the opening of the chapter embodies a temporal unfolding of events, how events are organized in time: from the early resistance against discontinuing her studies, to her present status as writing her master's thesis, and reaching into a future with an active work life. Narratives encompass beginnings, middles, and endings. Although the ending in this story is quite open, it offers an imaginary future closure.

Second, there is a main character pursuing a goal, an education, overcoming obstacles along the way, including her own mental illness, her father's cancer and death, and the chaos of her sister's psychopathology. The intentions of the character (completing her education and obtaining work) run as a thread through the story, tying together events, causes, and consequences on the road to reaching for her dream. Her intentions and wrestling with the barriers to her goals create a compelling story with real suspense. We are left to wonder what will happen next. Will she succeed on her path toward an active work life?

Third, the narrative integrates what Jerome Bruner terms the landscape of action with the landscape of consciousness.[9] The narrative portrays what happened in terms of actions, people, and places – the landscape of action. Weaved into the story are her dream images, emotions, evaluations, and thoughts – the landscape of consciousness. The narrative speaks to how she sees herself and other people and this inner world shapes her engagement with the external world. The landscape of consciousness encapsulates the subjective perspective of the narrator – her voice. The landscape of action anchors the narrative in the real world. Narratives integrate information across time, both external (what happened) and internal (what she thought and felt). As such, narratives are powerful tools for rendering the world and oneself comprehensible.

Fourth, the meaning of the narrative emerges from the configuration of events and mental states. In the story, her initial resistance to drop out of university is infused with meaning when embedded in a story where she has resumed studying and is hoping for a long work life. The meaning seeps through the lines, revealing that perseverance led her to the promised land of education. Imagine a different narrative. Suppose her story elaborated on repeated failures to pursue her studies – a narrative that she could have unfolded given the 10 years she needed to complete the courses. Then her opposition toward withdrawing from university would configure into a story about unrealistic expectations and self-deception. Alternatively, imagine her omitting the initial resistance episode from her life story. Then the message of endurance would be much less forceful. The crucial insight is that how individuals frame events in narratives makes a massive difference for meaning. Such framing includes selection, elaboration, and organization of the pieces in the narrative. Flowing from this idea, novel meanings can surface from alternative configurations. Some readers may argue that the protagonist in the story is very resourceful and that not all storytellers can spin a story of perseverance in pursuing higher education. We agree that resources may vary with implications for outcomes. However, if individuals do not story their various strengths, they fade to become almost invisible, with no potential to affect achievements and thriving.

Lived Story and Told Story

How do we understand the relationships between stories as we tell them (told story) and stories we keep in our minds and act (lived story)? This question is central to comprehending how therapeutic work with told stories may affect individuals' lived stories outside of therapy, an issue we return to in Chapter 15.

Above, we employed a verbally shared story to illustrate key characteristics, but stories also live in our minds. Individuals often share stories with friends, family, and colleagues as a part of bonding, teaching, and entertaining.[25,28] However, if the effects of narrative were limited to the minutes of telling, they would be trivial. After all, most of the time, individuals are not sharing or listening to stories. Many narrative researchers embrace the assumption that people also hold narratives in their minds.[8,29,100] Individuals dream and fantasize in stories, organize memories into narratives, and make sense of their emotions by embedding them in narrative.[11,23,24] As people reflect on their day, they craft stories about salient incidents such as the dinner with a friend and the phone call from a parent. As their minds roam toward the future, they envision possible events in narrative terms, like their upcoming vacation and a major task at work. When engaged in a long-term project, such as supporting a child recovering from illness, people continually ponder significant episodes, consider how one incident led to another, and spin possible futures that may flow from current actions. In their minds, they create ongoing narratives, meshing actions with reflection. In Dan McAdams' words: We live by stories.[101]

It is an unresolved debate whether the stories people weave in their minds and live by, what we term lived story, are truly narrative or lack the key qualities of narratives reviewed above. David Carr has argued convincingly for the similarity between lived narrative and told narrative.[102] He suggests that reflections about ongoing projects, such as pursuing education, are temporally structured. Individuals recognize that they are initiating a project, that they are underway, and that they will (hopefully) complete the project in the future. They reason about how one event may lead to another. They imagine a future where they tell the story and understand that this telling depends on maneuvering events into place in the present. They may even picture telling the story to a particular audience. In Carr's terms, "we are constantly striving, with more or less success, to occupy the storytellers' position with respect to our own lives" (p. 16).[102]

Telling the story shapes the story. For example, conversational contexts propel individuals to emphasize vital elements and fade out noise in storytelling.[103] To consider how told narrative interacts with experience, we capitalize on Donald Polkinghorne.[104] According to his analyses, experience is prenarrative (what we term lived narrative). In experience, people link actions to intended outcomes ("I will enroll in one course this semester in order to work toward obtaining my degree"). These intentional structures, encompassing temporal and causal relations between events, constitute prerequisites for told narrative. However, experience lacks a coherent plot, as the clatter and clamor of mundane happenings obscure the picture. When individuals verbally story their experience, they transform it through configurations that reveal meaningful plots. At the same time, using language folds culture-bound categories into understanding experience and oneself. For example, feeling chosen by God and receiving divine messages from the television may only instigate negative self-understandings when labeled as schizophrenia with its accompanying cultural meanings. Despite these transformations, the told story is grounded in experience. Simultaneously, the told narrative amplifies selected aspects of experience and brings to awareness previously veiled meanings, reshaping experience.

Despite David Carr's and Donald Polkinghorne's disagreements on whether experience is narrative or prenarrative, both inspired our view. Experience is often, but not always, intertwined with reflections about intentions and temporal-causal connections between past, present, and future events. Such reflections include verbal thoughts and the cultural meanings they carry (e.g., "I have schizophrenia and that means I am weak"). It constitutes a rudimentary narrative structure, what we label lived narrative. This stands in contrast to "raw" experiences where reflection has not imposed any narrative structure at all. In Chapter 6, we return to experiences that defy narrative structure (chaos "narrative"). Due to the push for clear plot, verbally conveying experiences can transform lived narratives into more coherent stories, creating novel meanings. Verbal sharing may unfold in a variety of contexts, including conversations with friends, psychotherapy, or diary writing. As individuals tell stories (told narratives), they step outside their role as protagonist, gaining a new perspective as author. Consequently, telling may grow insights about lived narrative that would otherwise remain in the dark. Consistent with this notion, several of our participants appeared to gain insights while telling their stories to us. Here is an example from a young woman with schizophrenia, recently hospitalized for the first time. She described past chapters about her illness causing her to lose a sense of who she is, then she reflected on her future chapters: "*Well, I guess it has to be love and children and becoming a parent and identity development. Wow, there is a lot of identity in this. It is funny how you see some other things when you, like, go through it all.*" Such insights in turn amplify narrative structuring of remembered and imagined future events that mesh with ongoing reflections and actions, potentially altering lived narratives. To return to our participant quoted at the beginning of this chapter, she clearly lived a narrative of perseverance in pursuing education. She continued her studies despite troubles and hurdles. Telling her life story in our study may have brought her lived narrative into focus, configuring a more coherent and themed story reaching toward the future. The telling may integrate her memories and aspirations into a tighter story, thereby molding future reflections and actions, further propelling her toward her dream of a long work life and personal recovery. In short, lived narrative and told narrative interweave.

When Stories Turn Self-Defining: Narrative Identity

So far, we have discussed the nature of stories but not the identity functions of the particular class of narratives that comprises extended life stories. Dan McAdams, who is a key figure in the field of narrative identity, has proposed that people understand who they are through reflections on how their remembered past is connected to their present situation and the future as they imagine it.[8,27,101] Individuals craft stories of their lives, and these stories are important to their identities. Narrative identity interacts with other psychological processes, such as personality, which together with life circumstances frame the possibilities of narration.[27,105] In other words, individuals do not create their narrative identity in a vacuum as a purely self-composed piece of art. It unfolds within a dynamic, but not unlimited, space of possibilities and is anchored in concrete life events.

Most people do not write their autobiographies or sit their friends down for days to share a full account of their life stories. Rather, we carry life stories in our minds and share them in a piecemeal fashion with friends, colleagues, family, and therapists. Much of the time, life stories live quietly. However, in times of crisis and transition, the story may move to the forefront, demanding attention.[106] When individuals create their identity through narrative, they bridge their present self to a past self – a self that may sometimes feel like a stranger to the person they are today.

Narrative identity braids different selves, from the past (the self as schoolgirl), the present (the ill self), and the future (the self as mother), into an overall picture of evolutions from one self to another.[27] How could the participant we quoted at the beginning of the chapter change from requiring years of hospitalization to being symptom-free, studying at university, and hoping for an active work life? How can she reconcile her past ill self with her present recovering self? Creating believable and compelling stories explaining these transformations provides a sense of self-continuity across time.[107] She may be a different person now, but she is also the same, and she recognizes the sameness because she can story the journey undertaken by her past self to arrive at her present self. As individuals narrate their lives, they imbue them with meaning and purpose.[101] Events did not just occur randomly. Rather, as our participant tells her story, she saturates her actions with meaning and her purpose becomes clear. This illustrates how life stories constitute psychological resources. However, as we illustrate later, life stories may also be a psychological liability when purpose is defeated, and meaning is bleak.

As is clear from above, narrative identity provides continuity, purpose, and meaning. However, narrative identity does not just organize people's inner worlds, it also shapes action. An influential study on redemption stories and adaptive action exemplifies this idea. In their study, William L. Dunlop and Jessica Tracy asked recovering alcoholics to share the story of their last drink.[108] They discovered that participants who told redemption stories were more likely to maintain their sobriety at a later point. Redemption encapsulates sequences with negative events resulting in positive outcomes.[109] Presumably, narrating the last drink as the final slip (negative event) before one leaves alcoholism behind to pursue a better life (positive outcome) guides future actions consistent with the redemption story. It becomes a lived narrative of recovering from alcoholism. As such, redemption stories are adaptive models for narrating negative events to enable change.[110] However, it is important to keep in mind that not all stories of suffering and defeat can be spun into redemptive versions.[111]

The raw material for life stories is remembered past and imagined future events.[107] Individuals think of their lives as consisting of periods, both past periods ("my school years") and future periods ("my retirement").[112] These periods comprise chapters that endow life stories with overall coherence ("my school years," "moving to Copenhagen," "my years of hospitalization," and "work life"). We have shown that individuals use chapters to create coherent life stories. As they organize the past and future into series of chapters, a basic life story skeleton emerges.[113,114] (see Appendix 3 for an illustration).

Nested within each past and future chapter are memories and imagined future events belonging to that period. For example, the chapter of education contains memories of events that took place as a part of that chapter (receiving acceptance letter, first day at university, and failing exam). Some of these memories and imagined future events serve as symbols of themes and goals with enduring significance and become key scenes in life stories.[101,115] Using Jefferson Singer's term such memories have become self-defining.[116] Returning to the quote from the opening of this chapter, our participant envisioned a key future scene where she ends her work life chapter when passing away. The imagined future event symbolizes the recurrent life story theme of persistence and her goal of having a work life.

Susan Bluck and Tilmann Habermas suggested that life stories encompass reflections about connections between events and between events and the self, termed autobiographical reasoning (<u>after</u> high school (event 1), I took a gap year (event 2), <u>because</u> I needed time off from school).[22,29] These links explain how individuals affected events (I decided to take a gap year) and how experiences in return changed individuals (the gap year made me more mature). Such self-event connections are at the root of how experiences mold identity. This is illustrated in the following quote from a participant with bipolar disorder, who took a gap year after high school when she was in a stable period, traveling with a friend (note that this is relatively common in Denmark). She reflects on how this travel chapter shaped her positively: *"My friend and I travelled to Australia and Africa for about half a year. It was amazing. Things happened to me during that time. Through meeting people and experiences, I matured, grew more relaxed, more complete in a way."*

When individuals craft life stories they endow some experiences with significance, while they dismiss other remembered and imagined events as trivial. They braid key scenes and chapters into temporally and causally connected storylines from which focal life themes surface.[29] These themes can be implicit, between the lines, as the theme of perseverance in the opening quote of this chapter or individuals can explicitly state themes, as in the following excerpt from a participant with borderline personality disorder. The participant's mother lived overseas and had left him with an aunt, about whom he tells:

> *She couldn't cope with me. Because already back then, I was really frustrated and had a lot of stuff that I hadn't worked through . . . . I was too wild for the other kids and ran off from kindergarten. The teachers couldn't manage me,*

and my aunt thought it was too much, so I was sent back to my mother. It has a negative effect when someone gives up on you, right? The stay as such was positive, but being discarded, that was negative. It has affected me ... and it was just one of the times I was discarded.

In the example, the participant links his stay with his aunt to the theme of being discarded, a theme running as a red thread through his story. Such themes bring forth identity conclusions about who one is ("I am discarded by others") that shape the person's engagement (or lack thereof) with the world.[117]

Grounded in this literature, we analyze the life stories of individuals with mental illness to answer our two main questions: How do individuals narrate the consequences of their psychiatric disturbance and story well-being into their identity? We present the themes that emerge and their accompanying identity conclusions in Chapters 9–12.

The Narrative Ecology

Constructing narrative identity is an ever-evolving process saturated with cultural and social contexts. Kate McLean has proposed that narrative identity is embedded in a narrative ecology comprised of stories voiced by concrete others and culturally shared stories.[118] Individuals keep stories about their parents, their partners, their children, and their friends. Together with David Pillemer, we have termed these vicarious stories to underscore that individuals can draw lessons from stories transmitted by others, that personal and vicarious stories interact.[43,119] In parallel with our research, Robyn Fivush and her group have demonstrated the importance of vicarious stories for parents, also termed intergenerational narratives.[120] This is illustrated by one of our participants with borderline personality disorder, who knitted her mother's story into her own: *"My mother couldn't take care of me. She had no clue about infants because she didn't grow up with her own mother. It was like weird, weird, weird, that family constellation. Completely crazy. It goes back for generations."* Later she again talks about her mother's story in relation to her own:

A lot of what I experience today, I really feel her pain, a lot of what she lives, I can see that we have many parallels. Find the one to break the social heritage .... But I'll say that we did break it, all three of us, because none of us children, my siblings and me, have given up regarding our own children and sent them away.

The quote illustrates an important idea in research on vicarious stories. That is, they intertwine with and shape personal stories, both as individuals model their personal narratives after close others' stories and as they resist them. For example, Kate McLean and her colleagues found that adult children often reported learning lessons about themselves from stories parents had told about their own lives.[118] Vicarious stories may become even more vital when individuals encounter events not easily accommodated into their narrative. In his book, *The Wounded Storyteller*, Arthur Frank suggested that he needed other people's illness stories: "That is the book's consistent message about why suffering needs stories: To tell one's own story, a person needs others' stories" (p. xi).[121] We return to his insights about narrative and illness in Chapter 6.

Individuals gather a treasure trove of vicarious stories from conversations where stories are shared to bond, empathize, entertain, and teach. Furthermore, conversations open up personal stories to negotiation with conversational partners.[28] Such coauthoring is perhaps most crucial in childhood where primary caregivers regularly invite their children into interactive storying of events and slowly scaffold their narrative skills. Caregivers guide children to share narratives through questions but differ in how they engage in such conversations. Research by Robyn Fivush, Elaine Reese, and colleagues has revealed that children of caregivers who ask questions that invite children to expand on and express their own perspective, later tell richer narratives compared to children of caregivers who ask less elaborative questions.[122] Such studies imply that interactions with caregivers sculpt children's budding narrative identities.[123] Later in the life cycle, conversations with friends, partners, and children continue to influence narrative identities. For example, friends may ask questions to invite reflections about the meaning of events and offer support for exploring difficult emotions. Or they may be distracted, inattentive listeners. Research reviewed by Monisha Pasupathi indicates that audiences shape how individuals later remember events and tell their stories.[26]

Under some difficult circumstances, there may be no supportive audience for the stories individuals live by. No listeners are willing to hear the stories or audiences actively suppress stories to keep them hidden.[122] Some of our participants told stories indicating that their voices had been silenced: "*There was the rape that was hard. . . . I have had to keep it a secret for two years. It has been really hard to bear on my own*" or "*I wasn't bullied, but I was ignored, I would say. I had no friends at all, not at all. No one wanted to talk to me.*" Others hinted that caregivers had been hostile audiences, coauthoring a self-defeating story for the participant: "*Because my father always said: 'You* can't manage that.' If I said I wanted to be a social worker, then that was too big a dream. All the time at home, being labeled as someone who couldn't manage." While we need more research to cast light on the influence of silencing and aggressive audiences, it is safe to conclude that significant others coauthor both positive and negative narrative identities.

Grounded in the literature on coauthoring and vicarious stories, we suggest that individuals who have survived neglect, silenced trauma, bullying, and loneliness, as some of our participants have, may grow up with a dearth of supportive coauthors to their stories. Additionally, they may have few positive vicarious life stories available as templates for personal life stories because their family and peers have either shared few stories or highlighted stories of defeat. The implication is that their narrative resources are depleted and that their narrative identities may make them vulnerable to psychopathology. While this is not a focus for our life story analyses because we did not collect the life stories prior to the occurrence of psychiatric disorder, we revisit the idea of narrative identity as a vulnerability to mental illness in our theoretical framework (see Chapter 14).

Cultural stories comprise an additional layer of the narrative ecology.[118] Culture refers broadly to ways of world-making that define what life is like, what a person is, and how to live well.[124] It involves shared belief systems and practices, including storytelling practices, both at broad levels (countries) and narrow levels (hospital wards).[122] Cultural stories include actual narrative products, such as films and books. The film story of John Nash and the autobiographies we analyzed in Chapter 1 are examples of cultural stories about mental illness. Less concrete, master narratives are shared cultural story templates constraining and shaping concrete stories.[109,118,122] They reveal themselves through their appearance in cultural stories, personal life stories, and vicarious life stories. It is beyond the scope of the present book to provide a review of master narratives and we suggest that interested readers turn to other sources.[125,126] Rather, we give two examples that we believe are particularly relevant to our purposes and emphasized by Kate McLean and Moin Syed in their influential framework for master narratives: redemption and cultural life scripts.[127]

Redemption is a pervasive master narrative concerning story structure.[109,127] As we alluded to earlier in describing the study of recovering alcoholics, redemption stories can be personal.[108] However, individuals model such personal narratives after a culturally shared master narrative that is highly valued in the United States (and maybe in other cultures). For example, the film story of John Nash represents a redemption story as he struggles with schizophrenia toward an ending where he receives the Nobel Prize and delivers a moving speech to his wife.

Cultural life scripts refer to master narratives of the life course that have been extensively researched by Dorthe Berntsen, David Rubin, and colleagues.[127,128] They reasoned that since individuals internalize cultural ideals about life, one way to elucidate such master narratives was to ask individuals about events in "the typical life." From their studies, they concluded that people recognize these cultural ideals as a kind of recipe for the typical life, what they termed the cultural life script. This script is comprised of important life events and their predicted timing, such as school, work life, marriage, and children. These culturally sanctioned ideas seep into individuals' life stories by highlighting certain milestones that individuals should reach at certain times in their lives, many of which take place in adolescence and young adulthood.

Although the cultural life script, redemption, and other master narratives shape life stories, individuals do not simply copy master narratives into their own story. Rather, they relate their stories to master narratives, either implicitly by reproducing them or explicitly by noting divergences.[127] Some quotes from our participants illustrate the latter process. As a response to a standard interview question about whether one of her chapters had changed her in positive ways, a participant with major depressive disorder responded: "*I don't think so. I don't think it is positive. It hasn't made me stronger or anything.*" Clearly, she is negating the what-doesn't-kill-you-makes-you-stronger redemption master narrative. Another participant seemed to negotiate the cultural life script in her reflections about lagging behind in education:

> *I feel like, how to put it, that you are being pushed a bit by society. People around me ... because I took two gap years, which is a long time, and then I started and then I became ill. Now I'm in my fourth year not studying or anything. I really feel a lot behind. But I have started thinking that, well you are only 23, it will be OK.*

The quotes indicate that some individuals with mental illness may fall out of popular master narratives. We wonder what they risk falling into.

As acknowledged above, master narratives are a slippery concept as they only emerge through personal, vicarious, and cultural stories, but we speculate that when struck by mental illness, some individuals could fall into a darker set of master narratives. Such master narratives may include negative and inaccurate stereotypes about the mentally ill. As we touched upon in Chapter 3, these stereotypes revolve around people with mental illness as weak, as out of control, and as dangerous.[20] Furthermore, the academic literature on mental illness reviewed in Chapter 3 is dominated by trauma, deficit, vulnerability, risk of relapse, and cascades of costs. Healthcare professionals know this literature by heart, and it may constitute a negative master narrative of mental illness, with the following storyline: Vulnerability and trauma leads to mental illness with repeated relapse and difficulties with social roles. This preconception certainly seems to infuse some interactions between healthcare professionals and service users (as evidenced in several quotes in the book). Given that healthcare professionals often see individuals in crisis and not when they cope well, these selective encounters reinforce negative master narratives that may require resistance to avoid problematic interactions between staff and service users.[129] Otherwise, such master narratives may come to dominate the narrative ecology of severe mental illness, framing how individuals story their identities.

Our analyses above, including lack of supportive coauthors and adaptive vicarious stories as well as destructive master narratives, imply that the narrative ecology of individuals with mental illness may be a dark place. We would like to emphasize that many individuals with mental illness grow up with loving parents, siblings, and friends. Further, when close others and healthcare professionals reproduce bleak stories, this is not intentional. Rather, good intentions may be overruled by powerful toxic master narratives that block alternative versions. We believe that these ideas merit attention as possible explanations for why some individuals with mental illness struggle to craft adaptive life stories fostering well-being and return to this idea in Chapter 14, where we develop our narrative framework of mental illness.

The Contribution of the Present Book

As we review in Chapter 6, research has linked narrative identity to mental illness and well-being. However, this literature has not addressed our first question concerning how individuals story the consequences of their psychiatric disturbance; that is, how they create causal links between mental illness and who they are.

As proposed by Monisha Pasupathi and colleagues, the contours of self-event connections may be affirmative, empowering, and vitalizing versus destructive, degrading, and doubtful.[130] The autobiographies we analyzed in Chapter 1 revealed that the authors often interpreted their mental illness as causing negative changes in their self-understanding. However, a few stories identified positive consequences. Recall Kay Redfield Jamieson who reasoned that her bipolar disorder made her feel life more strongly.[14] Initial readings of our participants' life stories indicated that they also identified both detrimental and beneficial outcomes of their mental illness. Consequently, we coded the life stories for both positive and negative consequences of mental illness. We describe the coding system in more detail in Chapter 7 and in Appendices 5–6.

Regarding our second question concerning experiences participants narrate as bringing well-being, we coded the parts of their life stories that included positive emotions, meaning, personal growth, positive relationships, and the other aspects of subjective and psychological well-being. When individuals with mental illness synthesize well-being experiences into their life stories, they are slowly composing positive identities as someone capable of finding love and peace, and able to learn and grow. As such, the analyses provide insights about how individuals with mental disorders may experience well-being and grow positive identities, both aspects of personal recovery identified in Chapter 4.

Understanding life stories as folded into a many-layered narrative ecology is significant because it opens our eyes to the truth that life stories are constrained by the possibilities of culture and relationships.[118] When our participants narrate the effects of mental illness and well-being experiences, the stories reflect not only their lived stories but also the narrative repertoire available through vicarious and cultural stories. Still, life stories do not just passively reproduce master narratives or previously heard stories. As individuals story their lives, they imaginatively knit together their experiences with master narratives and vicarious stories in ways we do not entirely understand. Hence, every life story is unique. In Chapters 9–12, we showcase the sprawling array of stories disclosed by our participants to expand the narrative reservoir available to individuals living with mental illness, their close others, and healthcare professionals. In other words, we hope that the stories shared by our participants in this book will serve as vicarious stories contributing to a warmer climate in the narrative ecology of mental illness.

Summary

- Narratives are a basic mode of understanding and individuals are continually embedded in narrative webs as protagonists in and authors of their own stories and as supportive characters in and coauthors of close others' stories.

Summary

- Narratives comprise temporal unfolding of events depicting protagonists who attempt to overcome obstacles in pursuing their goals.
- Narratives integrate the landscape of action with the landscape of consciousness as they encompass both descriptions of what happened, intertwined with mental states such as intentions, emotions, and interpretations.
- The meaning flowing from narratives depends on the configuration of events and mental states.
- Individuals verbally share narratives (told narrative) and weave narratives in their mind that guide action (lived narrative).
- Told narratives are grounded in lived narratives and at the same time told narratives may transform lived narratives.
- Life stories are a source of identity and meaning as they tie together the remembered past with the present and the imagined future.
- Individuals craft their narrative identities through selecting, organizing, and interpreting material from autobiographical memory and imagined future events.
- Narrative identity is embedded in sociocultural processes, a narrative ecology.
- Through conversations, significant others coauthor the stories individuals share.
- Individuals know stories about family and friends, also termed vicarious stories, which may shape personal stories.
- Master narratives serve as templates for storytelling.
- There may be a negative narrative ecology of mental illness comprised of inaccurate stereotypes, of negative master narratives arising from research drawing a grim picture of life with mental illness, of nonsupportive or absent coauthors, and a dearth of adaptive vicarious stories.
- The life story analyses in the book focus on themes and identity conclusions emerging when individuals narrate consequences of their mental illness and well-being experiences.

CHAPTER 6

Narrative Identity, Illness, and Well-Being

How does illness affect storytellers? And can individuals narrate their identities in ways that make them vulnerable to psychiatric disorder and low well-being, hindering personal recovery? These are the central questions we address in this chapter. We turn first to prominent research yielding insights about how illness disrupts stories and apply these insights to psychopathology. Second, we present a range of approaches that center on the idea that narratives may be at the root of mental disorder and effective psychotherapy. We then discuss research on connections between narratives and well-being. Finally, we introduce studies directly targeting how individuals experience the cost of mental illness and events important to well-being. Throughout we elaborate on how this literature informed the present life story analyses. In Chapters 14 and 15, we synthesize the ideas from this chapter with our life story analyses to develop a conceptual framework that we use to develop a guide to repair the identity damage from mental illness and grow personal recovery.

Narrative Identity and Illness

Illustrating how illness can cut through the threads of narratives, one of our participants depicted the impact of her bipolar disorder:

I enjoy high school. I like my class and my brain is challenged. I learn and discover so much exciting stuff. But the first year I feel the darkness of depression for the first time. A cloud passing. It lasts a short month, relatively mild, and it passes. I become "myself" again. In the third year, it turns bad. For a period, I am all full of energy and grand thoughts, and I am constantly on the move. Very little sleep. But it changes suddenly, and I become severely depressed in the late winter months. Everything seems meaningless, hopeless. I burn myself with cigarettes. I am hospitalized in the spring for two months. I can't stand living at home. I have difficulties with my mom especially. In the spring, I leave home. I postpone my high school exam and complete it later. I do well, really well, but the price is another hospitalization. I have totally lost my balance. I turn so many negative thoughts and images inwards and I am cruel to myself. The illness knocks me out and I can't imagine that I will be well again. I feel knocked off course.

This example illustrates a central idea in Arthur Frank's important book on how illness affects narrative, where he identified several ways to story illness.[121] Below, we zoom in on the chaos "narrative," the restitution narrative, and the quest narrative. Propelled by his personal experience of suffering from cancer, Frank describes how illness cuts into the fabric of the stories individuals live. As reviewed in the previous chapter, individuals live and tell stories where they knit together the remembered past with their present and imaginary future. When illness intrudes, it disrupts these ongoing narratives. The stories no longer hold. The imaginary futures individuals were navigating toward are lost, replaced by the unknown. In a journey metaphor employed by Frank, individuals lose both the map and the destination.

Illness is chaos. It undoes the plot of the lived and told story and overwhelms storytellers. According to Frank, such chaos defies verbal storying. Rather, chaos "narratives" are lived. Daily life is anarchy, havoc, and confusion that do not translate into orderly stories with temporal structure and plot. Chaos "narratives" surface verbally when individuals stammer through experiences with little sense of meaningful connections between events. No protagonist pursuing goals, no author to voice what it all means. Recall Carr's idea from the previous chapter that individuals strive to occupy the role as storytellers in their own lives.[102,121] The turmoil of illness steals that role. When chaos "narratives" are shared, they are hard to listen to as the chaos transmits to the audience. Think back to the quote at the beginning of Chapter 2, where one of our participants portrayed how his therapist discovered his hallucinations and initiated hospitalization. Chaos seeps through the lines in his story. While chaos "narratives" may subside as initial crisis fades, for chronic and recurrent conditions, as severe mental illness can be, chaos continues to lurk at the edge of the story. As will become evident in our life story analyses (see Chapters 8–12), one often-voiced cost of mental illness is an uncertain future. In severe mental illness, chaos may threaten to return.

People need stories to structure the chaos of illness.[121] However, narratives must resist the theft of agency from illness and the passive role sometimes fostered by traditional, paternalistic healthcare systems. When acute illness strikes, individuals may become unable to care for themselves and pursue their goals. They can even lose the freedom of choice, as is evident when coercive treatment is used. In such cases, healthcare professionals take on major responsibility for a time and care for individuals to the best of their abilities. While state-of-the-art treatment is often collaborative, ill individuals face the peril of losing agency, that stories trap them in roles as passive victims.

Frank acknowledges that personal narratives are unique but argues that they are also similar in many ways. In his book, he elaborates on two categories of stories that individuals unfold to navigate the tornado of illness. Primarily analyzing somatic illness, like cancer, he suggests that the standard medical master narrative may inspire personal stories. Following this master narrative, individuals may story their illness as restitution narratives, which are highly valued by healthcare systems, and include becoming ill, receiving treatment, and recovering and back to normal. This story type fits some illnesses and many advantages flow from it. For example, it structures illness into a series of treatment steps to be overcome, promising happy endings that sustain hope. However, the backside is that it leaves individuals little room for storying their suffering. In addition, the restitution master narrative is poorly suited to prolonged or recurrent illness courses, where the "recovered and back to normal" ending is fragile in the shadow of potential future episodes. We speculate that the restitution master narrative may fit few individuals with severe mental illness. For example, some mental illnesses, such as personality disorders, have no clear-cut beginning and end. Perhaps most importantly, the "back to normal" ending may sometimes seem out of reach. This is in line with our analyses where one cost of mental illness often surfacing in the life stories of our participants was a loss of their former self and a keenly felt loss of a "normal" life (see Chapter 10).

Storytellers may also narrate their illness as a quest, a journey through suffering.[121] In quest narratives, individuals do not go back to "normal." Their illness transforms them. They draw new maps for their life and travel to new destinations. Protagonists in quest stories are not action heroes. Rather, the heroism comprises perseverance in the face of extreme suffering, living through pain, damage to bodily functions, and loss of life. The protagonists bear witness to the anguish of illness and share its ravages with others. They lend their stories to others who are caught in chaos "narratives" or poorly fitted in restitution narratives. The quest narrative parallels the redemption story we described in Chapter 5, where negative events (the illness) are storied with positive outcomes (helping others).[109] However, Frank emphasizes how even heroes in quest narratives live with reminders of the illness and fear of recurrence, suggesting that quest narratives are not purely redemptive. Still, stories of personal recovery, as we touched upon in Chapter 4, could resemble quest narratives.

Other scholars agree that illness disrupts ongoing narratives and that individuals need stories to render their illness experiences comprehensible. Lars-Christer Hydén's insightful review of illness narratives emphasizes that narratives help create meaning in the face of illness.[131] While this meaning-making function is generally adaptive, chronic illness calls into question individuals' life worlds, accompanied by a lost sense of self. Individuals craft stories of illness to make sense of their suffering and reconstruct their identity. They revise their stories to explain why they became ill and what illness did to them. This is a risky time for storytelling. Individuals now view life from the vantage point of illness. For some individuals, the remembered past may take on a darker shape. After all, it led into the present state of illness, impelling them to retell their past in order to make sense of this new ill self. New chapters of vulnerability can emerge as central to defining the self and toxic interpretations of inadequacy and worthlessness may become foreground. These self-defeating stories in turn shape the experience of symptoms and suffering.

Despite the peril that illness narratives are composed to depict the self as vulnerable, inadequate, and worthless, narratives can serve adaptive functions. Weaving illness events into coherent stories renders experiences communicable to others, transforming the turmoil of illness that audiences may reject into tell-able tales. Further highlighting the communicative function, Rita Charon suggests that illness narratives play important roles in the relationship between healthcare staff and patients.[132] Currently, technical descriptions of illness and scientifically established treatments are center pillars in medical practice. Founded on significant discoveries in medical research, healthcare staff can cure or relieve a range of medical conditions. While the benefits of this approach are enormous, Charon argues that healthcare professionals can become dominated by this technical approach to the point where they ignore the subjective side of suffering as noise and distraction. She suggests that patients tell illness stories to regain their status as persons in a medical world that risks reducing them to mechanical beings. Wary of a system devaluing relationships as patients are tossed from one expert to the next, Charon proposes that healthcare professionals could turn to narrative medicine, that is, "medicine practiced with the narrative competence to recognize, absorb, interpret, and be moved by the stories of illness" (p. vii).[132] By witnessing suffering communicated in illness narratives, healthcare staff may ease the pain. We return to narrative medicine in Chapter 15, where we outline a narrative intervention to aid personal recovery and discuss the benefits our approach may hold for professionals.

Both Arthur Frank and Rita Charon underscore that bodies are at the nexus of illness narratives.[121,132] We will not foreground the body in the life story analyses. This choice does not reflect that our participants are mentally rather than somatically ill, leaving bodies irrelevant. On the contrary, our participants storied their bodies into their identity. We read stories of bodies that were beaten and raped; stories of individuals cutting and starving their bodies; stories of what drugs, medicine, and medicine withdrawal did to bodies; stories of bodies held by caring others; and stories of bodies enacting dreams. However, this theme will fall into the background as we carefully unfurl answers to our two main questions: 1) how individuals narrate the consequences of mental illness and 2) how they story sources of well-being into their identities.

Narrative Identity and Psychotherapy

The literature reviewed above mostly centers on somatic illness, expounding on how illness disrupts ongoing narratives and how narratives may mend the rupture and communicate personal suffering. However, the focus is different when considering the science of narrative and mental illness. As illuminated by Hydén, research and theory in this area revolve around the idea that narratives may cause illness.[131] That is, problematic stories, or the absence of stories, may be a part of the explanation for mental illness. The upshot is that constructing or reconstructing stories may be at the heart of effective psychotherapy.

Psychotherapists with otherwise very different convictions have argued that reauthoring narratives are among the active ingredients in therapy.[117,133,134] In his classic book, *Narrative Truth and Historical Truth*, Donald Spence disputes the then deeply held conviction that effective psychoanalysis cures through unearthing historically accurate causes of present problems.[134] It is not vital that psychoanalysts dig out repressed, but historically accurate, childhood memories and the mystic transformations they have undergone to give rise to neurosis. Rather, the crucial factor is that interpretations facilitate construction of coherent and comprehensive narratives. These narratives should link present problems meaningfully with past events and foster adaptation. Whether these events really occurred the way individuals remember them or caused the problems is less relevant. The healing power flows from narrative truth, not historical accuracy.

Consistent with Spence's notion that individuals need narratives to explain the source of their mental illness, but leaving the intricacies of psychoanalysis behind, many, but not all, of our participants crafted stories grappling with the causes of their illness. Recall our participant from Chapter 3 who linked his delusions that poison seeping through the walls would destroy his brain to witnessing a close friend grievously hurt in a traffic accident and later pronounced brain-dead. Many of our participants followed diathesis-stress thinking when storying the roots of their mental illness as transmitted genetically through family members or brought about by vulnerabilities and the far too many traumas in their lives. The need to explain the emergence of mental illness is strikingly evident in this participant with schizophrenia who at the time of the interview recalled no traumas in her early years and struggled to find a suitable explanation:

> Well, nothing really happened that stands out. Because my parents were not divorced, and I haven't had any grandparents that died in my lifetime. We haven't even had a dog that died. I wasn't bullied, have always had friends, have had an easy time in school. All those basic things that simply just worked. But when I think back to my childhood, I was extremely sensitive.

She then elaborates on her sensitivity. Later she revisits the lack of explanations in reflecting upon a depressive episode in adolescence: "*With depressions, there is not always a trigger, but it would have been nice if there had been something, if you had been exposed to something. Of course, it is not good to be exposed to something, but something concrete to blame. A cause. It can be frustrating, it has been to me at least, lacking something to blame.*" We note that Spence's influential ideas revolve around narrating the causes of the problem. He has less to say about employing narratives to grasp the consequences of mental illness and the climb to recovery.

Although from a very different theoretical standpoint, Michael White and David Epston agree with Spence that narratives are at the nexus of psychotherapy.[117] Anchored in the ideas from narrative psychology reviewed in Chapter 5, they suggest that individuals experience problems when their narratives do not represent the richness of experience, hindering choice and opportunities. In other words, the transformation from experience to lived and told narrative has gone awry. The source of problematic narratives may stem from constraining master narratives overshadowing aspects of experience. For example, master narratives about the mentally ill as weak and vulnerable may seep into personal narratives and rob them of agency, outshining experience of mastery. Telling impoverished narratives depleted of agency may become self-fulfilling prophesies preventing individuals from exerting influence on important outcomes and pursuing valued goals. Based on this understanding, the central aim in therapy is to scaffold reconstruction of narratives wherein individuals evolve into empowered protagonists. White and Epston outline several routes therapists may travel to support their clients in restorying their lives. One example is listening for and elaborating on unique outcomes to create alternative and more adaptive stories. Unique outcomes are incidents that run against the dominant self-defeating story. Individuals may not recognize these incidents as unique; rather the events have been ignored as irrelevant because the existing narrative eclipses potential contradictions. One of our participants with borderline personality disorder shared bleak chapters about being abandoned by her biological father, bullied in school, continuing social conflict, a son with ADHD, obesity, and divorce. However, her final chapter depicts her present job:

> *I simply have the best boss in the world ... I know that he thinks that I am simply great out there and they are just happy with me, right ..... As soon as I enter the shop, then I feel free, because I feel well. I feel safe. That is really important to me. To feel safe in one's workplace and that you get along with your colleagues. It has clearly meant that he has allowed me a space of freedom in my life, in my everyday life, which means that I can bear it.*

Her last chapter ran counter to all her previous chapters with their themes of defeat, helplessness, and social discord, thereby illustrating the idea that even very dark stories may leave room for some light. Narrative therapists may invite her to expand on how she contributed to the emergence of this safe and happy space in her life.

It is worth mentioning that Spence on the one hand and White and Epston on the other hand hold contrasting ideas, despite their shared conviction that narratives matter.[117,134] For one, Spence values coherence and comprehensiveness in narratives, whereas White and Epston accentuate agency. In addition, White and Epston mainly discuss how problematic narratives limit present opportunities and are less concerned with coauthoring narratives to explain the root of the problem. Furthermore, the authors diverge in their thoughts about the role of therapists in restorying clients' experiences. Spence seems to allocate the responsibility with the psychoanalysts who possess unique skills and knowledge, which allow them to suggest interpretations that configure experiences into narrative truths. Explicitly denouncing therapists as authorities, White and Epston assign expertise to the client. The therapists do not have access to the clients' experiences, which is the foundation for change. Consequently, the therapists' role is to nurture the client's voice in reauthoring a new story.

In alignment with insights from Spence as well as White and Epston, Paul Lysaker and colleagues further developed the idea that narratives matter in psychotherapy by proposing that a key task is to facilitate narrative repair.[135] This encompasses crafting coherent illness narratives that allow individuals to comprehend their current problems as well as processing losses, traumas, and negative emotions. Complementing these stories of suffering, individuals need stories of happiness that highlight strengths and capabilities that may pave the way to a desired future. Crucially, revised narratives must be enacted to be helpful. If they live only in the interaction between the therapist and the person with mental illness, not changing daily life, they are poor narrative repairs. Clearly, these ideas bear affinity to our two main questions and we return to how narratives may be employed to recover from mental illness in Chapter 15.

Narrative Identity and Mental Illness

Systematic research on how narrative affects and is affected by mental illness is gradually building. Currently, most interest centers on individuals with schizophrenia who are generally recognized as struggling to craft coherent stories of their lives. Paul Lysaker and colleagues have proposed that schizophrenia is associated with difficulties in synthesizing complex information to create coherent self-understandings. Studies by this group have confirmed that individuals with schizophrenia tell less coherent stories of their illness compared to individuals with other conditions.[136] Other scientists have extended this research and shown that individuals with schizophrenia struggle with telling coherent and meaningful stories.[137–139] Furthermore, individuals with schizophrenia story their lives with low mastery and interpersonal difficulties.[140] Reviewing this literature, Henry Cowan and his collaborators concluded that "the narrative identities of individuals with schizophrenia-spectrum disorders are distinguished by three features: disjointed structure, a focus on suffering, and detached narration" (p. 1).[141]

It is possible that schizophrenia is unique in its connection with narrative identity disruptions. Indeed, schizophrenia is generally considered the most severe mental illness accompanied by profound disturbances in self and identity.[142,143] Still, individuals with other mental illnesses could evidence similar problems with narrative identity. This may especially be the case if suffering from mental illness is a part of the explanation for less coherent life stories with little room for agency as indicated by Arthur Frank's analyses of how somatic illness affects narrative.[121] Budding research indicates that individuals with other types of mental illness also craft negative narrative identities, when compared to individuals with no known psychopathology. For example, Tim Dalgleish and his team discovered that individuals with major depressive disorder story their past selves with more negative attributes.[144,145] Jonathan Adler and colleagues showed that individuals with features of borderline personality disorder told stories characterized by themes of low communion and agency.[146,147] These themes concern the overall messages transmitted in the stories, that is, how individuals imbue their lives with meaning. Agency themes comprise autonomy, mastery, and achievement, whereas communion themes encompass intimacy, caring, and belonging. Individuals with borderline personality disorder emphasized themes of isolation, conflict, and alienation as well as powerlessness, defeat, and failure. Majse Lind and her collaborators confirmed this pattern in their recent literature review.[148] Another type of diagnoses, drug addictions, may likewise be accompanied by troubles with agency and communion themes.[32] As we point out in Chapter 7, we see similar problems with narrative identity in our studies of individuals with bipolar disorder, schizophrenia, major depressive disorder, and borderline personality disorder. This led us to anchor our findings in the transdiagnostic approach to mental illness[50,53] (see Chapter 2), suggesting that themes of low agency and communion as well as negative meaning constitute a negative narrative identity that may characterize individuals suffering from several mental disorders.[38] We note, however, that this conclusion glosses over massive individual variation.

Presently, it is an open question whether a negative narrative identity heightens vulnerability to mental illness or is a result of the major disruptive force of mental illness. Inspired by the literature reviewed above, we accept both possibilities as viable. As suggested in the previous chapter, traumatic early parts of life may rob individuals of narrative resources, such as supportive coauthors and adaptive vicarious stories, contributing to negative narrative identities, which could constitute a vulnerability. This line of thinking concurs with traditional diathesis-stress models[58] (see Chapter 3) in that negative narrative identities are present before and contribute to the eruption of mental illness. At the same time, mental illness can ignite chaos in the same way that Frank suggests somatic illness does.[121] From this perspective, the eruption of mental illness severs the threads of ongoing narratives and individuals may restory their past centering on trauma and vulnerability to explain their mental illness. In other words, negative narrative identity follows from mental illness and may become a self-fulfilling prophesy hindering personal recovery. In our life story analyses, we focus mostly on how individuals narrate their life *after* mental illness. We address how they interpret the consequences of their illness and incorporate well-being into their narrative identities. Thus, our approach is grounded in the idea that mental illness alters ongoing stories and that narrative identity may be an important tool to regain a life worth living. However, we note that some individuals suffering from mental illness may lack narrative resources, and this has implications for how to effectively employ narratives in the pursuit of well-being and personal recovery. We return to this insight when presenting our conceptual framework in Chapter 14 and address it as a potential obstacle to narrative repair that may be tackled by employing our guide for narrative repair (see Chapter 15 and the case story in Appendix 8).

A skeptic may argue that narrative identity is superfluous, that the real problem is the trauma. That is, the bullying, the neglect, the abuse, the isolation. However, as should be clear from the previous chapters, events are not just events. Events, also traumatic events, influence mental illness and well-being according to how they are storied, how meaning is extracted. It matters what the subjectively construed narratives say about the protagonists and the worlds they inhabit. This is a hard point to prove empirically, but some studies lend support to the idea that narrative identity matters and that psychotherapy may be effective by altering narrative identity. In an ambitious study, Jonathan Adler followed individuals in psychotherapy over several months.[149] After each therapy session, participants were invited to write a narrative about therapy and how it impacted their sense of self. They also completed measures of psychopathology. The study showed that clients who wrote narratives emphasizing agency themes tended to improve in the following sessions, testifying to the possibility that narrative identity is involved in overcoming mental illness. Consistent with this idea, other researchers have found that psychotherapy targeting problematic narratives alleviates self-stigmatization and depression.[150,151]

Despite the growing interest in narrative identity and mental illness, there are currently few clear-cut answers about their interaction. However, this picture is rapidly changing as researchers conduct inventive studies to illuminate the liabilities and possibilities of narrative identity. For our present purposes, we note that individuals with mental illness in general story their lives as low on communion and agency themes. As we show in

Chapters 8–12, these broad themes also play out in how individuals narrate the costs of mental illness. In our analyses, we dive deeper into an array of subthemes and build a richer framework for understanding identity problems resulting from psychopathology.

Narrative Identity and Well-Being

Researchers have paid considerable attention to the question of how narrative identity may foster the good life.[30,31,94] We draw on this research here because it informed our life story analyses and our guide for narrative repair (see Chapters 8–15). A diversity of studies, reviewed by Jonathan Adler and colleagues, has explored how features of narrative identity relate to well-being.[31] There is sound evidence that individuals who narrate their lives with more themes of agency and communion fulfillment experience improved thriving. Importantly, narrative identity uniquely predicts well-being after considering other factors, such as personality traits. We exemplify these themes in the following excerpt from one of our participants with major depressive disorder. She storied her divorce and subsequent marriage to highlight both agency and communion:

> *I started noticing that there was also room for what I felt and what I wanted and what I thought [agency theme]. It has ... we have experienced a lot together, my husband and me. We are good at being with each other. One day, when the kids have moved out, I think we will be well. Like, we have had crises, major crises, but no more than we have been able to find our way back and find our feelings. I also feel ... when I think about it, if I had become ill when I was married to my ex-husband, I wouldn't have the support I get from my current husband [communion theme].*

Furthermore, individuals who describe important events elaborating on positive meaning, such as learning, growth and insight, tend to thrive.[94] Particularly powerful versions of positive meaning, redemption stories, are also linked to improved well-being.[30,152] As a mirror image of these results, individuals narrating events suffused with negative meaning experience less happiness. This is also the case for the dark twin of redemption, contamination stories. That is, individuals who story positive events with negative outcomes tend toward low well-being.[152] The implication of this strand of research is that while meaning may be preferable to chaos "narratives," not all meaning is equal. Tragedies may be a celebrated literary genre but living and telling tragedy stories are liabilities to the good life.

Finally, there is evidence that telling more coherent stories is beneficial. For example, Dana Baerger and Dan McAdams coded life stories for coherence.[153] This included whether individuals told the stories to orient the listener toward the background context, unfolded temporal and causal connections as well as an evaluative stance, and synthesized story elements into a larger whole. When analyzing their participants' responses, the researchers found that individuals who shared more coherent stories enjoyed higher life satisfaction and happiness.

Why would individuals who narrate their lives more coherently, emphasizing how events gave birth to learning, growth, and insight, and elaborating agency and communion themes, experience higher well-being? One possible explanation is that told stories shape lived stories. Consequently, individuals who tell such stories seek out experiences fostering happiness. For example, telling a story that embellishes agency themes may propel individuals toward persistence in self-chosen projects feeding aspects of well-being such as autonomy and environmental mastery. Furthermore, the subjective sense of meaning and purpose arising from coherent life stories that nest experiences of growing, mastery, and belonging is in itself an aspect of well-being. Bringing key scenes of intimacy to mind reevokes feelings of love and gratefulness, strong positive emotions that are part and parcel of well-being. Consequently, life stories can give rise to happiness as they configure both inner worlds of meaning and outer worlds of action.

However, it is also possible that individuals who live happy lives simply tell happy stories, and that narrative identity plays no role in shaping good outcomes. Rebutting this criticism, researchers underscore that life stories connected with well-being are not simply happy stories. Rather, they depict protagonists as learning from failure, overcoming difficulties.[152] Narrative identity as related to the good life is not only about joy, love, and enthusiasm, it is also about how difficult events are incorporated into the life story. What do we know about strategies for narrating negative events to preserve thriving?

As reviewed by Kate McLean and colleagues, studies suggest that narrating negative events may be especially crucial to well-being.[28] The reason for this is that negative events often challenge positive beliefs about the self, such as worth and ability. A quote from one of our participants illustrates how she narrates bullying as destroying her sense of worth: *"But it was mainly the bullying that dominated and then because I wasn't really Einstein either, I had difficulties remembering and getting things into my head .... It really dominated me, back then. It has probably affected the person I am today. Low self-worth.*" Consistent with the idea that storying negative events is central to thriving, scientists have shown that children who are raised by primary caregivers who scaffold expressive and explanatory stories of negative events experience higher well-being.[28] Tilmann Habermas provides a careful analysis of how narrating negative events serves to express and understand difficult emotions.[11] These ideas are consistent with the expressive writing paradigm developed by James Pennebaker and his group, who have shown beneficial effects of writing in emotionally expressive ways about traumatic events.[154,155] In general, this research indicates that narrating negative events and the associated difficult emotions to promote understanding while not undermining the value of the self is adaptive for well-being. The potentially adverse effects of silencing touched upon in Chapter 5 are in line with these ideas.

On the other hand, the traumatic events may be "overnarrated." Dorthe Berntsen and colleagues set out to study the potentially harmful effects of constructing traumatic events as central to narrative identity.[156] They developed a questionnaire to measure the centrality of traumatic events, including statements like the following: "This event is a reference point for how I understand myself and the world." Robust research demonstrates that individuals who agree with such statements suffer from more symptoms of psychopathology and lower well-being.[157] These findings parallel Arthur Frank's notion that illness may swallow identity.[121] That is, if trauma and illness become the core of narrative identity, leaving little space for other storylines, individuals suffer doubly. Not only are they victims of trauma and mental illness, they also define who they are.

These ideas provide pointers for how to employ narratives to counter negative effects of traumas. However, we note that researchers are still in the dark concerning many issues about narrating negative events and that we lack systematic studies of whether individuals with mental illness reap benefits of storying their traumas and illness. With these caveats in mind, the literature indicates that narrative exploration of both toxic consequences of suffering from mental illness as well as experiences leading to well-being may be fruitful for individuals with mental illness. Expanding a negative narrative identity focused on mental illness and trauma by braiding in other storylines may allow individuals to surface as protagonists with unique strengths and facilitate healing and growth. We provide practical guidance for how to support exploration of such alternative storylines in Chapter 15.

Studies of Subjective Consequences of Mental Illness and Sources of Well-Being

The researchers whose studies we reviewed above have mainly examined general patterns in how narratives relate to mental illness and well-being. In such quantitative studies, researchers formulate hypotheses about expected relationships between features of narrative identity, mental disorder, and well-being (e.g., "more coherent narratives are related to better well-being"). They then elicit narratives from participants and employ standard coding systems to assess the degree of coherence, meaning, or agency in each narrative. Highly trained coders assign each narrative a numerical score, for example 1, 2, 3, or 4 as a measure of coherence. Subsequently, researchers use statistical methods to relate these narrative numbers to measurements of well-being or mental illness. Critically, the general patterns discovered in such studies apply to broad groups of people; they may not hold for particular individuals. So, on a group level, individuals with schizophrenia tell less coherent stories compared to individuals with no known mental illness. However, some individuals living with schizophrenia may story their lives as or even more coherently than some individuals with no known mental disorder.

Research based on statistical testing of hypotheses is a strong method because it disciplines our data collection and analyses to reduce the risk of confirming strongly, but falsely, held convictions. This quantitative approach is less well-suited when the territory is unmapped because it depends on formulating hypotheses about expected relationships. When little is known, open-ended approaches that permit exploration and discovering the unexpected are called for. In our life story analyses, we employ a more open-ended approach to elucidate how individuals interpret identity consequences of their mental illness and identity-salient sources of well-being. Although we are the first to tackle these questions from a narrative identity perspective, other researchers have explored first-person perspectives on mental illness. Such studies do not necessarily embrace the assumption that narratives are vehicles for understanding the consequences of mental illness or pathways to a life worth living. Nevertheless, the insights emerging from such studies may inform our life story analyses. A systematic review of studies is beyond the scope of our book, but we present selected studies to provide comparisons for considering the generalizability of the themes emerging in our own life story analyses. We suggest that interested readers seek out supplementary reading.[158–161]

Stephen Lally's study of how mental disorder and hospitalization challenge self-understanding is particularly relevant for our purposes.[162] To illuminate this issue, he interviewed 60 individuals hospitalized with a variety of psychiatric disorders. He asked questions about their mental condition, focusing on how experiences had affected their self-understanding. From the analyses, he identified several phases of how mental illness affected participants' self-understanding. Although they would at first resist the identity of being mentally ill, over time they accepted it as a part of the self. This acceptance came with a sense of lost time and feeling unable to fulfill culturally prescribed developmental tasks such as marriage and education. As participants began to identify with other patients, they experienced alienation from their friends and family who carried on with their lives outside the hospital. Considering their work abilities reduced and receiving their diagnosis of severe mental illness comprised other negative milestones. Lally described a late stage of identity engulfment where "patients come to view themselves as mentally ill and see this as an all-encompassing, permanent view of the self" (p. 262), during which they mourn their lost selves. While clinicians perceive acceptance of illness as crucial to improvement, Lally's study indicates that some individuals may become as disabled by their tortured identities as by their symptoms.

Other interview studies have highlighted a range of costs experienced by individuals with mental illness,[163–165] including social costs (e.g., forced to give children up for adoption, social isolation, disrupted relationships, poorer sexual functioning, stereotyping); self-harm (e.g., drug abuse, suicide attempts); negative consequences for education and employment with the accompanying financial problems; despair over lost opportunities; loss of identity and self-esteem; worries about effects of medicine; loss of self-control and predictability. Nevertheless, Erin Michalak and colleagues found that although individuals with bipolar disorder mostly identified negative consequences, some also pointed to the positive impact of their illness, such as forging closer relationships.[165]

Expanding upon potentially helpful experiences, the themes emerging from these studies include tackling mental illness head on (e.g., taking the illness seriously, seeking knowledge about it, accepting it, learning self-management, and maintaining autonomy despite the need for support); socializing with peers; social support; establishing routines to create order in the chaos of illness and reduce uncertainty; exercise and caring for pets; as well as hope and optimism about the future. These themes foreshadow several of the answers to our two main questions concerning identity stories about consequences of mental illness and sources of thriving, and we revisit them in Chapters 8–12.

The Contribution of the Present Book

Researchers in life stories, mental illness, and well-being have generally examined broad agency and communion themes as well as positive meaning, and in this book, we provide more fine-grained analyses that specifically target what narrative identity reveals about the impact of the illness and sources of thriving. Studies of first-person perspectives on mental illness have elaborated on costs and how well-being may be achieved. However, these studies have not taken a narrative identity perspective and as such may have missed insights about costs and happiness that only become apparent as individuals reflect on their life stories and the identity conclusions they carry.

We elicited full life stories from our participants, while spotlighting the parts important to elucidating personal costs and well-being when living with mental illness. Our life story analyses, presented in Chapters 8–12, address these issues as we unfold themes emerging from our participants' narratives. At the same time, the literature on narrative, illness, and well-being reviewed in this chapter is ripe with insights that echo themes in our analyses. First, severe illness disrupts ongoing narratives leading to a sense of lost future, loss of former self, and loss of the "normal" life (we return to these themes in Chapter 10). Second, individuals with mental illness generally story their lives with lower agency and communion themes. These broad themes are similar to findings from previous qualitative studies targeting the personal impact of psychopathology, and they also emerge in the identity costs of mental illness identified in our analyses (see Chapters 8–12). Third, individuals enjoying higher well-being story events as bringing about insights, learning, and growth, and configure events as suffused with high communion and agency themes. These broad themes are consistent with prior qualitative studies and are recognizable in the more nuanced subthemes we identify in our life story analyses of well-being sources.

Our life story analyses both extend and found inspiration in ideas reviewed in this chapter. In Chapter 14, we synthesize our life story analyses with this literature to build a narrative identity framework for understanding mental illness and personal recovery. In Chapter 15, we propose a guide for narrative repair, which individuals can employ to cope with identity problems arising from mental illness and work toward well-being and personal recovery.

Summary

- Severe illness disrupts individuals' ongoing narratives, leading to a sense of lost former and future self, and creates chaos that needs storying to become comprehensible. The past is restoried to explain the current ill self.
- Narratives of illness can communicate suffering; both other ill individuals and healthcare professionals may benefit from these narratives.
- Some approaches to psychotherapy assume that narratives are at the root of effective therapy, with the implication that the primary goal of therapy is to facilitate adaptive stories.
- Researchers have demonstrated that individuals suffering from schizophrenia construct less coherent stories.
- Other studies have shown that individuals with a range of mental illnesses narrate their identities as low on themes of agency and communion.
- A negative narrative identity may comprise a vulnerability existing prior to psychiatric disturbance.
- In the present analyses, we focus on life stories after mental illness eruption, that is, how individuals create their narrative identities to reflect consequences of psychopathology and sources of well-being.
- Robust research shows that features of narrative identity are related to well-being, including coherence; positive meaning of learning, growing and insight; and themes of high communion and agency.
- Storying trauma provides a way to express and understand difficult emotions, but adverse effects may arise from narrating trauma and mental illness as a central defining quality of identity.
- Exploratory studies of first-person perspectives on mental illness have uncovered multiple negative consequences of living with mental illness as well as domains of well-being.

CHAPTER 7

How Did We Collect and Analyze the Life Stories?

In this chapter, we share an overview of how we collected the life stories from our 118 participants and how we analyzed the stories to answer our two main questions. Readers less interested in the mechanics of science may find the chapter a little dry and prefer to consult the summary at the end, while those who wish to learn more details may consult Appendices 4–6. Tine Holm, Majse Lind, Rikke Amalie Agergaard Jensen, and Anne Mai Pedersen collected the narratives as a part of their PhD projects, therefore we present each project including the main results as background for the present analyses. The brief descriptions do not do justice to the massive work involved in collecting the stories or the goodwill our participants extended to us in sharing their traumas, illness memories, happy moments, and dreams during the hours-long interviews. These stories are the true center of gravity in the book.

Tine Holm's Project on Life Stories in Individuals with Schizophrenia

Tine Holm was the first in our group who set out to study life stories in individuals with psychopathology. Based on the literature reviewed in Chapter 6, Tine Holm decided to examine whether individuals with schizophrenia displayed difficulties in crafting life stories. To this aim, she interviewed 25 individuals with schizophrenia and 25 individuals with no known psychiatric illness (the control group). During the interviews, she asked participants to tell their life stories, allowing approximately 15 minutes. She then invited participants to outline chapters in their life stories and answer questions about different qualities of the chapters. Finally, she elicited up to three self-defining memories from participants. To assess whether the participants with schizophrenia showed cognitive deficits that might explain potential difficulties with constructing life stories, she tested all participants on cognitive functions and found that the two groups did not differ (see Table 7.1). She found that while participants with schizophrenia had as much chronological order in their chapters as the control group, they self-reported their chapters as more negative.[36] She also compared the open-ended life stories from the two groups and showed that the narratives of individuals with schizophrenia were dominated by themes of low agency and communion. However, she found little evidence that they struggled to tell their life stories chronologically.[35] Finally, Tine Holm demonstrated a dearth of self-defining memories in the time following psychiatric diagnosis,[34] consistent with first-person reports that mental illness goes hand in hand with a loss of self (see Chapters 1 and 6).

Majse Lind's Project on Life Stories in Individuals with Borderline Personality Disorder

The idea that less adaptive mentalization is at the root of borderline personality disorder[65] (see Chapter 3) inspired Majse Lind's project. She wondered whether mentalization problems would be apparent when individuals with borderline personality disorder told both personal and vicarious life stories. To answer this question, she interviewed 30 persons initiating psychotherapy for borderline personality disorder and 30 persons with no serious mental illness. She asked participants to describe up to 10 chapters in their personal life stories and answer questions about emotional tone and meaning while orally elaborating on their answers. Then she invited them to engage in a similar vicarious life story task, describing the life of a parent (see Table 7.1). Majse Lind discovered that individuals with borderline personality disorder rated both their personal and their vicarious life stories as more negative and with more negative meaning than the control group.[40] Contrary to expectations, the clinical group did not evidence less complex meaning in their personal life stories. However, the themes in both their personal and vicarious life stories revealed low agency and communion fulfillment. She further confirmed that her participants with borderline personality disorder struggled with aspects of mentalization, displaying difficulties with emotions and empathy as well as identity disturbance.

Majse Lind decided to examine whether the life stories would change as a result of psychotherapy. Thus, she interviewed most of her participants one year later and found that individuals with borderline personality disorder now constructed their personal life stories with more themes of agency.[39] The general take-home point is that narrative identity is more

Table 7.1 *Overview of samples and methods in the four projects*

	Sample size and demographics	Diagnoses central to study	Comorbid diagnoses	Symptom levels	Functional level and psychological measures	Life story measures
Tine Holm's project	24 outpatients; 11 women; mean age = 36 years; mean years of education = 16; most received disability benefits; most lived alone.	ICD-10 diagnoses of schizophrenia (21) or schizoaffective disorder (3).	Not checked.	Pp were assessed on positive and negative symptoms and displayed low to moderate symptom levels. Pp had higher self-reported depression and anxiety symptoms compared to the control group indicating low to moderate symptom levels.	The pp with schizophrenia did not differ from the control group on measures of neurocognition.	Oral life story on past lasting approx. 15 minutes; up to 10 past chapters (not included in present analyses); up to 3 self-defining memories with follow-up questions on emotional and identity features.
Majse Lind's project	30 outpatients; 28 women; mean age = 30 years; 23% had terminated education after elementary school, the remaining had completed high school and/or other further education.	DSM-IV diagnoses of borderline personality disorder.	Comorbid personality disorders, including antisocial, histrionic, obsessive-compulsive, avoidant, and dependent.	Pp scored higher than the control group on self-reported depression symptoms indicating low to moderate symptom levels.	Pp scored higher than the control group on alexithymia, and identity disturbance, but lower on empathy. No group difference on emotional intelligence.	Pp asked to orally describe up to 10 chapters in past life story and follow-up questions concerning emotional tone and influence of chapter on self.
Rikke Amalie Agergaard Jensen's project	20 outpatients with schizophrenia spectrum disorders; 14 women; mean age = 31 years; mean years of education = 13. 20 in- or outpatients with major depressive disorder (one with	ICD-10 diagnoses of schizophrenia (17) or schizoaffective disorder (3) or major depressive disorder (19) or bipolar disorder, depressive episode (1).	Not checked.	Pp with schizophrenia were assessed on positive and negative symptoms and displayed low symptom levels. Pp with major depressive disorder were assessed on	Pp were assessed on psychosocial function and scored lower than the control group, indicating manifest difficulties in functional level. The pp with	Pp asked to orally describe up to 5 past and 5 future chapters in life story; follow-up questions concerning emotional tone, whether chapter

Table 7.1 (cont.)

	Sample size and demographics	Diagnoses central to study	Comorbid diagnoses	Symptom levels	Functional level and psychological measures	Life story measures
	bipolar disorder); 12 women; mean age = 33 years; mean years of education = 13.			depressive symptoms and displayed moderate to severe symptom levels. Both groups had higher self-reported depression and anxiety symptoms compared to the control group, but pp with major depressive disorder scored higher than pp with schizophrenia.	schizophrenia did not differ from the control group on measures of neurocognition; the pp with major depressive disorder scored lower than the control group on 2 of 5 measures.	illustrates self, and influence of chapter on self.
Anne Mai Pedersen's project	24 clinically remitted outpatients; 23 women; mean age = 33 years; mean years of education = 15.	ICD-10 diagnoses of bipolar disorder, but no current affective episode.	Systematic information on co-morbidity not available on full sample.	Pp self-reported symptoms of mania and major depressive disorder and all scored below clinical threshold, except for two whose scores indicated mild to moderate depression.	Individuals with bipolar disorder reported lower levels of subjective well-being compared to the control group.	Pp completed questionnaires where they were asked to describe up to 10 chapters in their past life story and 10 chapters in their future life story; follow-up questions concerning emotional tone, whether chapter illustrates self, and influence of chapter on self.

Note that pp refers to participants and that for Tine Holm's project we list the 24 pp who provided material for our analyses (one pp was lost due to technical difficulties).

negative, less agentic, and less communal in borderline personality disorder and that growth in agency themes may be involved in regaining psychological health.

Rikke Amalie Agergaard Jensen's Project on Life Stories in Individuals with Schizophrenia and Major Depressive Disorder

Based on Tine Holm's and Majse Lind's findings, it was starting to dawn on us that relations between schizophrenia, borderline personality disorder, and narrative identity may not be disorder specific. Taking this one step further, Rikke Amalie Agergaard Jensen designed her study to directly compare two groups with different mental disorders: schizophrenia and major depressive disorder. She also thought that examining future extensions of life stories was crucial to richer insights into narrative identity and psychopathology. Zeroing in on these questions, she interviewed 20 individuals with schizophrenia, 20 individuals with major depressive disorder, and 20 individuals with no known psychiatric disorder. Each participant described up to five past and five future chapters in their life stories. For each chapter, they answered questions about emotional tone and meaning while elaborating their answers orally. In addition, Rikke Amalie Agergaard Jensen assessed cognitive function and depressive symptoms (see Table 7.1). As expected, she found that compared to the control group, the two groups with mental disorders rated the content and meaning of their past chapters as more negative.[37] When she examined themes, the two clinical groups had in common that past chapters were lower on agency and communion.[38] In short, the past was storied as bleak. Surprisingly, the pattern was different for future chapters. While a few individuals saw no chapters in their future, those individuals with psychopathology who did project themselves forward in time described chapters no less positive, agentic, and communal than the control group. Rikke Amalie Agergaard Jensen speculated that crafting future narrative identities to reflect positively on the self could be one path toward hope and personal recovery.[37,38]

Anne Mai Pedersen's Project on Life Stories in Individuals with Bipolar Disorder

In parallel with Rikke Amalie Agergaard Jensen's research, Anne Mai Pedersen reasoned that toxic life stories could explain why individuals suffering from bipolar disorder experience poorer well-being even during the calmer periods between affective episodes. Consequently, she designed a questionnaire, which instructed participants to describe up to 10 past and 10 future chapters and answer questions about emotional tone and meaning for each chapter. Furthermore, the questionnaire included measures of well-being. In close collaboration with clinical psychologist Krista Nielsen Straarup, Anne Mai Pedersen recruited 15 women with bipolar disorder and 15 women with no known psychiatric illness to complete the questionnaire (see Table 7.1). Echoing Rikke Amalie Agergaard Jensen's results, she found that participants with bipolar disorder wrote about past chapters with more negative content and meaning as well as themes of unfulfilled agency and communion needs.[41,42] Against expectations, but consistent with Rikke Amalie Agergaard Jensen's study, the future chapters described by individuals with bipolar disorder did not differ from the nonclinical group on positive tone or agentic and communal themes. However, participants with bipolar disorder viewed this hoped-for future as less probable than the comparison group. A few were even unable to craft chapters for their future. Finally, the group with bipolar disorder reported lower well-being and this was related to their more negative narrative identity. An ongoing study examines whether life stories told by individuals with bipolar disorder differ from those shared by individuals with chronic somatic illness. For the analyses in this book, we harvested the life stories of the first nine participants recruited for this project.

Analyzing Life Stories to Illuminate Consequences of Psychopathology and Sources of Well-Being

The participants in the four projects shared their life stories in different formats (past versus future, chapters versus self-defining memories versus free format life stories, written versus oral). Obviously, these method differences may affect what we can uncover in the life stories about consequences of psychopathology and sources of well-being. Still, we collapse all life stories in the analyses. When we analyze and discuss the life stories in the next chapters, we weight our conclusions relative to how consistently answers emerge across the four projects. Additionally, we keep method differences in mind when interpreting the results. For now, it is helpful to hold on to the overall robust pattern across the four projects. The life stories shared by our participants were in general coherent and elaborated, although there were exceptions. They revealed narrative identities with a past revolving around diminished mastery and self-determination along with interpersonal strife and isolation. Despite this bleak past, the participants who could imagine their future constructed happier prospective chapters. Still, participants felt uncertain about their possibilities for reaching this desired future. This picture is relevant as a background for the analyses presented in the next chapters.

To analyze the life stories for answers to the questions we pose in this book, we developed our own coding manual and procedure. During this phase, we were inspired by Steinar Kvale's engaging discussion of methodology in his influential book *Interviews*.[166] Following his lead, we first clarify our standpoint with respect to underlying assumptions about the nature of knowledge (epistemology). Because our two research questions concern how individuals with mental illness narrate the costs of their disorders and events fostering well-being, we adopt a phenomenological stance in analyzing the life stories. That is, our main goal is to discover themes in narrative identity, not to engage in interpretations uncovering unconscious motives or intricate language games. Although our stance is phenomenological, we also adopt assumptions from constructivist thinking that are part and parcel of narrative identity research, especially the notion that verbal thought and social sharing bring culturally bound categories and master narratives into play.[28,104] As argued in Chapter 5, narrative is an essential medium of knowledge, which is particularly suitable to cast light on subjective experience.[9,10] From our perspective, the verbal narratives we elicit in the interviews are grounded in lived narrative, the stories individuals tell in their minds and act in daily life. We assume that language is an inherent aspect of lived narratives as individuals verbally reflect on their ongoing stories. At the same time, the life story telling that our participants engaged in during the studies may bring new meanings[104] (as reviewed in Chapter 5). From a hermeneutic perspective, we adopt the idea that interpretation is at the core of understanding human endeavors. However, we are not interested in surfacing meanings hidden to our participants. Rather, individuals' *own* interpretations are at the heart of this project, although the themes and identity conclusions we develop also reflect our analyses of the stories. As such, many of our assumptions align with Jonathan Smith's interpretative phenomenological analysis,[167] although we employ an explicit narrative perspective on experience and meaning. Further discussions concerning the relation of our assumptions and analyses to other qualitative approaches are beyond the scope of the book.

More concretely, we analyze the life stories to extract common themes in how our participants narrated identity-salient consequences and sources of well-being. Identifying such themes allows insights into storylines that are frequent across individuals. Readers of this book can use this knowledge of common themes to assist their identification of subjective consequences and well-being experiences in the stories they tell and listen to. Borrowing Arthur Frank's term, the themes constitute listening devices, helpful to focus attention and make sense of stories.[121] At the same time, it is important to note that individuals may share stories that do not fit into these common themes and that infrequent meanings likewise yield valuable lessons about the perceived costs of psychopathology and pathways to thriving. In short, readers should bear in mind that our themes do not capture the whole picture.

Our analyses contain two parts. In the first part, we aim to provide an overview of how frequent different themes are with respect to how our participants interpreted the impact of their mental illness and sources of well-being when constructing their narrative identities. In Chapter 8, we summarize these analyses. In the second part, we identify subthemes nested within themes and organize these into four superordinate themes: relationships, self, functional level, and treatment (Chapters 9–12). Here the uniqueness of each story will shine clearly through the examples we provide.

The Coding Manual and Procedure

In this section, we present a summary of how we analyzed the life stories. Readers who prefer a more detailed account may read Appendix 5 instead. The analyses contained five steps (see Figure 7.1 for an overview).

In step 1, we engaged in open reading of the life stories to discover themes concerning personal impact and sources of well-being, focusing on all life story parts that included 1) negative consequences of mental illness, 2) positive consequences of mental illness, and 3) experiences associated with well-being, meaning, and value.

In step 2, we discussed these themes in the group, checked the themes by coding life stories, and further adapted them into our coding manual containing 28 common themes (see Table 7.2).

In step 3, we coded all life stories according to the manual (see Appendix 6), marking all relevant segments in each life story, and counting how many participants showed evidence of each theme. The themes were not mutually exclusive. If a participant shared a story revealing several themes, we coded them all. For example, the following life story segment was coded with both education and positive memories as sources of well-being, since the educational success in itself brought positive feelings and because she actively used the memory of this success to restore self-worth:

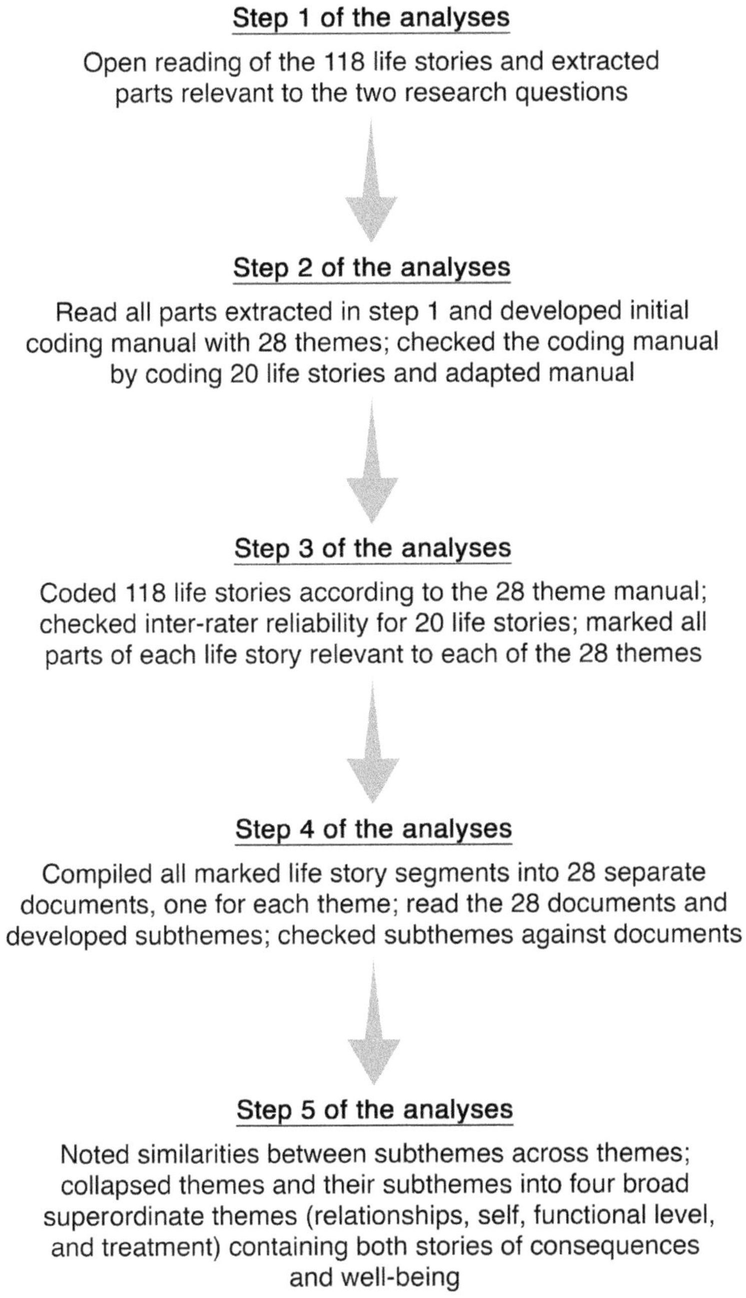

The Coding Manual and Procedure

Step 1 of the analyses

Open reading of the 118 life stories and extracted parts relevant to the two research questions

Step 2 of the analyses

Read all parts extracted in step 1 and developed initial coding manual with 28 themes; checked the coding manual by coding 20 life stories and adapted manual

Step 3 of the analyses

Coded 118 life stories according to the 28 theme manual; checked inter-rater reliability for 20 life stories; marked all parts of each life story relevant to each of the 28 themes

Step 4 of the analyses

Compiled all marked life story segments into 28 separate documents, one for each theme; read the 28 documents and developed subthemes; checked subthemes against documents

Step 5 of the analyses

Noted similarities between subthemes across themes; collapsed themes and their subthemes into four broad superordinate themes (relationships, self, functional level, and treatment) containing both stories of consequences and well-being

Figure 7.1   Overview of the analyses

Table 7.2 *Themes extracted under each of the three focus areas*

Negative consequences	Positive consequences	Sources of well-being
Work	Insights about self	Work
Education	Showing strength	Education
Social relations	Improved self-care	Social relations
Stigmatization	New social relationships	Others with psychopathology
Treatment	Caring for others	Treatment
Self and identity	Other	Personal qualities
Loss of positive states		Positive memories
The bleak, uncertain future		Goals and dreams
Cognitive functions		Leisure activities
Everyday functions		Living space
Other		Other

Note that "Other" comprises descriptions not codable under any of the other themes.

> *So I am pretty happy about my four A grades because then I can't be that stupid. When my voices say: "You are no good, you can't get anything right, you are stupid and lazy, no one has any use for you, and you should kill yourself because the world would be a better place without you." Then I can simply say, well I did get my four As and I also have other good grades.*

These three steps comprised the initial part of our analyses with the purpose of providing an overview of how frequently our participants narrated different consequences and well-being experiences into their identity (see Chapter 8). After conducting this initial analysis, we realized that we could paint a more nuanced and richer picture by in-depth analyses distilling subthemes. Hence, we continued the analyses in two more steps.

In step 4, we started out by creating 28 separate documents, one for each theme. These documents consisted of all life story segments marked as a part of step 3 (one document for negative consequences for social relations, one document for leisure activities as a source of well-being, etc.). We then analyzed the 28 documents for subthemes. Returning to the example above, where one of our participants used her positive memories of educational success to counter her negative voices, this illustrates at least three subthemes: 1) self as agentic (she actively uses her memories of educational success to regain self-esteem), 2) self as valued (she values herself as an academic achiever), and 3) education and work as fostering well-being through the self (education constitutes the context for the emergence of this valued and agentic self).

Finally, in step 5, we noted relationships between subthemes across themes and collapsed these into four superordinate themes: relationships, self, functional level, and treatment. For example, the subtheme of being different/not "normal" arose across the themes of negative consequences to self, loss of positive states, and goals and dreams (see Table 7.3 for an overview of superordinate themes, themes, and subthemes). We decided that there was a useful message in presenting stories of consequences and well-being together within the same superordinate theme, showcasing contrasting stories. We present these in-depth analyses of subthemes and their associated identity conclusions in Chapters 9–12. We provide illustrative examples to allow readers to evaluate the validity of our subthemes and to offer vicarious stories of mental illness for readers to learn from. When selecting quotes, we preferred examples that were elaborate, yet representative of the subtheme. We attempted to present quotes from as many participants as possible, including participants from all four studies and of all genders. We translated quotes from Danish to English and edited them slightly to improve readability. This included deleting some repetitions and filler words that are part and parcel of speech, but not written language. We strove to keep the quotes close to our participants' voices, and hence their tone differs from our written academic language.

The Limits of the Analyses

There are features of the method that limit the conclusions and here we discuss the most central. We note briefly that most of our participants were women, reflecting the gender distribution within the diagnoses of our participants as well as women generally volunteering more often for life story studies. Although we analyzed the life stories of 30 men, the pattern of results may apply more to women. The participants may also differ in other ways from the broader population of individuals with mental illness, with the implication that results may be less relevant to some groups.

Table 7.3 *Superordinate themes, themes, and subthemes in narrative identity*

Superordinate themes	Themes	Subthemes
Relationships	Negative 1) Social relations 2) Stigmatization Positive 3) New social relationships 4) Caring for others Well-being 5) Social relations 6) Others with psychopathology	Negative 1) Relationship strain 2) Lack of understanding and stigmatization 3) Relationship rupture 4) Withdrawal and loneliness Positive 5) Positive social consequences Well-being 6) Receiving help and support 7) Gaining self-worth from relationships 8) Acceptance and understanding 9) Togetherness 10) Safety and stability 11) Love 12) Giving to others
Self	Negative 1) Self and identity 2) Loss of positive states 3) The bleak uncertain future Positive 4) Insights about the self 5) Showing strength 6) Improved self-care Well-being 7) Personal qualities 8) Positive memories 9) Goals and dreams	Negative 1) The ill self 2) Loss of previous self 3) The negative self 4) The self as different 5) The bleak, uncertain future self Positive 6) The positively changing self Well-being 7) The valued self 8) The accepting self 9) The agentic self 10) The growing self 11) The dreaming self
Functional level	Negative 1) Work 2) Education 3) Cognitive functions 4) Everyday functions Well-being 5) Work 6) Education 7) Leisure activities 8) Living space	Negative 1) Struggles with education and work 2) Loss of basic everyday life and cognitive functioning Well-being 3) Education and work as fostering well-being through self 4) Education and work as fostering well-being through relationships 5) Well-being through leisure activities 6) Well-being through living space

Table 7.3 (cont.)

Superordinate themes	Themes	Subthemes
Treatment	Negative 1) Treatment Well-being 2) Treatment	Negative 1) Unclear and negative diagnoses 2) Inadequate access to needed help 3) Negative aspects of treatment Well-being 4) Diagnosis as helpful 5) The growing and agentic self in treatment 6) Beneficial relationships in treatment

Note: Headings indicate negative consequences of mental illness (Negative), positive consequences of mental illness (Positive), and sources of well-being (Well-being).

Here, we mention two characteristics of the participants that we think may have shaped the themes extracted in the analyses.

First, as in much psychiatric research, the participants likely represent relatively well-functioning individuals with mental illness, since high functional level increases the likelihood of volunteering for studies and perhaps in particular studies as demanding as ours. This is supported by observations that the samples with schizophrenia performed relatively well on cognitive tests and were rated as well-functioning in one study[36,38] (see Table 7.1). Still, our participants suffered from severe mental illness as evidenced by massive hospitalizations and frequent suicidality. Nevertheless, the results may apply less well to individuals with severe mental illness displaying lower functional levels.

Second, all participants lived in Denmark and two cultural issues are worth highlighting due to their potential shaping of the results. The first issue concerns the extensive Danish welfare system,[168] including free university programs and health care, state-financed economical support during education and unemployment, and possibilities for flexible employment or early retirement (a type of disability benefits) due to mental illness. Compared to individuals living in countries with less extensive welfare systems, the Danish model could in principle buffer the negative consequences of mental illness, as long as welfare is offered without compromising individual needs. However, psychiatric health care in Denmark is presently severely underfinanced compared to somatic health care. Consequently, the potential beneficial effects of the Danish welfare system may be less pronounced than assumed at first glance. The other issue relates to the secularity of Danish culture.[169] Danes rarely participate in religious activities (except for transitional events such as marriage and funerals) and mostly consider themselves weak in faith. We suspect that life stories told by individuals from highly religious cultures may have included more themes colored by faith than we observed in our samples.

The method used to elicit life stories may naturally shape what participants share, as may the situational context of the interview,[28] which in this case was research interviews/questionnaires presented as examining life stories in individuals with mental illness. How can we know that the themes extracted from the life stories would also surface if the participants had shared their life stories in a different context, for example in an informal conversation with a friend or family member? The short answer is that we do not know. Variations in method and context may very well shape what individuals share as consequences of psychopathology and what they story as central to thriving. However, we do believe that our method has advantages that allow individuals to share a broad range of experiences. The participants told their life stories in open formats. While they were asked to describe their life stories as chapters in three of the studies, thus scaffolding a certain structure, the participants determined the content of the chapters. In two of the studies, we prompted participants to elaborate on the positive and negative consequences of their chapters and on future chapters, which likely facilitated reflections central to our research question concerning consequences of their mental illness and well-being sources, but with no leading questions concerning specific themes. Consequently, we assume that the material shared by our participants reflect what they felt was important to their life stories and who they are.

A final limitation concerns the analyses of life stories. We have already mentioned some of these above as a part of describing the analyses. However, our influence on the data analyses begins when we ask our two questions and identify themes. We had already content-coded the life stories for broad agency and communion themes (although these are not a part of the present analyses) and knew about research in the area. In fact, someone not familiar with our backgrounds may correctly deduce from the themes that we study identity, autobiographical memory, well-being, emotion, and future cognition. Clearly, we read the life stories with our own unique pair of glasses. However, others should still be able to discover similar themes when familiar with our coding procedure. To allow readers to check our analyses, we show representative and illustrative examples from the life stories.

In this chapter and the associated Appendices 4–6, we have put our methodological cards on the table. As much as we desire science to provide unambiguous answers, limitations are inherent to research. For all the reasons given above, readers need to carefully consider the analyses we present in the next chapters before jumping to conclusions about mental illness in general or one person in particular. However, the analyses provide insights that together with existing research and future studies illuminate how narrative identity suffers in the face of mental illness and how narrative identity may serve as a source of well-being.

Summary

- The life stories we analyze were collected in four different projects where participants were asked to describe their full life stories, past and future chapters in their life stories, and/or self-defining memories.
- We developed a coding manual by reading through all statements concerned with consequences of mental illness and well-being experiences.
- The coding manual contains 11 themes of negative consequences, 6 themes of positive consequences, and 11 themes of well-being experiences (see Table 7.2).
- We read the life stories and noted themes present for each individual.
- For each theme, we created documents with all relevant descriptions from our participants and extracted subthemes from these documents.
- Finally, we collapsed the themes and subthemes into four superordinate themes of relationships, self, functional level, and treatment.
- There are limitations to the present analyses, including that participants represent well-functioning individuals with mental illness who live in a nonreligious country with extensive welfare support. The implication is that the themes we present in our analyses may differ from how other groups would narrate their experiences.
- Additionally, the study context as well as our background probably influenced the themes we extracted.

CHAPTER 8

Overview of Narrative Identity Themes from the Initial Analyses

In this chapter, we provide an overview of our initial analyses including the frequency of identified narrative identity themes. We examine the personal consequences of mental illness incorporated into narrative identity. Next, we consider what the participants' stories reveal about identity-salient sources of well-being, meaning, and value. Our approach of combining life stories with thematic analyses of the segments relevant to our two research questions differs markedly from qualitative interview studies where participants are directly asked about consequences and well-being (see Chapter 6). When we collected the life stories, we did not directly target impact of psychopathology and sources of thriving. Rather, we simply asked participants to share their life stories and let them decide what they found important. Hence, the themes we identify in our analyses reflect what participants chose to elaborate on when they constructed their narrative identities. In other words, we elucidate the damage mental illness does to narrative identity and narrative identity as a resource for well-being and personal recovery.

Throughout we relate our discoveries to existing literature, drawing attention to broad similarities and divergences. We also point out differences in findings between diagnostic groups. In Chapters 9–12, we dive deeper into the stories, unfolding the subthemes as organized into the superordinate themes of relationships, self, functional level, and treatment.

Narrative Identity Themes: Negative Consequences of Mental Illness

When we invited our participants to freely tell their life stories, shedding light on how they construct their narrative identity, what negative consequences flowing from mental illness did they share? In Table 8.1, we display the subjective costs of mental illness. The first thing to notice is that the negative impact of psychopathology is pervasive. When storying their identities, our participants described their mental illness as causing

Table 8.1 *Percentages (frequencies) for negative consequences of mental illness from a narrative identity perspective*

Negative consequences	Total	Schizophrenia spectrum disorder[a]	Borderline personality disorder[b]	Schizophrenia spectrum disorder[c]	Major depressive disorder[c]	Bipolar disorder[d]
Social relations	60% (71)	42% (10)	60% (18)	70% (14)	75% (15)	58% (14)
Stigmatization	9% (11)	17% (4)	10% (3)	15% (3)	0% (0)	4% (1)
Self and identity	58% (69)	38% (9)	57% (17)	80% (16)	75% (15)	50% (12)
Loss of positive states	27% (32)	21% (5)	17% (5)	40% (8)	35% (7)	29% (7)
The bleak, uncertain future	43% (51)	21% (5)	20% (6)	65% (13)	65% (13)	58% (14)
Work	28% (33)	25% (6)	23% (7)	40% (8)	20% (4)	33% (8)
Education	36% (42)	29% (7)	30% (9)	40% (8)	10% (2)	67% (16)
Cognitive functions	15% (18)	13% (3)	0% (0)	25% (5)	20% (4)	25% (6)
Everyday functions	20% (24)	25% (6)	10% (3)	10% (2)	30% (6)	29% (7)
Treatment	50% (59)	79% (19)	43% (13)	60% (12)	15% (3)	50% (12)
Other	41% (48)	33% (8)	37% (11)	55% (11)	45% (9)	38% (9)

Note: Total and divided by study and diagnosis displayed in the following order: Studies led by Tine Holm,[a] Majse Lind,[b] Rikke Amalie Agergaard Jensen,[c] and Anne Mai Pedersen[d]. Note that "Other" comprises descriptions not codable under any of the other categories.

cascades of negative effects. They suffer not only from symptoms and functional impairment, but also from subjectively felt effects of psychopathology. These consequences are integral parts of their narrative identities, their sense of who they are, where they come from, and where they are going. The prominence of negative consequences apparent in their narrative identities aligns with insights from personal recovery approaches. A key task is recovering from the identity costs of illness that stand in the way of well-being.[5] Below, we expand on the types of negative effects our participants experienced and narrated as important to identity.

Our participants often portrayed the toxic impact of psychopathology within the superordinate theme of relationships (see Table 8.1). This echoes voices from the autobiographies that inspired the present book (see Chapter 1)[1,12–14] and the qualitative studies reviewed in Chapter 6.[162–165] Furthermore, when our participants story their mental illness as negatively influencing relationships this is in tune with survey findings, which show that psychopathology comes with a range of social costs (see Chapter 3).[17,71] Most important from the present point is that costs to relationships bear implications for narrative identity and we pull these to the forefront in Chapter 9. It is surprising that so few of our participants shared experiences of stigmatization (9 percent). However, recall that individuals construct life stories by selecting some experiences as important to identity, whereas other events are de-emphasized. Possibly the narratives gravitated toward other damaging social experiences. Furthermore, stigmatization (and self-stigmatization) are not terms often employed in everyday speech, and in our coding, we strove to be true to the phenomenological approach and stayed close to the wording of our participants. Hence, some negative consequences may reflect stigmatization, although our participants did not explicitly describe their experiences in ways that allowed us to code them as such.

The high proportion of participants who storied mental illness as toxic within the superordinate theme of self (see Table 8.1) generally parallels the empirical findings on narrative identity and psychopathology, other qualitative studies (see Chapter 6),[141,148,162] and the autobiographies quoted in Chapter 1.[1,12–14] When our participants crafted their stories, they often included negative self-views, bleak and uncertain futures, as well as loss of positive states. Our participants told tales of lost hopes and dreams, the unreachable "normal life," and a future threatened by reoccurrence and functional decline. What is remarkable is the prominence of these themes. This points to the massive impact of psychopathology on narrative identity. Our methodology probably partly explains the pervasiveness of these themes. Exemplifying the influence of method, the participants in Rikke Amalie Agergaard Jensen's and Anne Mai Pedersen's studies were asked directly to narrate future chapters and naturally shared more reflections on their projected future stories than Tine Holm's and Majse Lind's participants, who did not receive this prompt (but still spontaneously included reflections on their future). In short, the questions we asked shaped life story construction and hence the themes growing out of our analyses.

Our participants narrated their illness as causing problems within the superordinate theme of functional level, often including work and school (see Table 8.1). This resonates with other qualitative studies where individuals describe their psychiatric disturbance as interfering with educational achievement and job performance as well as quantitative studies demonstrating negative impact on vocation and education (see Chapters 3 and 6).[17,71,163,165] Some of our participants also told stories revolving around functional impairments in basic everyday tasks and cognitive abilities. In Chapter 11, we elaborate on the identity meanings our participants ascribed to these functional losses.

Half of our participants storied negative consequences from treatment of their illness (see Table 8.1). This encompassed side effects of medicine, the shock of being hospitalized and diagnosed, and problematic interactions with healthcare staff. It is perhaps not surprising to professionals that stories of adverse treatment surface in our analyses. However, it is worth pausing to consider the full implications. The suffering of individuals with mental illness is not limited to frightening symptoms, functional losses, relationship strain, and damage to selfhood. When they seek treatment, it comes with a high price for many of them, which may help explain why some are ambivalent, critical, and noncooperative in treatment. It is important to note, however, that just as many participants shared stories of treatment as a source of well-being. We elaborate on this in the next section.

Finally, many participants narrated toxic consequences of their illness not captured by the coding system we initially developed. We do not elaborate further on these stories, but not because they are insignificant. Rather, the choice reflects our limited possibility of exploring themes shared by fewer participants. To provide readers with a taste of this, we notice that several stories concerned how mental illness led to suicidal behavior. In addition, our participants narrated self-harm, drug abuse, violence, financial losses, and weight changes as negative consequences of their illness. Finally, some participants shared reflections about the devastating impact of their psychiatric disturbance in the language of broad negative identity conclusions such as "*a complete failure*" and "*my life is one big mess.*"

Generally, participants diagnosed with different psychiatric disturbances did not differ greatly in how they storied the costs of their illness and made it a part of their identity. Since we coded personal consequences in relation to all mental illnesses mentioned in the life stories (e.g., we coded the negative consequences of major depressive disorder that a participant with borderline personality disorder had experienced earlier in her life), the study is not well-suited to locate disorder-specific costs. The upshot is that there may be disorder-unique consequences even though these were not apparent in our data.

There were some group differences, which we believe reflect a mix of method variance between studies and potential diagnostic divergences. We have already mentioned that the study methods probably explain group differences in how often participants elaborated costs for their projected future narrative identity. We also think that method differences were the reason why fewer of Tine Holm's participants with schizophrenia narrated their illness as impacting self and identity. In the other three studies, we explicitly asked participants to answer questions about how chapters reflected on their self, whereas this was not the case in Tine Holm's study. Consistent with the idea that social context shapes narratives,[28] our participants probably composed their stories with reference to study prompts. On the other hand, some group differences may reflect disorder-specific costs. This could be the case for the absence of costs to cognitive functioning in participants with borderline personality disorder as well as the few negative consequences with education and treatment themes shared by participants with major depressive disorder. These are questions to pursue in future research. Most noteworthy are the similarities across diagnoses, indicating that many individuals with a range of psychiatric disorders struggle with identity problems emerging directly from their illness or indirectly through the illness's impact on relationships, education, and vocation, as well as from treatment.

Narrative Identity Themes: Positive Consequences of Mental Illness

Our participants were much less likely to narrate positive consequences of their illness. As we show in Table 8.2, the percentages for these themes were substantially lower than the percentages for most negative consequences. This aligns with the autobiographies we were inspired by where we also observed that silver linings were rare (Chapter 1).[1,12–14]

Table 8.2 Percentages (frequencies) for positive consequences of mental illness from a narrative identity perspective

Positive consequences	Total	Schizophrenia spectrum disorder[a]	Borderline personality disorder[b]	Schizophrenia spectrum disorder[c]	Major depressive disorder[c]	Bipolar disorder[d]
Insights about self	27% (32)	8% (2)	23% (7)	50% (10)	45% (9)	17% (4)
Showing strength	8% (10)	8% (2)	10% (3)	0% (0)	20% (4)	4% (1)
Improved self-care	13% (15)	0% (0)	13% (4)	15% (3)	35% (7)	4% (1)
New social relationships	3% (3)	4% (1)	3% (1)	0% (0)	5% (1)	0% (0)
Caring for others	8% (10)	8% (2)	3% (1)	25% (5)	10% (2)	0% (0)
Other	3% (4)	0% (0)	10% (3)	5% (1)	0% (0)	0% (0)

Note: Total and by study displayed in the following order: Studies led by Tine Holm,[a] Majse Lind,[b] Rikke Amalie Agergaard Jensen,[c] and Anne Mai Pedersen[d]. Note that "Other" comprises descriptions not codable under any of the other categories.

Additionally, the gap between positive and negative consequences mirrors the study by Erin Michalak, who demonstrated that while some participants alluded to positive effects of their illness, negative impacts dominated.[165] This implies that individuals with mental illness working to gain well-being could concentrate storying on other domains of life, as the costs of mental illness likely outweigh positive consequences. We stress this point because a naïve reading of the narrative literature invites the idea that mental illness can be restoried as redemptive. Relatedly, the concept of personal recovery advocated by Retta Andresen and colleagues comprises a sense of having grown from the experience.[3] While it is possible that redeeming mental illness can benefit some individuals, we caution against it as a general strategy,[30] especially early in the illness course. The sharp imbalance between negative and positive consequences signals that strong redemption stories may fit experience poorly. That is, insisting on a story where the suffering ends in pure happiness and growth is not beneficial if it clashes with circumstances in the individual's life. Such discrepancies between experiences and told stories may signal a lack of insight and acceptance, paving the way for imagining unrealistic future stories. Rather, we suggest that sources of well-being are more easily discovered and storied into identity through highlighting relationships, achievements, and leisure activities, while interpreting their significance for personal strengths and resources. A useful metaphor may be that individuals can benefit from painting a picture where mental illness (silver linings or not) is just one figure among many other brighter motifs. We give practical guidance toward this aim in Chapter 15.

Although positive consequences were scarcer, a substantial proportion of our participants interpreted their mental illness as yielding insights about themselves (see Table 8.2). To a lesser extent, participants talked about becoming better at caring for themselves and showing strength in mastering their illness. Finally, a few of our participants shared reflections about gaining compassion for others in difficult life circumstances and new social relationships as a result of their psychiatric disturbance. The interpretations of beneficial effects flowing from mental illness resonate with research on positive meaning reviewed in Chapter 6.[31,94]

The positive outcomes are similar to those established in studies of benefit-finding[170] and post-traumatic growth.[171] Both concepts refer to perceiving positive sequels to difficult life events, ranging from illness and abuse to accidents and natural disasters. As such, benefit-finding and post-traumatic growth overlap with redemption stories in their similar negative-to-positive structure.[152] Researchers have discovered that individuals often find benefits or experience growth as improved self-understanding, gaining strength, and deeper social relationships.[172] Clearly, some of our participants story the positive impact of their illness mirroring these general strategies for interpreting negative life events. One possible explanation is that redemption master narratives mold storying of diverse negative life events, including mental illness.[127] Still, since relatively few of our participants narrated their disorder as leading to positive outcomes, we suggest that under the present cultural circumstances mental illness does not lend itself easily to redemption, although with time, the support of caring others, and successful treatment such positive meaning may surface. We also note that the lack of emphasis on positive outcomes may reflect a general scarcity of redemptive mental illness stories in our culture, possibly because fear of stigmatization prevents sharing personal stories of psychiatric disturbance and personal recovery.

The participants in Rikke Amalie Agergaard Jensen's study especially voiced beneficial outcomes, probably due to the interview prompts. For each chapter, she explicitly asked participants in an open-ended manner whether the chapter illustrated positive personal characteristics or had changed them in positive ways (she posed similar questions about negative characteristics and changes). Likely, these questions invited more reflections on potential valuable consequences of psychopathology. We return to the idea that open-ended questions can guide how individuals think about their life stories in Chapter 15, where we discuss narrative strategies for working toward well-being and personal recovery.

Narrative Identity Themes: Sources of Well-Being, Meaning, and Value

Our participants shared many moving and invigorating stories saturated with well-being, meaning, and value. As we display in Table 8.3, these originated from a range of domains. Several themes are mirror images of those for negative consequences. Accordingly, while mental illness may come with a steep price for narrative identity as it is constructed in the context of costs to relationships, education, and vocation as well as costs from treatment, individuals can recover well-being as they engage with their social worlds and construct more adaptive narrative identities.

The experiences our participants story into identity as bringing value, meaning, and well-being are not unique to mental illness. Massive research documents well-being benefits of supportive relationships, leisure activities, and education.[173–175] In short, our participants find thriving in

Table 8.3 *Percentages (frequencies) for sources of well-being from a narrative identity perspective*

Sources of well-being	Total	Schizophrenia spectrum disorder[a]	Borderline personality disorder[b]	Schizophrenia spectrum disorder[c]	Major depressive disorder[c]	Bipolar disorder[d]
Social relations	85% (100)	83% (20)	97% (29)	80% (16)	80% (16)	79% (19)
Others with psychopathology	11% (13)	13% (3)	7% (2)	35% (7)	0% (0)	4% (1)
Personal qualities	76% (90)	67% (16)	80% (24)	100% (20)	80% (16)	58% (14)
Positive memories	26% (31)	13% (3)	40% (12)	35% (7)	35% (7)	8% (2)
Goals and dreams	69% (82)	29% (7)	53% (16)	90% (18)	90% (18)	96% (23)
Work	40% (47)	38% (9)	43% (13)	50% (10)	30% (6)	38% (9)
Education	53% (63)	67% (16)	73% (22)	45% (9)	15% (3)	54% (13)
Leisure activities	45% (53)	54% (13)	40% (12)	40% (8)	45% (9)	46% (11)
Living space	15% (18)	17% (4)	13% (4)	25% (5)	10% (2)	13% (3)
Treatment	51% (60)	54% (13)	63% (19)	55% (11)	20% (4)	54% (13)
Other	13% (15)	13% (3)	17% (5)	20% (4)	10% (2)	4% (1)

Note: Total and divided by study displayed in the following order: Studies led by Tine Holm,[a] Majse Lind,[b] Rikke Amalie Agergaard Jensen,[c] and Anne Mai Pedersen[d]. Note that "Other" comprises descriptions not codable under any of the other categories.

well-known places. Central to the present analyses is that individuals with psychopathology bring these resources for thriving into their narrative identities with adaptive identity conclusions. We dive into these meanings in Chapters 9–12.

Relationships as a superordinate theme nested a multitude of well-being stories (Table 8.3). This parallels other qualitative studies showing that relationships serve a variety of adaptive functions (see Chapter 6).[163–165] While relationships to other individuals with psychopathology were narrated as facilitating thriving, fewer participants endorsed such relations as they constructed their narrative identities. This underscores that a wide array of relationships can foster the creation of narrative identities undergirding thriving when individuals live with mental illness. Personal recovery approaches spotlight relationships as crucial when they portray recovery as reconnecting with the social world and engaging in valued social roles.[3,5,86] To illuminate how relationships both help and hurt the narrative identities of individuals with mental illness, we provide detailed analyses of this contrast in Chapter 9.

While our analyses of costs show that mental illness may erode selfhood, steal hope and dreams, and lead to an uncertain subjective future, most of our participants simultaneously storied their personal characteristics, their subjective future, and, to a lesser extent, positive memories as parts of a good life (see Table 8.3). This highlights narrative identity, with its extension from the remembered past to the imagined future, as a potentially rich resource for facilitating happiness in individuals with mental illness. Developing a positive identity and gaining hope are at the heart of personal recovery[86] and, in Chapter 10, we showcase our participants' stories to elucidate the narrative identity processes involved.

Our participants often narrated the superordinate theme of functional level, including work, education, and leisure activities, with well-being and some of our participants emphasized the importance of living space (Table 8.3). Thus, while their life stories were ripe with costs stemming from vocation and education, these contexts concurrently hold promise for creating narrative identities that support thriving. We complement this insight with the observation that many of our participants storied events outside the culturally valued realms of education and vocation as fostering well-being, meaning, and value. That is, they shared richly detailed stories about how leisure activities such as creative projects, sports, and traveling fueled happiness. We highlight this because healthcare professionals, who are strongly engaged in their jobs and treasure education, may overlook leisure activities as sources of positive identity and thriving. The cultural life script comprises several socially celebrated education and vocation milestones, such as graduation and first job.[128] Some individuals with mental illness may for a time lose hold of these culturally dominant sources of value and meaning because their illness interferes with school and work attendance.[17] However, this need not rob them of opportunities for well-being, if they can discover other sources, such as leisure activities, and narrate them into identity in adaptive ways.

About half of our participants storied events related to treatment as contributing to well-being, value, and meaning (Table 8.3). The theme encompassed experiences from therapy, warm relationships with support persons and staff at psychiatric group homes, and being diagnosed. As this theme will be of particular interest to readers working in the healthcare system, we analyze treatment stories featuring well-being in Chapter 12, contrasting these with personal costs experienced as a part of treatment. Here we expand on how such positive and negative treatment experiences have implications for narrative identity.

Others mentioned sources of well-being that did not fit within the established themes. These included unique experiences that we will not discuss further.

Mirroring the picture for consequences of mental illness, we found few group differences. Still, the groups diverged within some themes. Probably due to the method differences we have already discussed, Rikke Amalie Agergaard Jensen's and Anne Mai Pedersen's participants more often disclosed goals and dreams as they were asked directly to describe future chapters in their life stories. There is also some indication that Majse Lind's and Rikke Jensen's participants more often narrated positive memories as bringing well-being in the present. This could reflect that they both gave interview prompts inviting participants to reflect on how past chapters affected them. Possibly indicating diagnostic differences, the participants with schizophrenia more often shared well-being stories about relations to other individuals with psychiatric disturbances. Finally, similar to diagnostic group differences in negative consequences for education and treatment, individuals with major depressive disorder less often narrated these domains as fostering well-being, value, and meaning. Because group differences were generally minor or likely due to methodology, we do not elaborate on these in the remaining chapters. Rather, we focus on similar sources of happiness in the narrative identities of individuals with different diagnoses.

The Next Chapters

The discovery that individuals with mental illness craft narrative identities that unfold multitudes of costs supplements diathesis-stress models and existing research into the burden of mental illness. To deepen this insight, we expand our simple model from Chapter 3 to illustrate often-narrated consequences of mental illness with their meaning and identity implications in the next chapters. This model complements those constructed by diathesis-stress researchers, who delineate the causes of psychopathology, focusing on trauma and vulnerability (see Chapter 3).[6,7,58,64]

While it is tempting to include narrative identity sources of thriving in the same model to provide a simpler picture, we decided against this. Our participants did not first story consequences of their illness and then move on to depict experiences fostering well-being. We could discern no final stage of eternal happiness and growth. Rather, interpretations of costs and stories of happiness interweaved. Consequently, a model implying that individuals construct their narrative identities with well-being occurring at some delimited stage, differentiated from personal costs, would be misleading. This picture fits severe mental illness as a recurring problem for identity that individuals need to cope with during periods of their lives. Hence, we develop our narrative identity models of well-being sources separately from our models of consequences for narrative identity. The models will comprise routes to happiness shared by our storytellers.

Before moving on, it may be helpful to retrace our steps. We started out by identifying two questions that have received little attention in mainstream research on mental illness: 1) What do life stories reveal about subjective consequences of suffering from mental illness? and 2) What do life stories reveal about experiences bringing well-being when living with mental illness? We argued that analyzing life stories would provide substantial answers, because this would reveal how individuals narrate their identity as affected by mental illness and identity-salient sources of well-being. As narrative identity is the compass individuals use to steer the course of their lives, the findings have broad implications for understanding what it is like to live with and recover from mental illness. In our initial analyses, presented in this chapter, we provided an overview of the frequency of themes concerning consequences (negative and positive) and well-being experiences. In the following chapters, we draw out subthemes identified in the second part of the analyses. Recall that our analyses provide answers at both the level of experience (what do individuals experience as costs and paths to well-being) and the level of identity (how do the costs of mental illness color identity and how is identity involved in thriving). We interpret how the subthemes implicate narrative identity as damaged by mental illness and as a resource for gaining well-being. Throughout we relate the subthemes to central concepts from earlier chapters.

In the next chapters, we present the subthemes within each of the four superordinate themes as identified in steps 4–5 of our analyses (see Table 7.3). In Chapter 9, we expand on the meaning of relationships in narrative identity, including how our participants storied costs to relationships and stigmatization, positive consequences for relationships, and relationships as sources of well-being. In Chapter 10, we travel further into selfhood, including harmful effects, the bleak and uncertain future, as well as loss of positive states. We contrast this with positive consequences for the self as well as stories of well-being featuring personal characteristics, positive memories, goals, and dreams. In Chapter 11, we explore functional level encompassing education, work, basic everyday tasks, and cognitive abilities, illuminating the negative identity meaning our participants construct from these functional losses. We contrast this with how they story well-being into their identities in the context of education and work, leisure activities, and living space. In Chapter 12, we conclude with analyses of how participants imbue healthcare experiences with both positive and negative meaning for their identity, depicting both the costs and well-being benefits flowing from psychiatric care.

The chapters give voice to our participants and we prioritize extended quotes from their life stories. Their tales expand the narrative ecology of mental illness, allowing us to witness both the suffering and the potential for a good life. Stories speak to the heart. Hence, while we systematically develop and present the subthemes as a part of the scientific endeavor of model building, we implore readers to let the stories sweep them away. Allow the stories shared by our participants to resonate with your own stories.

Summary

- Subjective negative consequences of mental illness as represented in narrative identity were pervasive.
- Many of our participants crafted narrative identities with themes reflecting costs of mental illness on relationships, self, and identity, as well as their subjective future.

- About half of our participants incorporated negative effects of treatment into their narrative identities and a substantial proportion shared themes of toxic impact on vocation, education, and everyday and cognitive functioning.
- Fewer participants constructed narrative identities where mental illness caused positive effects, but the most common affirmative interpretation was that the illness improved self-understanding.
- Our participants included a variety of well-being experiences in their narrative identities; the most prominent themes were relationships, personal characteristics, goals, and dreams.
- A substantial number of participants also shared well-being stories within the thematic categories of treatment, vocation, education, leisure activities, positive memories, and living space.
- There were few diagnostic group differences, and some of these are likely due to study methodology.
- In the next chapters, we elaborate on subthemes and identity implications, collapsing the themes into four superordinate ones: relationships, self, functional level, and treatment.

CHAPTER 9

Relationship Themes in Narrative Identity

In the present chapter, we elaborate on subthemes within the superordinate themes of relationships and the implicated identity conclusions, first with respect to the massive costs of psychopathology and the few positive consequences for relationships, and second with respect to how social bonds were storied with well-being, value, and meaning. We comment on subthemes emerging in several life stories and relate these to central concepts from Chapters 4–6, but we devote the majority of the chapter to quotes from participants who elaborated on a subtheme. The quotes are rich and often illustrate several subthemes, underscoring that they are not mutually exclusive. Rather, our participants constructed multiple identity meanings from each relationship experience.

Subthemes Concerning Negative and Positive Consequences for Relationships

Many of our 118 participants shared stories saturated with relationship losses. The toxic consequences emerged across bonds to parents, siblings, friends, romantic partners, and children as well as groups. When mining the narratives for the steep price our participants paid, we discerned four subthemes: relationship strain, lack of understanding and stigmatization, relationship rupture, and withdrawal and loneliness. These subthemes suggest that the low communion themes found in the life stories of individuals with psychopathology (reviewed in Chapter 6)[141,148] may stem partly from how they experience and interpret the impact of their illness. We expand on the subthemes below together with positive personal consequence of mental illness and provide an overview in Figure 9.1.

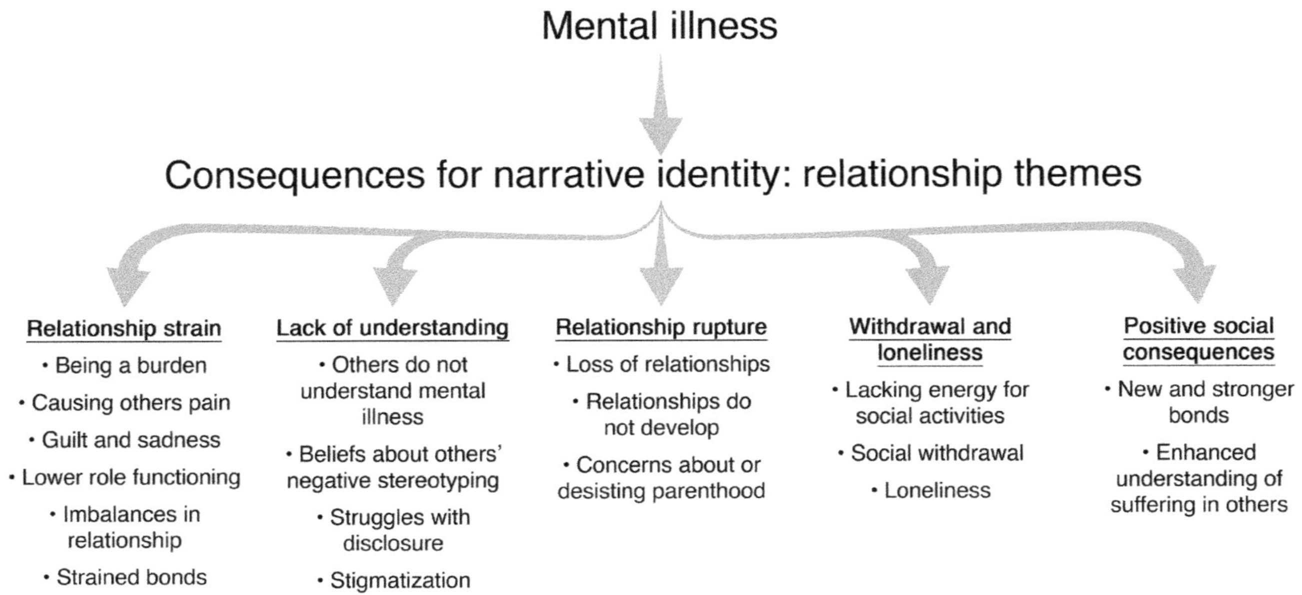

Consequences for narrative identity: relationship themes

Mental illness

Relationship strain
- Being a burden
- Causing others pain
- Guilt and sadness
- Lower role functioning
- Imbalances in relationship
- Strained bonds

Lack of understanding
- Others do not understand mental illness
- Beliefs about others' negative stereotyping
- Struggles with disclosure
- Stigmatization

Relationship rupture
- Loss of relationships
- Relationships do not develop
- Concerns about or desisting parenthood

Withdrawal and loneliness
- Lacking energy for social activities
- Social withdrawal
- Loneliness

Positive social consequences
- New and stronger bonds
- Enhanced understanding of suffering in others

Figure 9.1 Consequences of mental illness for narrative identity: relationship themes

Relationship Strain

Participants storied their mental illness as turning them into a burden for other people to bear, sometimes straining their social bonds. They disclosed how their disorders had caused close others deep pain, and they felt sad and guilty about the suffering their parents, siblings, friends, and partners underwent. Some described vivid scenes conveying this subtheme. One of our participants with schizophrenia who had multiple suicide attempts behind him, told us about escaping from the hospital to kill himself by stepping in front of a train:

> *I had actually planned when that train would come and so I laid down [on the rails] but then I didn't make it in time. I thought okay, fair enough, I'll lie here and sleep on the rails and wait for a morning train. But the police were looking for me, and my mother. I was found and brought back. I remember that I was . . . that I went to bed the morning after I had been out all night, where my mother snuck up in bed to me and just lay there embracing me. I also remember that she cried for the first time, you know, cried about something I had done. That was really hard . . . . . My close others, when I think about this period, when I think back, how important it is that they are offered some help. They have experienced some very ugly things with me, and I simply think that everyone struggling with a child or a close other, they should really be offered some help, because these experiences are also really traumatic for them. I think about parents watching their child close to dying many, many times, you know. My parents have thankfully coped really well.*

Participants narrated their mental illness as an obstacle to fulfilling their roles as parents, siblings, friends, and partners, leading to a sore conscience and imbalances in relationships. One participant struggled to complete education for several years and was then diagnosed with schizophrenia. He reflected:

> *All the other friends I have had during the other school periods, I don't talk to them at all. Not those from the residence hall either. It is difficult to keep in touch and stay focused. I think it has something to do with me feeling insufficient as a person and then it is difficult to manage friendships and keep them going and like . . . being there for them when it has been so difficult for me to keep control of myself. It has probably become such unequal friendships.*

A participant with bipolar disorder shared a chapter concerning imbalance in her romantic relationship. Before her diagnosis, she repeatedly experienced work-related stress and wondered why she could not manage as well as others:

> *Job and stress affected my private life so that I never had the energy to help out at home. My partner worked, did everything at home and cared for me during my illness . . . . The relationship was under a lot of pressure and during diagnostic clarification, [name of partner] also had to help even though I felt bad about it.*

When our participants braid experiences with this subtheme into their narrative identities, drawing causal connections between their illness and strained relationships, they may derive identity conclusions such as "I am a burden," "I cause other people pain," and "I can't fulfill my social obligations."

Lack of Understanding and Stigmatization

Our participants shared stories explicitly or implicitly concerned with other people's lack of understanding. They directly stated that other people had difficulties comprehending how affected they were by their illness, as in this example from one of our participants with borderline personality disorder. She is married with two children and, in the chapter, she feels besieged by negative life events. One of her children is diagnosed with ADHD, her mother passes away, and she is forced to close her toy store, both a job and a hobby to her. She then talks about her ensuing down period:

> *Lack of understanding from everyone around you about what is going on and everything. Because I have always been in good spirits, been a kind of superwoman. Then suddenly I am just lying there and all those people I have always helped, they are not there, because they simply don't know what to do. It is almost like they fear dealing with it. So that is a period where I have felt very alone and very challenged about the children growing up.*

This subtheme also comprised beliefs that other people viewed them negatively because of their illness. This ranged from others in general to family and friends, as illustrated here by a young participant with schizophrenia, who described early life story chapters characterized by strained parental relations, difficulties with school, and pervasive anger. He was diagnosed after 10th grade and expressed his thoughts about how his friends perceived him:

> *It often strikes me . . . when I am in a group of friends, then my thoughts start going: "he is the one who is mentally ill, he is the one who is totally crazy, he is the one who got the full package with the psychiatric hospital and medicine and doctors" . . . . It is really . . . it has been strange. I am fragile.*

Further, our participants struggled with disclosing their mental illness, sometimes being apprehensive about others' reactions. One of our participants with schizophrenia described a high school chapter portraying social withdrawal, loneliness, and the emergence of her illness. Later, she moved to a different city and notes: "*There are several people from my high school that have moved to [name of city] and I have met quite a few of them, but I don't want to say hi because of the whole "how are you" question, I just don't feel like answering that.*"

While the above analyses mostly concern our participants' *beliefs* about how other people may react to their mental illness, some participants also narrated experiences with direct stigmatization, most often in relation to education and work-life. This is evident in the stories shared by participants in previous chapters. Think back to the story from the opening of Chapter 5, where healthcare staff asked our participant to give up her study program in sociology. Or recall our participant from Chapter 4, who narrated the communication from the healthcare system in the following way: "*Now you get this diagnosis and then you have to take medication for the rest of your life and that is what you have to live with. Then you can get disability benefits when you are 18 and that is your life,*" a message she clearly resented. A participant with borderline personality disorder entitled one of her chapters "*starting psychiatric treatment*" and shared the following: "*It has been a real hell. Because I was tossed between all sorts of diagnoses from ADHD and depression to everything . . . and that meant that they didn't think I could complete high school, so that is negative.*" She later includes chapters about graduating from high school with good results, an experience she treasures as a source of self-worth and motivation for further education.

When stories with this subtheme become a part of how our participants define themselves, they may carry identity meanings concerning how other people view them: "other people don't understand me," "other people see me as crazy," and "other people think I can't manage." If these views of others are accepted as valid, they may turn into self-views: "I am crazy and I can't manage," and as such they constitute narrative identity processes implicated in self-stigmatization.

Relationship Rupture

Many of our participants told stories about how they had lost partners and friends because their mental illness overwhelmed other people. Sometimes participants constructed causal connections with the overall message that their illness changed them, which caused others to withdraw. One of our participants made her loss of friendships very explicit. She started her life story with chapters about having a happy childhood, enjoying high school, and starting further education where she socialized with other students. Then schizophrenia erupted to make her life take a downward turn:

> But also, that perhaps from having many friends, losing some of your friends, because there are people who can't really handle that I have become so ill. Yes, there are normal people and I actually really like being with normal people because then you just have your own illness, then you don't have to think about all other sorts of things. Because it can get too much, when everyone is ill, right? But it is also hard, some of those you used to hang out with, you know, like old friends from my residence hall. They can see how much you have changed. The one they know has suddenly turned into someone else. But you can understand them because it is difficult to tackle stuff like that.

Several participants also storied breaches in romantic relationships as resulting from their mental illness. Furthermore, our participants narrated their illness as hindering romantic development. This quote is from a middle-aged participant with schizophrenia holding an office job:

> I have never had a girlfriend for example, and it's not because ... I don't feel that I have problems talking to girls or have, how to explain it, problems in relation to the opposite sex. But I have been poor at entering into a relationship with a woman. I have never dared to make that jump. That is probably one of the things that cause me some pain...

Relatedly, some participants voiced concerns that they were not attractive partners due to their mental illness and that their illness led them into superficial and destructive romantic relationships.

Mental illness also had some of our participants question the possibility of parenthood, illustrating a loss of future possibilities for interpersonal relations. One woman with bipolar disorder shared chapters about chaotic years with hospitalization and educational failures. Then she elaborated on her current relationship chapter, and as she imagined her future, she wrote: "*I so much look forward to becoming a mother, to having children with [name of partner]. When I was most severely ill, I sometimes thought that it might not be a part of my life to have children. Those were hard thoughts, because I have looked forward to it for many years and wanted it in my future.*" Along similar lines, some of our participants storied decisions not to have children due to their illness, as disclosed by this young participant with schizophrenia, who lived with her partner:

> So far I have only told my three best friends and my partner. I think of keeping quiet for another few years before I tell my family. But I have known for four

> *years now that I am not having children. Because I don't think I will ever be completely well. I may get on remission, or in remission, but I don't think I will become completely well. And I don't think ... like I don't want what I have been through, to happen to a child.*

From stories with this subtheme, the following identity meanings may become salient: "I am too difficult to be with" and "I am unfit to care for children," contributing to the negative narrative identities individuals with mental illness may develop.

Withdrawal and Loneliness

Several of our participants interpreted their illness as causing them to lack the energy to engage in social activities and to withdraw from social events and relationships. This subtheme is expressed here by one of our participants, who storied difficult childhood and young adulthood chapters. Ending her life story with a more positive chapter including the relationship with her current partner, she still describes how she is battling the social consequences of a long-term major depressive episode: "*I don't have a social life, I cannot manage very many things, I can't see a way out of it . . . . I can't be with other people, and I feel more and more weird.*" A participant with bipolar disorder echoed this negative meaning. She described an early life with a wide social circle, then goes on: "*After I became ill, I simply couldn't be there for as many people and I have had to be there for myself. More egoistic perhaps . . . . Today my relations are very limited. I have some difficulty accepting that.*"

Loneliness also featured in the stories, as in this young participant with bipolar disorder, who experienced loneliness despite describing her friends and family as caring and supportive:

> *I became ill the first time when I was 19 years old with a moderate/severe depression. I don't remember much from when I became ill. I have had a lot of illness episodes since then . . . . It has affected me a lot socially, personally, and familywise. I find it difficult to remember periods where I have felt reasonably well. I associate myself with the illness. I have difficulties sorting out who I am. I become more self-critical, indifferent, deranged, lonely. I often don't want help and want to manage on my own. I hide how I feel. I don't feel up to anything, I lack joy and energy. I feel I am a burden to others.*

When our participants include this subtheme in their narrative identities, they may arrive at identity conclusions such as "I can't be with other people" and "I am alone." Together with the other negative identity meanings derived from the range of social costs depicted above, a narrative identity of social alienation may slowly build. If this comes to dominate and shape behavior, personal recovery becomes difficult. The subthemes we outline below carry warmer identities that can pave the way for seeing oneself as connected, a key process in personal recovery.[3,5,86]

Positive Social Consequences

Only a few participants made causal connections between their mental illness and positive relationship outcomes, like developing new relationships or strengthening already present social bonds. As we touched upon in Chapter 8, the rarity of such positive meaning or redemptive versions of mental illness may be explained by the poor fit with experience or the lack of redemptive master narratives for psychiatric disorders. The most vivid example came from a participant with schizophrenia, who experienced warm relations with other inpatients when first hospitalized:

> *I still remember exactly what it was like to enter this ward and be so scared and be so insecure and then these young people sat there, it looked entirely normal, sitting in the sofa, laughing. It was a very, very significant experience for me that they just said: "Come on over, well, are you the new one from ward 5?" and that they talked openly about their experiences and thoughts .... It was simply so strange that you have felt different and alone in the world, and all of a sudden then there are other people who know exactly how you feel. For me ... it was almost the biggest part of the hospitalization: meeting other patients and forming bonds with them.*

The example stands in some contrast to other participants who shared stories about the strains of relationships to other individuals with mental illness.

More often, the subtheme of caring for others emerged. Our participants tended to emphasize how their own mental illness expanded their ability to recognize suffering in others. Key words signifying this subtheme comprised understanding, helping, empathy, contribute, and becoming less judgmental, often in the context of mental illness in others. One of our middle-aged participants elaborated on chapters focusing on family life and her love for creative activities. As a part of telling about her major depressive disorder, she reflected that it impacted negatively on organizing social events for her family. Then she adds:

> *But I think the most positive thing is probably that I have gained a better understanding of having a mental illness and I also have the feeling that I am good at helping others. If I know that they feel bad, because I have experienced it*

myself, then I can put myself in their shoes: "Well, OK, then maybe we shouldn't be 20 people and maybe the person also doesn't like a lot of music."

Derived from such subthemes, our participants may construct identity implications of "I am not alone," "I understand suffering," and "I can help others who are in pain." Such interpretations may impel individuals toward engaging in peer support, one aspect of personal recovery in the CHIME framework.[86]

Subthemes Concerning Well-Being, Value, and Meaning from Relationships

The insights we share in the subsequent sections are in some ways straightforward. The aspects of social bonds that are storied with well-being, meaning, and value in our 118 participants' lives are well known from the scientific literature as part and parcel of healthy relationships.[173,176] It is also consistent with the general finding that the presence of communion themes in life stories is related to thriving (as reviewed in Chapter 6).[31] Central to our analyses are the identity conclusions that participants may derive as they make these subthemes a part of their narrative identities in ways that foster well-being. We also illustrate the meaning these relationship experiences are imbued with when storied against the backdrop of mental illness.

Our participants storied meaning, value, and well-being into a wide range of relationships, including friendships, romantic relations, parents, siblings, grandparents, children, colleagues, in-laws, other individuals with mental illness, groups and more. Across these relationships, we categorized the nourishment participants described into seven subthemes: receiving help and support, gaining self-worth from relationships, acceptance and understanding, togetherness, safety and stability, love, and giving to others (see Figure 9.2). These subthemes are neither independent nor exhaustive, but they capture storylines that several participants shared.

Receiving Help and Support

Our participants shared well-being stories featuring help and support from both close and more distant others. They often voiced in general terms that parents, partners, and friends were helpful and supportive. More specifically, they storied instances of practical assistance, such as buying food when they were out of money and lending them a place to stay. They emphasized that close others looked after them when they were themselves

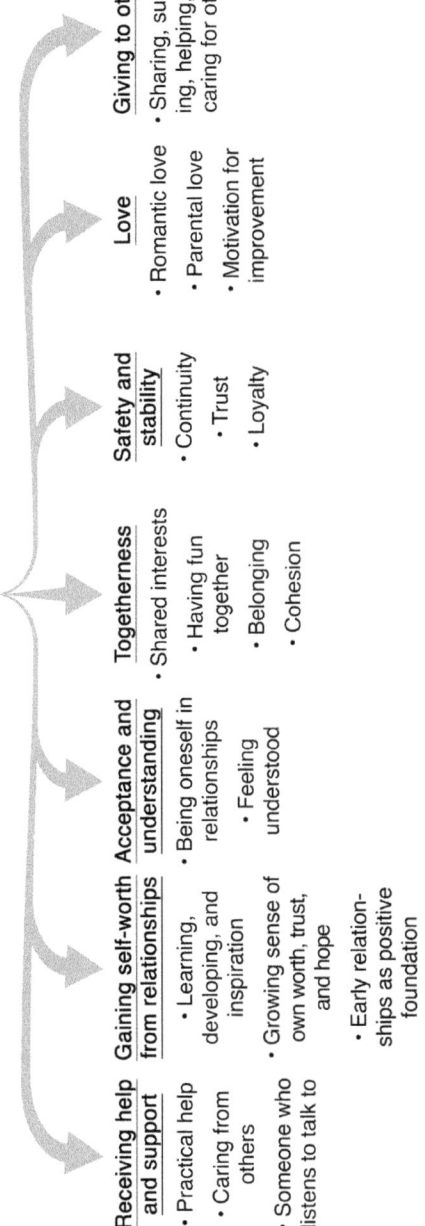

Figure 9.2 Well-being, value, and meaning in narrative identity: relationship themes

unable to. They also spoke about intimate others who listened and to whom they felt they could tell everything. Several participants vividly elaborated on these close, trusting relationships. One of our participants with schizophrenia dedicated her first chapter to one particular girl that she befriended. She talked about how they did everything together and laughed a lot. Then she said:

> *You know, I was 7 years old, when we met. It has clearly helped me that I have had such a close friend. Someone I could talk to about everything during my childhood, my growing up years, and my teenage years. I think it has given me trust in other people. I need to say that it really means a lot. Extremely so. I couldn't imagine ... I get a lump in my throat now. I cannot imagine a life without her at all.*

Several of our participants also storied support during episodes of acute mental disorder, such as hospitalization. They used terms such as *"was there for me."* One of our participants with bipolar disorder struggled with her illness while studying: *"The weather was grey, and the depression hit me like a train. The anxiety before the exam was immense, and I was on the phone with my dad as usual. He was encouraging and supportive. That always helped."*

Grounded in such subthemes, our participants may develop positive identity implications, including "I can trust other people to help and support me." Implicitly this also carries the meaning "I am worthy of help."

Gaining Self-Worth from Relationships

Affirmative identity meanings are even more explicit in this subtheme, where our participants interpreted relationships as nourishing their sense of worth. Some elaborated on how fulfilling their roles as parents established a sense of worth and pride. Several participants described perceiving others as role models, being inspired, developing in relationships, and learning from others. One of our participants with schizophrenia talked about a childhood with a strong bond to both parents, but also intense loneliness in school. He then depicted difficult teenage years with drug abuse, being the victim of an assault, and difficulties in school, which concluded with his first hospitalization. Exemplifying the importance of role models, he shared the following in a future chapter about cooperating with healthcare staff to reduce his medication:

> *I want to get out of it now. In a way, it will be great. It is a good thing I am looking forward to reducing my medication. I have talked to a lot of people who I know have also reduced it [medication]. I have worked with some people who*

> reduced their medication and some things come back. Some emotions, because it [medication] bottles up everything, also emotions and senses. My mother is also working on reducing her medication and she was like, the other day, yesterday, when we were waiting for the bus: "God, it smells like mushrooms." She couldn't do that before, you know. It is both emotions and senses sharpening . . . . I have talked to one of my colleagues in the group who is lecturing, and he has given me some really good advice. He says he thinks the last part of reducing medication is going to be most difficult. It was for him.

The quote also illustrates the importance of vicarious stories for shaping one's own story in desired directions (e.g., "*talked to a lot of people who I know have also reduced it*"). We revisit this insight in Chapter 15 as a part of our guide for narrative repair.

Our participants constructed connections between close others' belief and trust in them and growth of their own sense of worth, trust, and hope. A participant with borderline personality disorder was struggling in her first job in a school. While she was content with work, her self-care deteriorated at home. She then shared the following story about a colleague:

> At home everything just felt dead. And she was just there for me. In the beginning, she was the one who made lunch for me and made me bring it and came and picked me up in the evening and I slept at her place with her and her kids. She has three kids. You know . . . this person who did not need to care for me but did it anyway. When I know her basic story . . . it really made me believe that I could also be – because she has had some rough spots – I could also become a good person or something . . . . Because she has contributed to giving me the belief that I can also have kids one day. She has contributed to . . . like she has made some small seeds sprout inside me and grow, and like believes that there is something good in me. That I can do things. Like, I dare believe in life and in other people.

Several participants also noted how the sense that someone decided to be with them as a partner or friend nurtured their sense of worth as they emphasized the feeling of being chosen not by default, but because of who they are.

Some participants created links between early relationships with parents and grandparents and stable valued characteristics. One of our participants with major depressive disorder talked about growing up with alcoholic parents. She then decided to elaborate on a chapter revolving around her grandmother:

> I stayed with my grandmother, on vacation, which has done a lot of good . . . . Because she gave the caring and the safety that you needed, you know as a child,

the love and what you lack .... I think it's from her I have gotten the independence and the strength that I have needed .... I want to say as much as if I hadn't had my grandmother then I think I would have been completely lost. Because then I wouldn't have known what was good. That is, what is good in people and what is bad in people.

Growing from this relationship subtheme are identity meanings such as "I can become a good person," "I can learn from other people," and "I gain strength from caring others." These conclusions likely involve coauthoring processes where individuals construct their identity through the perspectives other people offer them.

Acceptance and Understanding

Acceptance and understanding in relationships featured as sources of well-being, value, and meaning in the narrative identities of some participants. They used terms like "*be myself*" and "*know me for who I am.*" One of our participants with schizophrenia told about growing up with an alcoholic mother and caring for her younger siblings. She was bullied in school because she was odd, and her psychological problems began in the late school years. She then talks about her new peers, interpreting their friendship as the source of her self-acceptance and self-worth:

I found out I had some really odd interests like them, and I had ... so I finally had some friends who understood me, and I could be myself. I did not have to try to be something I was not. I was allowed to be me, even if I was odd, so it began to be a part of my identity. It continued also when I lived in [name of city], I became more and more nerdy because then I started dating someone when I was 17, who was 25, who was studying to become a computer engineer, so I also developed an interest in computer programming.

Later in her life story, she says: "*That I have found myself and accepted myself and accepted myself as a nerd has meant that I am not bullied anymore. I have gained more self-worth, because there is room for me, and I can be what I am and there is nothing wrong with me.*"

Some participants explicitly narrated how a shared backstory of mental illness fostered acceptance and understanding in close relationships. One of our participants with borderline personality disorder grew up with a mother who was often very angry, and a brother limited by a severe anxiety disorder. She ended her life story with a chapter on her current romantic relationship:

I feel more normal, and we are really happy with each other. We are very good together and even if he has autism, then it's just two lovely, handicapped people together .... But because he has been through all these things, then he has a totally different understanding of our situation and we are really good at helping and supporting each other when we hit a down period. He has way fewer down periods than me. He has like adapted to his diagnosis. He is really good at helping me.

Supplementing the other subthemes concerning how relationships are linked to valued identity conclusions, the present subtheme adds the potential meaning "I can be myself."

Togetherness

Being, doing, and developing *together* emerged as characteristics of relationships that our participants narrated with value, meaning, and well-being. Key terms comprise shared interest, having fun together, cohesion, and belonging. Several stories centering on this subtheme concerned relationships to groups, including groups formed with reference to psychiatric illness. One participant with bipolar disorder described early chapters saturated with feelings of being different. This changed in the following chapter about her activities in a volunteer organization: "*I participate in many courses as a part of their leadership education. It is here I experience community, cohesion, and space to be who I am. As a part of the courses, I built good relations to other people and deep friendships that I still benefit from today.*" By emphasizing this chapter as a part of who she is, she constructs an identity as someone who can belong as a contrast to her other identity conclusions of being different.

At other times, our participants shared stories about valuing shared interests and activities in close relationships. This quote is from a participant with schizophrenia who completed an education as peer supporter and worked in a sheltered workshop for other individuals with mental illness at the time of the interview. She dedicated a chapter to her niece, whom she values highly:

My sister knew I was going through a difficult time and that I thought a lot about committing suicide. Then she said that I simply couldn't do that because I was to be a godmother for her first child, and she wasn't even pregnant then. It simply kept me going that I knew I was to be a godmother for her first child .... It's about being allowed to ... you know, I don't have kids of my own, so being a substitute mother for her and being her aunt .... I love being together with her and thankfully she loves being with me too. So that simply gives me zest for life. I know she likes me and doesn't want to do without me .... It is just something I can live on all the time, you know, that I have her. It is not

> *something that will disappear and she ... she is so good at making me feel special ... do creative things together, you know ... making sure to spend time with her, give her some experiences, and do things together and stuff.*

This subtheme grows identity implications revolving around the following: "I can be with other people," "I belong," and "I can enjoy doing things with other people."

Safety and Stability

Our participants often recounted safety, trust, stability, and loyalty in relationships as sources of well-being in their narrative identities. A participant with borderline personality disorder described her early life with a mother who suffered from mental illness and was unable to care for her. She was removed from her home by child protective services in her late school years and shared a chapter about the friendships she made in boarding school (note that it is common in Denmark to attend boarding school for a year around the age of 16). She said the following:

> *But at [name of school] it was just totally fantastic; it was really fantastic. We were together every weekend and we ... there was really, really cohesion without comparison. Which meant a lot to me, because it was the first time, I felt I belonged somewhere and with someone. We maintained that for some years. I actually still see some of them .... My body warms up and I feel that my body opens up when I talk about it. Because some of the strong friendships I have today stem from there. People who have followed me for 20 years by now and I have followed them, and we are still holding on. They are the only people I feel have been stable in my life – that is, the friends I have from back then.*

In contrast to valuing continuing relationships, some participants emphasized fresh beginnings and meeting new people in well-being narratives: "*It was fantastic to arrive at this new place where I had not been before. To start from scratch with new relations to new people. They did not know me, and I did not know them. So that was just what I needed: A fresh start.*"

In some stories, stable and trusting relationships anchored our participants when facing the ravages of mental illness. A participant with bipolar disorder recounted childhood and youth chapters of thriving with family, school, and friends. As she starts further education, her story takes a downward turn. She is battered by severe depression culminating in a suicide attempt. She then describes how her family stepped in to support her: "*I was hospitalized, and my father, brother and sister's boyfriend came to see me. First my father. They were in shock – they had no clue I was so ill. They were there for me and provided the care and presence that only they can because they are my family."*

The implications that seep into narrative identity from this subtheme include "I can feel safe with other people" and "I can maintain good relationships" in tandem with "other people will be there for me" and "my close others will hold on." Like other subthemes, this illustrates the interdependence in how self and others are interpreted, an idea embraced in several influential psychological theories.[118,177,178]

Love

Many of the life stories featured love, often in romantic relationships and in relation to children and family. Several participants disclosed poignant stories of falling in love. Not that all stories of romantic love ended happily. Indeed, as evident in our subtheme analyses concerning the personal costs of mental disorder, some loving relationships were lost to illness. Still, some participants shared glowing narratives of love. The following quote is from a participant with bipolar disorder who disclosed turbulent chapters about illness before she elaborated on the relationship with her current partner:

> *When I met [name of partner] and we became partners, something inside me clicked. We have been together for two years now. I have never loved someone as much as I love him, and I have always loved a lot. He gives me calmness and an inner warmth and joy, which is just wonderful. He is kind and good and loving and calm and listening. I think he is tailor-made for me. I feel completely safe with him and that has previously been a concern: Can I be completely safe with a man? . . . By loving me and expressing his love, he has also taught me to be good to myself.*

Note how she explicitly interprets this loving relationship as the cause of her growing self-care.

Our subtheme analyses of the negative consequences suggested that some of our participants interpreted their illness as causing poor perspectives for parenting. However, the narratives some of our participants shared about their children radiated love and joy. One participant with schizophrenia storied her early life with bullying in school and a nonsupportive mother. After some happy years traveling during early adulthood, she married and gave birth to two children. She shared the following as a part of her motherhood chapter where she interprets how her own childhood has affected her role as a mother:

> *The most important of the important is being a mother, right? It was my life project to have children and they are just so ... I know all mothers say that their children are just so ... but they are simply very precious .... No one has ever told me that they loved me, and my children should not doubt for one second that they were loved. In my role as a mother, I have taken my own childhood and turned it on its head and thought that all that doesn't work in me that is what I shouldn't do, I should do the exact opposite. When the kids were small, it was like: "OK mom, you can relax a bit." This is what I used to tell them: "I am a pioneer because I don't know the path I am walking, I don't know what it is like to be a mother, so because of that I probably do things too much sometimes, love you too much, chatter too much, am too caring, because I have had too little. You have gotten too much, so I count on you to find the golden mean."*

The significance of children as a source of value in the narrative identities of our participants was evident in reflections about taking control of mental illness and abstaining from suicide. Such reflections also referenced parents and siblings, romantic partners, and friends. Our participants storied the love and responsibility they felt for their children as a key bulwark to spiraling deeper into mental illness and suicide. One of our participants started her life story with remembering her happy time in school, followed by a dark chapter of her teenage years. When interviewed, she had just completed her education and is the mother of a child. She explicitly interprets her motherhood as a reason for wishing to get better:

> *Because it is now that I start dealing with the things that I should have dealt with the last five years or my whole life .... That's what makes me do it now [reference to treatment]. That I am a mother. That I have a responsibility for my daughter means that I have to get myself under control, so I can be a mother for her.*

A range of identity interpretations may emerge from this subtheme, such as "I can love and others can love me," "my love can make a difference for others," and "my love for others gives me a reason to get better."

Giving to Others

The subtheme of giving to other people housed stories of sharing, supporting, helping, and caring, in both the private and professional sphere. It also included utilizing their first-person experience with mental illness to aid fellow sufferers. The subtheme contrasts with imbalances in relationships emerging from our analyses of personal costs, underscoring the value derived from contributing to other people's happiness. Stories on this subtheme comprised both practical and emotional aspects of giving and caring. One of our participants with borderline personality disorder shared a chapter revolving around her relationship to her brother. She talks about the significance of having someone who shared her childhood experiences, although it shaped them in different ways, and her sense that they have always stuck together. She then says:

> When I was in high school and was partying, he went through some bad things that I talked to him about . . . . I can tell myself that I have always been there for him and I have always done things for him and I have always been . . . . It gives me some kind of self-esteem and satisfaction that I know that I do the best I can with my brother concerning help and support and fun and everything. It's not him as a person, it's probably more what I do for him. That may sound strange. But that's what gives me self-satisfaction. I support him and we do things together and he supports me.

It is worth paying attention to her explicit interpretation that helping her brother makes her feel good about herself.

The identity conclusions emerging from this subtheme may revolve around the following "I can help and support other people." Like the other subthemes, this illustrates the importance of healthy relationships and how they are interpreted to construct an adaptive narrative identity central for personal recovery. More specifically, the subthemes elucidate the narrative underpinnings of achieving connectedness and positive identity as steps toward personal recovery.[86] Individuals string together series of events and interpret their meaning to become someone who has the support of others, is accepted, can contribute, and love. In other words: They employ narratives to become someone who is recovering.

Storying Mental Illness and Personal Recovery: Relationship Themes in Narrative Identity

Relationships are ripe with identity meaning in the stories of our participants. When interpreting the effects of mental illness, they paint pictures of strained and ruptured bonds, withdrawal and loneliness, and other people lacking understanding of their illness, crafting narrative identities of social alienation. Meager silver linings appeared in some stories when our participants reflected on how their own experience with mental illness had grown their understanding of others, who struggle with psychopathology. These subthemes reveal an overabundance of negative identity conclusions emerging from the indirect effects of psychopathology on relationships.

Contrasting the wintry portrayal of how relationships and identity withered as consequences of mental illness, our participants literally warmed when storying how relationships related to happiness. A range of positive identity conclusions and possibilities of thriving seemed to grow from the subthemes of safety and stability, help and support, acceptance and understanding, togetherness, gaining self-worth, love, and giving to others. The subthemes revealed that relationships are rich reservoirs for the positive narrative identity necessary for a good life with mental illness.

The richness of relationship subthemes implies that when individuals with psychiatric disorder construct their narrative identities, positive and negative relationship experiences play a key role. Our participants storied relationships as signaling that they were burdens, caused pain, and of less worth or as conveying that they were lovable, belonging, contributing, and growing. As such, the subthemes reveal the narrative identity processes involved in perceiving oneself as connected and of worth, core aspects of personal recovery.[3,5,86] Consequently, working with narrative identity to support well-being and personal recovery could emphasize adaptive relationships and their affirmative identity implications. We suggest strategies for such work in Chapter 15.

Summary

- Participants' stories about harmful consequences within the superordinate theme of relationships included strained and ruptured relationships, lack of understanding from other people, and withdrawal and loneliness. When incorporated into narrative identity, these subthemes carry a range of negative identity conclusions, such as "I am a burden" and "I am alone."
- Positive consequences narrated as a part of identity included new and stronger bonds as well as enhanced understanding of suffering in others, allowing positive identity conclusions such as "I can help others who are in pain."
- Simultaneously, the life stories revealed how well-being accompanied relationships, encompassing help and support, gaining self-worth, acceptance and understanding, togetherness, safety and stability, love, and giving to others. The positive identity implications derived from these subthemes, such as "I can love and others can love me" and "I can help and support other people," may support thriving and personal recovery.

CHAPTER 10

Self Themes in Narrative Identity

In this chapter, we first examine how our participants storied direct effects of their illness on the self. The view that self and identity interact with mental illness has a long history. As early as 1911, Paul Bleuler described a disordered self as integral to schizophrenia.[143] Following this influential analysis, philosophers, psychologists, psychiatrists, and experts-by-experience have sought to map the complex interactions between mental illness, self, and identity. These contributions span philosophical analyses of how an impoverished self contributes to schizophrenia,[142] empirical studies of identity problems in borderline personality disorder,[179] and first-person accounts of how depression steals away identity.[180]

We extend this literature with our in-depth analyses of subthemes and identity conclusions surfacing when individuals with diverse mental disorders story consequences of their illness on selfhood. As discussed in Chapters 5 and 6, we argue that individuals make sense of themselves by constructing personal life narratives.[9,27,29] Building on this assumption, we mine our participants' stories for their reflections on how their illness affected who they are and where they are going. In contrast to theoretical accounts, which describe self problems as causal factors in the genesis of psychiatric disorder,[142,143] we illuminate first-person perspectives on consequences of mental illness for the self. Recall that narrative identity braids past, present, and future selves into a coherent tale depicting stability and change.[8] In the analyses, we present the diverse aspects of the self that enter and leave the scene when individuals with mental illness construct their narrative identities. Next, we go beyond costs and dive into the subthemes and identity meanings emerging from stories of how the self provides fertile grounds for growing well-being, meaning, and value. We share numerous extended quotes, often illustrating multiple subthemes.

Subthemes Concerning Negative and Positive Consequences for the Self

As revealed in Chapter 8, many of our participants storied their illness as influencing their selfhood negatively, and below we unpack the different subthemes and their implications for narrative identity. The subthemes encompass the ill self, loss of previous self, the negative self, the self as different, and the bleak, uncertain future self. We depict these subthemes in Figure 10.1 along with the positive impact on the self as narrated by our participants.

The Ill Self

Our participants storied their self as disappearing in illness; the self as robbed of control, choice, and self-care during illness; and the self as splintered, divided, confused, unbalanced, and chaotic. Phrases like *"my life disappeared in illness," "pushed into a corner of myself," "I am not good to myself," "split off from myself,"* and *"it feels like I am two different people"* portrayed the ill self. These interpretations of how their disorder affected them comprise specific instances of low agency themes characteristic of individuals with mental illness and may ignite self-stigmatizing views of being weak and out of control. The subtheme also reflects the identity engulfment described by Stephen Lally and the chaos "narrative" put forward by Arthur Frank (reviewed in Chapter 6).[121,162] One of our participants with major depressive disorder first described chapters revolving around her sister's illness and her daughter's handicap. She then elaborated vividly on her hospitalization, swallowed by illness and losing control:

> *I have experienced myself in a way that is very destructive. The values I thought I had in my life, you know, I have experienced how they were driven to the background, so that I did not have anything at all. The things that I thought were anchor points in my life, I have experienced how they disappeared . . . . I have been in a place where I have lost myself. Emotionally and intellectually, when I think back on it, I think it's the illness that overshadowed my understanding of how things were. You know, in a way I am now rediscovering myself. . . . But when I was very intent on hurting myself and trying to get away from life, I could sense that it was something I could not control, I got scared of myself.*

They also disclosed stories of secrecy, hiding and shielding from others, and sometimes themselves. One of our participants with borderline personality disorder elaborated on early chapters of being bullied in school,

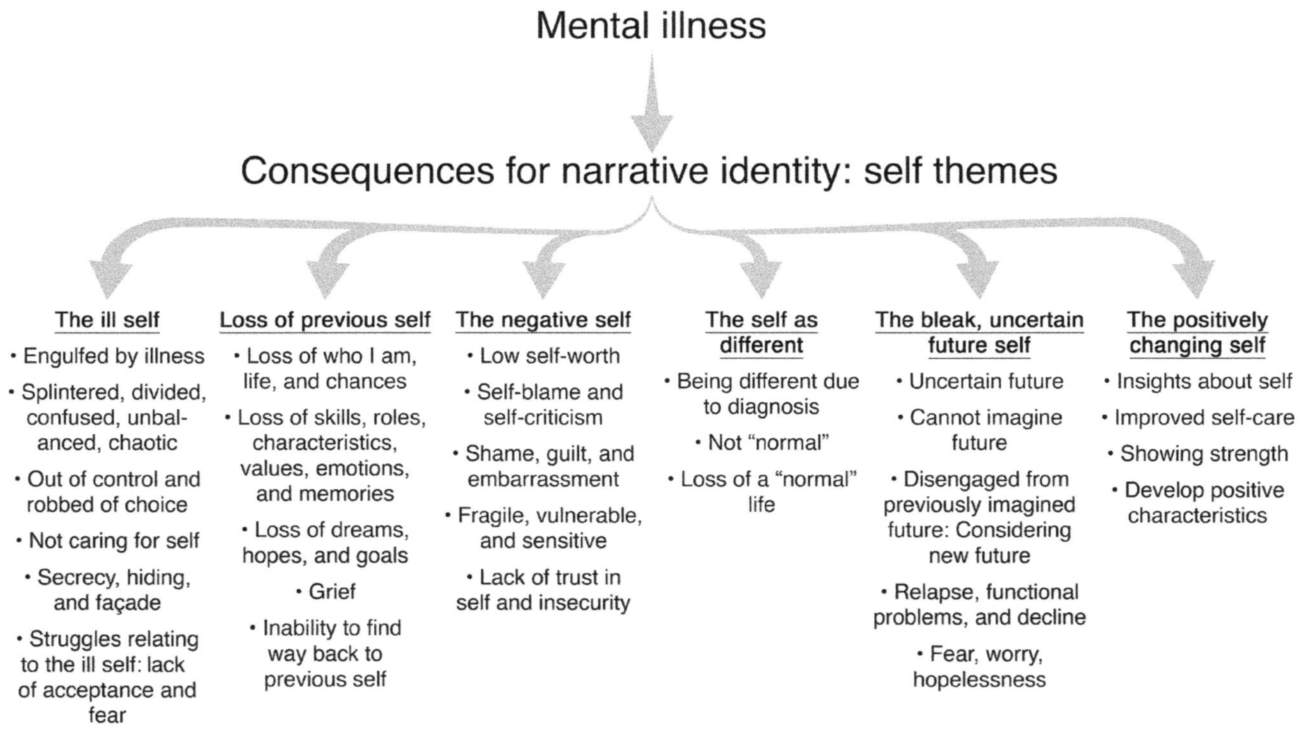

Mental illness

Consequences for narrative identity: self themes

The ill self
- Engulfed by illness
- Splintered, divided, confused, unbalanced, chaotic
- Out of control and robbed of choice
- Not caring for self
- Secrecy, hiding, and façade
- Struggles relating to the ill self: lack of acceptance and fear

Loss of previous self
- Loss of who I am, life, and chances
- Loss of skills, roles, characteristics, values, emotions, and memories
- Loss of dreams, hopes, and goals
- Grief
- Inability to find way back to previous self

The negative self
- Low self-worth
- Self-blame and self-criticism
- Shame, guilt, and embarrassment
- Fragile, vulnerable, and sensitive
- Lack of trust in self and insecurity

The self as different
- Being different due to diagnosis
- Not "normal"
- Loss of a "normal" life

The bleak, uncertain future self
- Uncertain future
- Cannot imagine future
- Disengaged from previously imagined future: Considering new future
- Relapse, functional problems, and decline
- Fear, worry, hopelessness

The positively changing self
- Insights about self
- Improved self-care
- Showing strength
- Develop positive characteristics

Figure 10.1   Consequences of mental illness for narrative identity: self themes

high school years, with partying on one side and depression on the other. Soon after she started working, she was hospitalized for suicidal ideation. She told the following as a part of a chapter on her work life: "*I have difficulties showing emotions. Like showing others that I am sad. So when I was at work, I just went outside to cry and then I came directly out with a big smile, like nothing was wrong.*" Later she expands on the same theme when hospitalized: "*Sometimes when people came visiting, I could easily keep up a facade. Like I did everything, pushed myself to play happy. When they left, I felt bad for a day because I couldn't take anymore.*"

When our participants narrated their ill self, some evidenced difficulties accepting themselves as suffering from mental illness. Listen to one of our young participants with schizophrenia who elaborated on education chapters:

> My time at university and my time in high school is what I use to define who [her name] is. If I could wish to be a person, then I know ... I have started recognizing that identity is not static. But when you are ill, all the time you hope to return to the old, the old self, the old [her name].

She entitled a later chapter "*University, life expectations, my hospitalization, black hole*" and said:

> I don't feel like myself. I feel like I was lost somewhere in all this. Maybe also expecting a change that didn't happen, it has just gone backwards. Identity crisis, I don't have, I don't know who I am, I don't know what I can get.... I still don't know what I am. I still feel I am missing myself and I have no acceptance of where I am. It's stuck. It's stuck because I dare not feel myself. I dare not accept where I am, and I am still simply just scared shitless. Because I feel that I am not doing anything. But, believe me, it is a full-time job to work with yourself and that is what I am doing presently. There are just a lot of loose threads that have not been pulled together yet.

Also reflecting toxic relations with their ill self, a few participants storied how they feared or preferred not to remember their ill self. The fear of the ill self also saturated some future chapters disclosed by our participants, which we expand on in the section "The Bleak, Uncertain Future Self."

Our participants made causal connections between their illness, losing themselves and losing control, having to hide and keep up facade, and struggling to accept. Individuals who shared stories featuring this subtheme may derive identity meanings such as "I am not myself," "I am out of control," "I am chaotic," "I cannot accept myself," and "I have to hide who I am."

Loss of Previous Self

Several of our participants reflected on having lost the person they were before illness, lost their identity. Some simply said that they had lost life and missed chances. A few participants explicitly named grief in this context. This echoes insights from Ellen Frank's interpersonal and social rhythm therapy where mourning the lost self is one aspect of treatment (reviewed in Chapter 3).[62] One of our participants storied his depressive episode as ruining his life. He described early adulthood chapters of work and marriage, both lost due to his illness. He was in the hospital for the third summer in a row and said: "*It is like someone completely different from who I was before I went down.*" As a part of his future chapter on reestablishing his work-life, he explicitly interpreted his loss of identity as stemming from change in social context: "*Like you lose a lot of identity in not being outside, having a job and a social network.*" The subtheme of relationship strain and rupture identified in Chapter 9 sometimes intertwined with this subtheme depicting loss of previous self.

Some spoke about attempting to travel back to this previous self, sometimes succeeding, sometimes failing. One of our participants with schizophrenia told us about a restlessness stemming from a childhood with many moves, from place to place, from school to school. She described an exchange year where she "*was totally out of control,*" abusing drugs and repeatedly jumping off from high places. She then shared this reflection:

> *Then I became a part of the psychiatric system and was hospitalized and that has actually been it, up to now. Lots of hospitalizations and medicine and living in psychiatric group homes and lying in bed for several years and not really get . . . you know, it feels like . . . in a way . . . that I have been split off from myself, a lot, so that I can't find my way back to who I once was.*

Some named the loss of specific positive values, characteristics, emotions, and memories. One of our participants with schizophrenia dropped out of part-time education because she always felt behind and lacked a social network. At the time of the interview, she had mixed feelings about receiving disability benefits:

> *It has been 50/50. I stress out easily and can't shoulder as much, so in that way it has been a relief. At the same time, it is frustrating in everyday life and over time not doing anything with your days. You know when you hear people say: "Oh, it must be great to get disability benefits." No, it is super boring, it is frustrating, and you feel like you are not doing anything satisfying with your life.*

Several of our participants interpreted their mental illness as causing the loss of previously held dreams, hopes, and goals. This included hopes and dreams they had held before becoming ill. One of our participants had planned to enter the military but was hospitalized with psychosis after completing high school. Relating his discharge from hospital, he said:

> *I was actually very happy about it, because it was a relief to come home. But, on the other hand, I didn't really know what I wanted to do with my life, because it was like turned upside down now. I was supposed to enter the military after high school, but then I ended up in the psychiatric hospital instead.*

When narrating the loss of dreams, hopes, and goals, participants sometimes explicitly compared themselves to others and cultural norms. As one of them articulated it: "*I wish I could do like the others who are studying and having children.*" This indicates the difficulties individuals with mental illness may face when they cannot shape their narrative identities from established master narratives such as the cultural life script.[128]

Some of our participants also shared stories of losing hope when relapsing. One participant with schizophrenia had planned to reduce her medicine intake following a stable period. Her symptoms returned, she was hospitalized, and her medication increased. She said:

> *I remember the evening I was hospitalized and entered the ward with my mother. I remember it was simply, I just felt kicked back. It was just "Okay, start all over with all this shit: Poisoned water, secret agents, suicide, and all that stuff." I really felt thrown back . . .. Losing faith, hope of everything, and just feel knocked over again.*

Others similarly interpreted repeated illness related failures as causing them to lose belief in the future.

As our participants reflected on their life stories, they reasoned that their illness had caused them to lose the person they used to be, their hopes and dreams, and the possibilities for a satisfying life. The subtheme echoes Arthur Frank's proposal that illness causes individuals to lose the map and destination.[121] Negative implications for identity drawn from this subtheme may be "I have lost myself," "I have lost my hopes and dreams," and "I cannot find my way back to who I used to be."

The Negative Self

The negative self came in different shades and was pervasive in the stories while often accompanying other subthemes. The negative self spotlights the narrative identity processes involved in self-stigmatization as our participants causally connected their illness to a range of negative self-attributes.[20] It appeared in direct statements about their worthlessness, blaming and criticizing themselves; emerged in emotions such as shame, guilt, and embarrassment; surfaced as lack of trust in themselves and feeling insecure; and leaked from narratives with negative evaluations of becoming too sensitive, fragile, and vulnerable. One of our participants was diagnosed with major depressive disorder following the loss of her mother and bullying at work. She interprets her disorder as causing her to become too fragile: *"I have had depression and anxiety. It is like, it doesn't take a lot to scare me and overturn everything. I am extremely sensitive to a lot of things and feel very fragile too. Even if it has also made me stronger, at the same time, I feel incredibly fragile. Feel like a figure made of glass sometimes."*

Another participant narrated how his close friend had died leading to pervasive suicide thoughts and failing at every turn in the educational system. He then depicted how mental illness robbed his trust in himself, eroding his worth:

> *That you are scared to try something new, even if you know that something bad can turn positive afterwards. But about ... when you have experienced a certain number of times that when you try something, you fail, then at some point in time, you get scared of trying something new. Especially when you feel bad, you dare not try anything at all. That is also a part of the negative self-worth, right .... It is a major sense of powerlessness to know, to recognize, that there are things you really, really, really want to do and then not have the resources or anything ... have the possibilities of going through with it ... and it can be things like education or things you need, but there is powerlessness when the illness takes over.*

The toxic identity conclusions emerging from this subtheme may include "I am weak," "I am worthless," "I am powerless," and "I cannot trust myself," reflecting the narrative identity processes involved in self-stigmatization.

The Self as Different

Some participants storied feelings of being different because of their psychiatric illness and boxed in when diagnosed with a mental disorder. This subtheme nests interpretations like *"don't fit in with most other people,"* *"made me more conscious that I am not normal,"* and *"I am different."* One of our participants with borderline personality disorder shared reflections on how diagnosis made her feel different and stigmatized:

> *Like this whole thing with diagnoses is really cool, because you need a diagnosis to get help and that is the way it is. But it is also really difficult because all of a sudden you are in a box and that's no one's dream. No one is probably thinking: "Oh, I wish I could be with one of those from [name of hospital]." I think it has been really difficult to accept that this is the way things are and that is how I am .... It isn't fun when you go out with people and they ask "what are you doing these days" and you have to tell them that you are on sick leave. It is simply incredibly difficult with the way our society is structured to have one [a diagnosis] and I believe personality disorder is the most difficult.*

This subtheme was also apparent when participants interpreted their illness as costing them a "normal" life. One of our participants storied her life with a safe childhood and a youth in high school full of parties and testing her parents' limits. When she started university, her illness entered the scene:

> *I haven't been good to myself either. I have always driven myself hard and pushed myself. It is the thing when you come from a family that is pretty normal. Then you are also forced to be fairly normal because you do what is expected of you. Have a job, study, or things like that. But you can't really transfer that to someone who is ill, and I couldn't live up to it either.*

This subtheme may give rise to identity meanings such as "I am different" and "I cannot live a normal life." Such implications are likely partly driven by divergences from cultural life scripts depicting the ideal life.[128]

The Bleak, Uncertain Future Self

When our participants projected themselves into future chapters, they saturated their stories with emotional expressions like fear, anxiety, worry, hopelessness, bitterness, hate, uncertainness, and apprehension. As we demonstrate later in this chapter, they simultaneously narrated their future selves with powerful positive emotions. We borrowed the concept of future selves from Hazel Markus[181] and consider the rich emotional layering as testimonies that our participants are strongly invested in these imagined stories of their future selves.

Several participants struggled to imagine the future, could not cope with the future, and explicitly interpreted their mental illness as making the future uncertain and unpredictable. This bears affinity to insights from previous research that illness disrupts ongoing narrative identity by stealing the future (see Chapter 6).[121,131] In the words of one of our participants with major depressive disorder: "*I think it is totally overwhelming. Right now, I don't think there is a future*" or a participant with schizophrenia:

"*The awareness that you don't know about tomorrow whether you'll hit rock bottom again.*" Some spoke about tackling one day at a time to cope with the uncertainty of the future. One of our participants with bipolar disorder had her first depressive episode while in high school. After two gap years working, she started university, but on reduced time due to her illness. She wrote the following about her future study chapter:

> *Hopefully this will be a positive chapter full of exciting reading, fun with friends and study peers, and interesting events. However, I am also a little worried since I find it difficult to imagine the chapter without illness episodes, which frightens me. In this chapter I hope to get to know myself (the stable me) and my illness better. I find it a little difficult to think about the future. I take it one day at a time. I dare not really have any hopes for the future because I'm scared that my illness will be in the way.*

She continued to construct a future chapter about her future self at work:

> *Again, I dare not really think about it. There are so many things that could affect me negatively that it seems almost unavoidable that I will become ill again. When I was 17, I didn't think I would make it to 18 and when I was 18, I didn't think I would turn 20. It seems weird to be in a future I wasn't prepared for. Hence, it is also difficult for me to imagine the future now.*

Some of our participants also related more benign stories about the uncertain future. They had disengaged from previously hoped-for futures and were in the process of composing new prospective chapters.

Many participants imagined their future stories unfolding into the ill self. Some talked about a generally negative future. Some voiced concerns with relapse, which they feared. They shared worries about pushing themselves too hard causing relapse by failure to monitor themselves. They disclosed images of being unable to fulfill roles as parent, partners, and employees. One of our participants with bipolar disorder portrayed a childhood with leisure, friends, and doing well in school. In her teenage years, mental illness emerged, and she attempted suicide. At the time of the study, she was in treatment, but disclosed her fear in a future chapter:

> *I would like to educate myself as a social worker. Later in the future, I'd like to marry and have kids. I'd like to live an entirely normal life. But I am scared. Can I complete an education, become a good wife, and am I fit to have children? I think a lot about whether I can get my illness under control.*

As reviewed in Chapter 6, psychiatric disorders may fit the restitution master narrative poorly. The implication is that the "getting well and back to normal" part of this master narrative cannot inform the future narrative identities individuals imagine.[121] Individuals with mental illness may reproduce or resist the negative master narrative of mental illness, while also struggling to fit other master narratives such as the cultural life script. This leaves them with little scaffolding for building positive narrative identities.[128] This stresses the importance of vicarious stories from peers in personal recovery as potential story models, an issue we return to in Chapter 15.[121,182]

Some participants storied futures with downward spiraling and functional decline, giving up, and even suicide. One of our participants with borderline personality disorder narrated her childhood as dominated by a scolding mother, being responsible for her younger brother, and bullying in school. She dropped out of high school and moved in with her aunt. She pursued education while threatened by her aggressive boyfriend and finally broke down. She hinted at her dread when she said:

> *I have to force myself to trust the physicians who are dealing with me and the social worker and my support person. I have given everything away and trust blindly that things will get better, it must not get worse. That is it. The consequence of that, it . . . it will end with me not being here. It has to get better.*

To the other subthemes, the bleak, uncertain future self adds identity conclusion reflecting further loss and discontinuity: "I don't have a future" and "my illness will return to shatter my dreams." All these identity meanings may need to be addressed and coped with to challenge their dominance of narrative identity and support personal recovery.

The Positively Changing Self

In the rarer instances when our participants interpreted their mental illness as bringing positive consequences, these were most often about insights and learning about themselves, becoming more aware, and understanding their own reactions better. These may reflect redemptive stories of mental illness as bringing positive meaning of learning and growth (see Chapters 5 and 6).[109] One participant with schizophrenia shared a school chapter about diving into a world of literature to cope with bullying and social exclusion. He developed high academic expectations, but his mental illness began to surface during high school and university, interfering with his achievement. He was studying when we interviewed him and as a part of navigating his new university program, illness, and treatment, he reflected: "*I have become much more conscious about what you can and cannot do with a mental illness – or with my mental illness at least. I am happy with that to a* very high degree. Also, because I can use it in my work when I give talks and as a member of [volunteer organization]."

Several participants explicitly tied expanded insight to enhanced caring for themselves. Some talked about prioritizing their own needs and downgrading their sense of social obligation. Other stories revolved around mental illness as a signal to change life circumstances to improve self-care. One of our participants storied the cause of her major depressive disorder as stemming from experiences with forgetting her own needs to help her family. She then reflected:

> *Of course it is a good thing to be there for others and help others. But it also has . . . it has been a kind of a revelation for me, that is, I have become better at saying no. That is the first thing. I have become better at looking after myself, I can tell. I have become better at paying attention to my feelings. That is: Can I manage that appointment? Or can't I? I am still practicing and working a lot with it, but I have improved.*

Relatedly, some participants also interpreted their mental illness as contributing to healthier help-seeking behavior. One of our participants described a chapter about enjoying his work with sales but had lost self-esteem after he was laid off. He was severely affected by a major depressive disorder at the time of the study but said: *"If I look back one year, then I couldn't ask for help and thought I could manage everything myself. Today then, well, I have become better at that. If I feel now that it is becoming too much, then I seek professional help."*

Some made connections between their illness and showing personal strength. A participant disclosed how she was left to live alone when she was 15, making her own living by stealing and dumpster diving. Soon after completing high school, she was hospitalized with psychosis. She then lived in a psychiatric group home for a period but decided to grow her creative talent and moved to a new city. Her talent was publicly acknowledged and she reflected:

> *This last year and a half I have really felt that I have gotten through some very difficult things . . .. The sense of having gotten so far in spite of all kinds of really tough stuff that happened and despite my continuing symptoms. It gave me a unique feeling that I . . . now I have reclaimed my independence even more or in a healthier way than earlier and have really been very full of joy and happiness. Especially the feeling of self-worth has been very strong this spring.*

Several of our participants shared stories where they interpreted positive characteristics as developing from their illness. These included becoming more patient, less stubborn, more relaxed, feeling less inadequate after meeting others with similar problems, changing their view of life, becoming wiser and more deeply reflective.

As a possible counterweight to the toxic identity conclusions emerging from mental illness, some individuals may derive brighter identity meanings from interpreting their illness as changing them in positive ways or as testifying to valued characteristics. These could take on a variety of forms, including "I have grown from my illness," "I know myself better after my illness," "I can manage my illness," and "I can take care of myself." This subtheme involves narrative identity processes implicated in empowerment and positive identity as parts of personal recovery.[3,5,86]

Subthemes Concerning Well-Being, Value, and Meaning from the Self

We discovered five subthemes in our analyses of how participants storied well-being, meaning, and value into their identities. While these stories featured the self in context (e.g., relationships, education), we here focus on aspects of selfhood (we cover the other superordinate themes in Chapters 9, 11, and 12).

Many participants weaved valued aspects of their selves into narrative identity, and several talked about acceptance and congruence when storying positive parts of their lives after the eruption of mental illness. We label these the valued self and the accepting self. Other stories emitted well-being, value, and meaning through narrating the self as influencing important outcomes, making good decisions, taking responsibility, and as learning, changing, and developing. These stories depict the self as the protagonist setting off to create a good world to live in (the agentic self) and the self as changing from engaging in the world (the growing self). These subthemes align with studies demonstrating that broad themes of agency in narrative identity are related to thriving (see Chapter 6).[31] In general, the subthemes mirror insights from a range of literatures, including psychological well-being (reviewed in Chapter 4) as well as research demonstrating that self-esteem, self-efficacy, and autonomy foster well-being.[90–92,183] Finally, a subtheme concerning the dreaming self surfaced from the future reflections disclosed by our participants. We provide an overview of these subthemes in Figure 10.2. Below, we extend the existing literature by analyzing how individuals with mental illness construct their narrative identities around these subthemes to derive adaptive identity conclusions crucial for thriving and personal recovery.

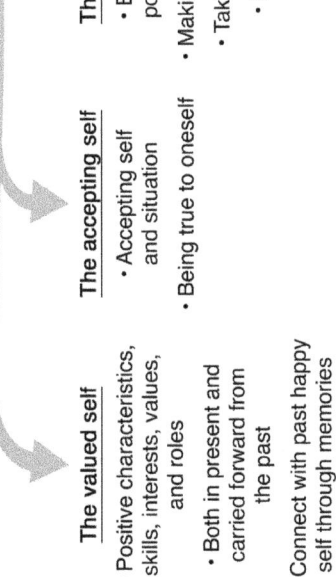

Figure 10.2 Well-being, value, and meaning in narrative identity: self themes

Our participants' stories reflect commonly recognized aspects of the good life. What is different is that they story the self as valued, accepting, agentic, growing, and dreaming in the face of challenges flowing from mental illness. Some stories explicitly featured the self as a source of thriving, while struggling with mental illness and engaging with treatment. Some stories focused on other domains or life periods where psychiatric disturbance was dormant. This suggests that individuals with mental illness can story thriving into their lives, both in terms of how they relate to their mental illness but also in terms of how these positive aspects of the self are constructed from stories unfolding in contexts such as relationships, vocation, and education.

The Valued Self

When our participants reflected on their life stories, they shared multiple valued aspects of their selves arising from diverse life domains. As demonstrated in Chapter 9, they sometimes storied this good self as arising from loving and caring relationships. Participants spoke about carrying treasured aspects of the self forward from a distant past chapter or the cherished self-image emerged from chapters closer to the present. This subtheme arose from explicit interpretations of how experiences revealed or spurred the growth of valued characteristics and were voiced as positive identity meanings: "*I am very creative,*" "*I have become a really open-minded person,*" "*it made me stronger,*" "*very sensitive and very empathic,*" "*I became a quite optimistic person,*" "*the trusting approach I have adopted,*" "*it taught me to be much more self-reflective,*" "*as a person I have always had a sense of humor,*" and "*being very independent.*" They also comprised interests, skills and talents, and roles and values, such as "*I managed to be a good mother,*" "*I have become better at drawing,*" "*to read and to enjoy the experiences you get through books,*" and "*I like when people have a humble approach.*" One of our participants with schizophrenia identified a chapter related to his job, describing how he cherishes the autonomy and responsibility. He then constructed a positive connection between a treasured aspect of his self ("*I like to listen*") from his past and his more recent work experience:

> I like asking questions. So way back from when I was very young, I have been more interested in listening to people than speaking myself. So, when people come here, I think I use that ability to work with them in ways that make me understand them better than others may have in the past. I show active listening.

Some participants talked about sunny remembrances in stories of thriving. They said: *"Those are good memories"* or *"I look back upon it as a happy time."* They found happiness in evoking past selves and making these a part of their narrative identity. A few explicated ambivalences arising from such positive reminiscing. They were bittersweet visitors from the past, the person they were, and that time was now gone. Exemplifying this, one of our participants with major depressive disorder told us about a chapter working abroad. He then said:

> *It was a fantastic time. I often think back upon it when I reflect on my past. A time where I made lots of money and had a lot of fun and knew lots of people. It was definitely a big, a good time in my life . . .. That time is also gone. I can't use any of it. Nothing but the memories.*

At the same time, a few participants interpreted happy memories to promise the possibility of change and kindle a small hope that things might turn better, that they could reconnect with lost aspects of the self. One of our participants with borderline personality disorder disclosed a life story suffused with suffering and strain. Her mother was mentally ill, and our participant was removed from her care. She struggled academically and was bullied in school. Her sexual boundaries were repeatedly transgressed, and she became somatically ill. Still, she describes a mostly positive chapter about kindergarten:

> *That was when I was happiest, I think. It is a real happy memory. Like kindergarten affects all chapters. Yes, in a positive way. But it was because then I started school and then I didn't feel so good . . .. So it wasn't like very good. Because it didn't last. Of course, it has been positive in the way that I have had something positive. I knew it could become positive again in some way.*

The identity implications of incorporating past positive selves into narrative identity may be: "My past gives me reason for hope" and "I can be happy."

Integrating valued selves into narrative identity both through self-stability connections ("I have always been. . .") and through self-change connections ("I have become more. . .") and tying these to ongoing experiences ("I use this in my. . .") is likely involved in personal recovery processes such as rebuilding a positive identity that enables well-being.[3,5,86]

The Accepting Self

Several of our participants shared stories about acceptance, congruence, and well-being. They spoke about *"allowing myself to be who I am,"* *"learn to live with it,"* and *"be true to myself."* The subtheme clearly relates to the relationship subtheme of acceptance that we elaborated on in Chapter 9. Sometimes stories revolved around accepting difficult situations. One of our participants with borderline personality disorder narrated a childhood dominated by her angry mother. When she reflected on her teenage chapter, she said:

> *A lot of people say: "You don't choose your parents, but you choose whether to keep them or not." But there are many people who don't know or remember this. I lost the last bit for my mother when I was 16. There was no saving it, that was it, I just have a crazy mother, that's it. Then it was simply about getting away from home. I wasn't really scared of her anymore, I accepted that she had to be there and even if she threw me out, the police would pick me up somewhere a few hours later, because she had called in and said that I had run away. It was that feeling: "OK, I have accepted that this is how it is for me." It gave me a kind of calm and clarity. It gave me a lot of clarity with respect to how do I handle this . . . . Because I accepted how everything was connected and I felt myself letting go of that eternal hope that my mother would become a good mother. I hoped so much that she was simply angry or something and that it would just disappear. But when I suddenly understood that there was nothing she was mad about, she was just nasty and that is the way she is. That meant I could put things in perspective and then I cut her off as soon as I left home. It has been positive for me to cut her off. That clarity has been very positive for me. I am really grateful that I had that experience.*

In some ways, this is a sad story. Still, our participant imbues it with positive emotion and interprets it as leading her toward helpful decisions.

The adaptive identity conclusions derived from this subtheme may comprise "I am true to who I am" and "when I accept things, I get better." Narrating the ability to accept and the positive impact of acceptance into identity may propel individuals toward continued work on acceptance, one aspect of personal recovery.[86]

The Agentic Self

Many participants narrated well-being into their identities through agentic narratives about setting desired life changes in motion, arriving at good decisions, mastering life, and seizing responsibility. One of our participants storied how she pursued an education in the creative domain, which she had to give up because it triggered severe manias and depressive episodes. She was in a relationship, which was strained by drug and alcohol abuse on both sides. She then wrote:

> *Before we part, he urges me to do something about my alcohol abuse. I contact the Center for Treatment of Alcohol Abuse and they assess me through a series of conversations. After some consideration, I decide to stop drinking. They conclude that I can benefit from their day treatment program and I am accepted into a six-week intense treatment course. It is an important decision for me. An active choice in the direction of a healthier life. The alcohol stop is still on and if everything works out as I hope, it will last. It gives me well-being and I feel more balanced.*

Some participants narrated how memories of coping with challenges inspired them to tackle later situations. In the words of a participant with borderline personality disorder, who shared a chapter about doing very well in high school and pursuing further education: "*When I think about taking an exam, then I just have to think about how it turned out in high school. So it has given me the desire to study.*" Through narrative identity she connects her present self with a past resourceful self needed for educational success.

Illustrating this subtheme in relation to mental illness, a participant with schizophrenia shared a vivid story of taking charge of his recovery. He was studying and living with his girlfriend when he was hospitalized due to mental illness and described being heavily medicated for 10 years. He then said:

> *There, once the change happens, it's when I start some work courses and some cognitive therapy and something about ... yes, like "Who is driving the bus?" [referencing self-help sources] and get some control on changing your life, your situation. The moment I get the possibility of changing my situation – what I think you call empowerment in American – but the moment I start getting the opportunity to shift my situation, it happens relatively fast. I start reducing medicine at some point in time, and then it happens even faster, when you have the energy. When you don't sleep 18 hours a day, then you have more time to move forward, so to speak. I work with different therapeutic tools. Then I begin, first I take a job, I don't know if that place still exists, I was creating their website, it was like a sheltered workshop. Then I start working at [name of company] a couple of years ago, like 8 hours, and do that for a long time, to figure out whether I can do these things again. After having done that for a while, I start studying again. I have done that since. I also teach a bit in the psychiatric system.*

Our participants causally linked together events taking place over extended time intervals, clearly illustrating how narrative processes are involved in the emergence of an agentic self. Such stories support identity meanings such as "I can make good decisions," "I can handle difficulties," and "I can change my life for the better," crucial for empowerment that is a key part of personal recovery.[3,5,86]

The Growing Self

Many of our participants shared stories where they interpreted the self as changing, developing, and learning, aligning with the research on positive meaning reviewed in Chapter 6.[94] We note again the overlap with the relationship subtheme of gaining worth from relations to loving others (see Chapter 9) and the adaptive identity implications arising from these subthemes ("I can learn from others"). They learned about themselves, the world, and other people. They acquired skills, in life and in school. They became more optimistic, more social, and better at coping. And our participants treasured these stories of growth. One participant with borderline personality disorder identified a chapter revolving around her job with childcare, which she storied with both challenges and development:

> *It has been extremely significant to me. It has emotionally been very mixed because it has been hard. I have worked with children with handicaps, autism and ADHD and stuff. I struggle to do it professionally because I get emotions mixed too much into it. That is, I care too much about the children. It is something I must consider as an educator, it has to be professional. I think that will be difficult, or difficult for me .... I think it has a very positive ... because I have developed in how one is with people and see people and respect people.*

Another participant storied his life around one massive change. He entitled his first chapter *"The first 30 years of my life"* and elaborated on his abusive mother, anxiety, and lack of independence and self-worth. He was considered for disability benefits due to his mental illness. He then continued with the following chapter, which he labelled *"Recovery"*:

> *It is about going from suicide thoughts to being like a well-functioning person today. Almost being braver than I have been before .... When I became ill, it was a necessary process for me to go through all that. There are many paths, like, I could also be sitting in a chair and not having anything to do. All I have done these past 10 years has been on the path forward. I have done a lot of things that have changed me. Like, in the beginning I couldn't walk the streets. My friend, he dragged me through the streets and now I don't have any problems being around people. Back then, I thought they could tell I had been ill. But I don't think that at all anymore. I also don't care if they ... I have discovered that people almost don't think about others. They think about themselves and how they appear in the public space and that thought has helped me to calm down.*

In the chapter, he also disclosed how he feels more like himself, how his self-worth has improved, and how he is seeking out opportunities for work.

Tying together the self of the past with the self of the present is at the core of constructing narratives of growth and development that support thriving. Making such narratives a central part of identity can bring implications such as "I can grow" and "I can learn" to the forefront, much needed for undertaking the major task of personal recovery.

The Dreaming Self

Our participants imagined themselves with happy futures. They employed rich emotional language when describing their projected future stories. They talked about hope, excitement, and calm; about looking forward to, enjoying, wishing, and dreaming. While fearing the ill self, they populated their future stories with hopes for education, jobs, children, traveling, leisure activities, grandchildren, romantic relations, social activities, everyday life, and living space. They projected their selves forward as becoming valued, growing, accepting, agentic, and "normal." They hoped to become more independent and courageous, and to rebuild trust, grow wiser, improve their self-esteem, self-knowledge, and self-care. In other words, their dreams were grounded in the subthemes that our analyses show are storied with well-being, value, and meaning while repairing some of the damage done by mental illness, that is, the negative self, struggles relating to the ill self, and the self as different. The identity meaning carried by this subtheme can be generally stated as "I can become..."

Several participants weaved mental illness into their future identity stories, recognizing that the ill self would probably be a part of these stories. This encompassed coping with their illness and limiting its impact on their lives, learning to live with their illness, becoming stable, reducing medication, employing treatment and assistance to achieve their goals, and getting well. Here we give one extended example from a participant who was sexually abused as a child and self-harmed for many years. After high school, he worked in a café, deteriorated, and ended up in hospital with a diagnosis of schizophrenia. When we interviewed him, he had been hospitalized 13 times and lived in a psychiatric group home. In his last chapter of the past, he elaborated on how he was working to get well, had reduced medication, and stopped self-harming. He then shared the following in his future chapters:

> *I am looking for another place to live. Because I feel that I am getting too well to stay here . . . . Because I am in the process of looking into where I can live. I'd like my own apartment. Not something within the psychiatric system, my own apartment and then with a support person. They said I could get that. It will be really exciting. I feel that I am getting better. The last bit will only come when I move away from here. I feel that when I move, I will start a new chapter . . . . I am really looking forward to moving. I have stayed with my mom over Christmas. When she had to go out, there were evenings where I had to cook dinner myself and enjoyed it. I am really looking forward to getting out on my own . . . . I'd like to prove to myself that I can do this alone, you know. I think it is positive that I have the courage to try life now – to get a life. I might get a bit lonely in the beginning, have to get used to it. It might be too difficult sometimes because here I know I can always see the staff if something is bothering me. But I don't see that as negative, I see it more as a challenge.*

In his next future chapter, he storied how he would reduce medicine even further:

> *I am really working on still being well when I get off my last medication, because then I am not on any medicine. But it will take some time and that is OK. As long as I feel as well as possible. But it will also be hard. The other times I stepped out of medications, it was incredibly hard. Because I developed withdrawal symptoms and I react drastically to changes in medication, so I quickly feel bad. But I feel that when we take it slowly as we do now, it will be OK . . . I will become more myself . . . . So, I think I will become another person, but still also myself, just me being happy and well.*

In two of his next three chapters, he projected himself into unknown territory and was less concrete in his descriptions. He dared dream about a girlfriend, even if he had not been in a relationship before: "*I'd also like if we could take a holiday together or something. I have never been on package holiday I would like to try that . . . . I think it is nice to have someone to share life with. But you also need the energy for it.*" He dreamed about finding a job maybe a few years into the future: "*Because I have often dreamed about like, what it would be like to have a normal everyday life like all other ordinary people. Go to work, and like it, and be happy and able to manage it.*" While few participants elaborated as many different chapters as this participant, many had future chapters with similar foci.

As we mentioned in Chapter 7, the quantitative analyses of future chapters revealed that our participants with mental illness storied their future as positive.[37,38,41] This led us to wonder whether the future narrative identities crafted by our participants were decidedly unrealistic. After all, they live with severe mental illness and the costs that accompany it. This is an important question, because future stories out of tune with past stories (lived and told) are likely to trap individuals in failure, disappointment, and passivity. Such future life stories will in the long run detract from, rather than contribute to, well-being. Several observations suggest that our participants in general did not lose hold of reality when projecting themselves into the future. Since our participants storied happy future selves revolving around subthemes that related to well-being in their past, they demonstrated good insight into what could bring thriving in the future. Furthermore, many participants accommodated their future chapters to their illness. They spoke about changing priorities, adapting everyday routines, choosing education and job wisely, and how to prevent or dam in potential future relapse. Thus, while the future stories brimmed with sunny outcomes, as is common for future life stories also in non-clinical populations, they still seemed tied to past stories for most participants.[184,185] They were about becoming, but still in continuation of what was.

However, some future life stories appeared less anchored in lived and told past stories. They contained good outcomes with little explanation of how the participant would move toward this future self. They seemed abstract and disconnected from the present situation and the past. This was the case in a young participant with a major depressive episode who identified past chapters focusing on her sports talents, strained family bonds, friends, and ex-boyfriend. In her first future chapter, she storied getting together with her ex-boyfriend again:

> *What means most to me is my ex-boyfriend, the guy I would like to get together with some day. Create a family. I like him a lot. I imagine that if I get together with him again one day then I'll get better, and then I feel well, so that's perfect for me. I have learned a lot of things that I can use. I'd like to treat him in a special way. Make sure that I stay in touch all the time, so he knows and understands that I am there for him and that I prioritize him first . . . . I look forward to it working out some day.*

She then identified a chapter entitled education: "*I'd like to work with people, and I don't know if I have high standards, but it will work out some day and I have thought about becoming a physician one day, so I look forward to it. When I get back on my feet one day then I'll work toward it.*" Although we cannot know without further probing, her future chapters appear disconnected from her past, with little elaboration of the pathways toward her desired future. This need not be an issue especially connected to psychopathology. Idealized and unanchored future chapters may cause trouble independent of mental illness. Here, we simply suggest that such chapters could signal that individuals need to work on their projected narratives to build hoped-for and attainable futures bringing happiness. This would support hope and optimism, crucial aspects of personal recovery.[3,5,86]

Storying Mental Illness and Personal Recovery: Self Themes in Narrative Identity

Our participants voiced multifaceted and diverse stories of how mental illness affected their self. Some portrayed a self engulfed by illness, as out of control, unable to care for itself, divided, splintered, and confused. Some hid their ill self from others, feared it, and found it difficult to accept. Before the ill self, there was another valued self, a self that some participants felt they had lost to mental illness and were looking to recover. Some also storied feeling different and losing the chance for an ordinary life. The ill self, the different self, and the loss of previous self may give birth to the negative self that many participants depicted, a self of shame, guilt, and embarrassment. A negative self that was too fragile, vulnerable, and sensitive. A sense that the self could not be trusted. Arising from these wounded selves were uncertain and unclear future selves, future stories of feared relapse, decline, and hopelessness. These subthemes may give rise to a variety of negative identity conclusions that could stand in the way of personal recovery if they come to dominate narrative identity (e.g., "I am out of control," "I am powerless," and "my illness will shatter my dreams"). Intertwined with these toxic selves were thinner storylines of positive change resulting from mental illness, often revolving around expanded insight and self-care, demonstrating strength by living through mental illness, and fostering positive characteristics. Such interpretations may bring more positive identity conclusions (e.g., "I can manage my illness") that could support personal recovery.

While mental illness was interpreted as depleting the self of resources, our participants also connected events and interpretations over time to bring forth the self as valued, accepting, agentic, growing, and dreaming. The richness and prevalence of these subthemes suggest that a variety of positive identity conclusions can be center pillars for building well-being and personal recovery. Storying experiences, sometimes from the far past, to highlight self-images that individuals like and can employ in daily life to steer toward desired outcomes they can grow from, may be a path to enhanced thriving. However, this storytelling was balanced with the very real struggles of the self as suffering from mental illness, including the engulfment, the fear, the resistance, the aversion, and the losses. To create future stories that are worth traveling to and possible to arrive at, individuals may require both storylines. They may need to make meaning of what mental illness did to their lives and their selves as well as integrating into the story the identity resources they can gather to build a life they wish to inhabit.

The stories in this chapter testify that narrative identity is crucial to understand the subjective side of mental illness. Taking a life story perspective revealed that mental illness was interpreted as changing the self, causing loss of selves as well as the appearance of the ill self, the negative self, the self as different, and the bleak, uncertain future self. Individuals may benefit from coping with these identity problems when working to recover from their mental illness. The stories also indicate that discovering, reviving, and strengthening the valued, accepting, agentic, growing, and dreaming self could be a promising strategy. We revisit these ideas in Chapters 14 and 15.

Summary

- Our participants storied mental illness as causing a variety of changes to the self, including an ill self, the loss of previous self, a negative self, the self as different, and the future self as uncertain and bleak. These subthemes carry a range of negative identity conclusions, such as "I am out of control," "I cannot be trusted," and "my illness will shatter my dreams" that are obstacles to personal recovery.
- Although rarer, stories where participants interpreted the illness as causing positive changes to selfhood comprised expanded insight and self-care as well as showing strength and developing positive characteristics.
- Stories of well-being featured subthemes concerning the self as valued, accepting, agentic, growing, and dreaming with possible identity implications including "I can change my life for the better," "I can learn," and "I can become."
- Constructing narrative identity to bring forward these positive aspects of the self may be important to personal recovery.

CHAPTER 11

Functional-Level Themes in Narrative Identity

Functional impairment in terms of reduced ability to work or study and care for oneself is part of the diagnosis of many mental disorders (note that relationships are typically included in functional level but that we analyze costs to relationships and their implications for narrative identity in Chapter 9).[51] As reviewed in Chapter 3, individuals with mental disorder are at risk for lower educational attainment, unemployment, and reduced work performance.[17,71] Furthermore, researchers have established that some mental illnesses, including schizophrenia, major depressive disorder, and bipolar disorder are accompanied by impaired cognitive abilities, such as difficulties concentrating and poorer memory.[186–188] In the present chapter, we explore the identity meanings of these functional impairments by analyzing how our participants story the costs of their mental illness on education, vocation, cognitive abilities, and basic everyday functioning (e.g., independent living). We provide an overview in Figure 11.1.

Despite the costs depicted in Figure 11.1, the well-being stories our 118 participants shared within the themes of schooling, work, leisure activities, and living space testify that when individuals create their narrative identities to incorporate successful functioning in these domains, this contributes to a good life. We present subthemes later in the chapter and display them in Figure 11.2.

We note that many of the subthemes we present in this chapter echo insights from Chapters 9 and 10. We believe this reflects that education, vocation, and leisure activities constitute the broader context for identity costs as well as opportunities for positive identity conclusions associated with well-being, also as these wider social circles scaffold beneficial relationships.

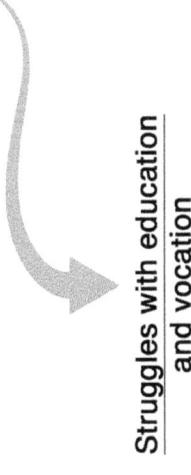

Figure 11.1 Consequences of mental illness for narrative identity: functional-level themes

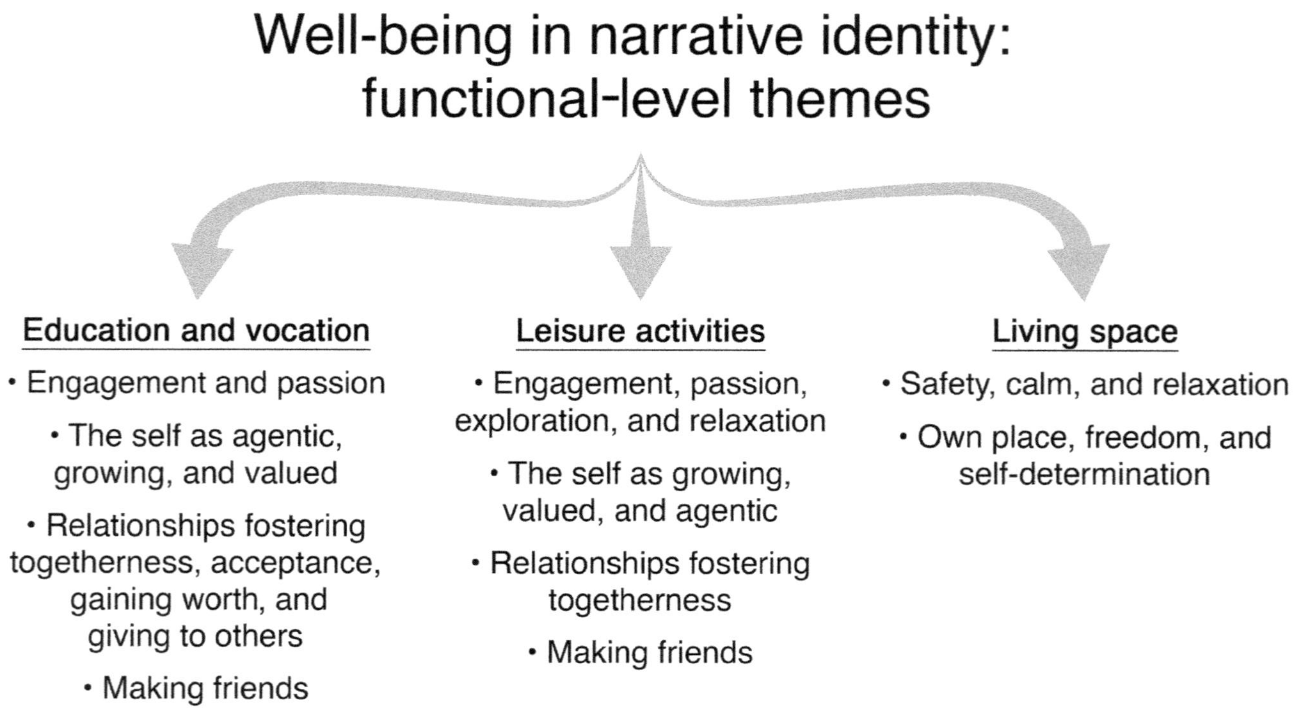

Well-being in narrative identity: functional-level themes

Education and vocation
- Engagement and passion
- The self as agentic, growing, and valued
- Relationships fostering togetherness, acceptance, gaining worth, and giving to others
- Making friends

Leisure activities
- Engagement, passion, exploration, and relaxation
- The self as growing, valued, and agentic
- Relationships fostering togetherness
- Making friends

Living space
- Safety, calm, and relaxation
- Own place, freedom, and self-determination

Figure 11.2   Well-being, value, and meaning in narrative identity: functional-level themes

Subthemes Concerning Negative Consequences for Functional Level

Struggles with Education and Vocation

As we showed in Chapter 8, many participants narrated their mental illness as robbing them of opportunities for education and vocation. Most mentioned it briefly, while others detailed the suffering they lived through when trying to obtain degrees or hold on to their jobs. Some participants interpreted reduced cognitive abilities, instability in daily functioning, and lack of energy as causing problems when pursuing education and vocation. An archetypical story, probably familiar to many experts-by-experience and healthcare professionals, was that schools and jobs elicited stress, anxiety, and relapse, leading to sick leave and educational dropout. Listen to the choir of voices struggling through primary and secondary school, high school, further education, and various jobs (excerpts from nine selected participants):

> *I stall socially and academically, suddenly perform worse than normal. Have poor attention, am inactive and unsure, but don't talk to anyone about it. A very dark and lonely period where I am also bullied more than I probably would have been if I had been OK.*

> *As I start high school, everything falls apart. I experience the pressure, get a bad case of OCD that controls me every waking hour of the day. It turns into a depression .... The depressions come and go several times a year and finally I drop out.*

> *High school was OK, that is, I started ... I still had psychological problems, and cut myself a lot, but I was just trying to get through it. I didn't get a very good exam, but I got through it;*

> *I have a study program where I just need to complete one rotten written assignment and started up again and I have been there for a week and now I have to go on sick leave again and that's not cool. I have been on sick leave for a year, and it has just been a battle to be in that program.*

> *In periods before exams (every second month), I have paralyzing anxiety and days with deep depression and loneliness. Anxiety due to performance, then just two hours of sleep, and then the depression. The depression sometimes kept me from going to school for several days.*

> *We had a test in biology where I was tested in something I really mastered, and I thought "yes." Then I just broke down, completely, I couldn't say a word, I just sat there and cried all the time during the test.*

> *I have realized that I can't hold a job. I just can't. Just a simple thing like coming here at 8:30 a.m.: My brain melts down.*
>
> *I am afraid to start education again and job and things like that. I have dropped that a bit, right now, that is. I have lost belief in myself.*

Our participants interpreted their inability to complete education and hold a job in one word: failure. A few employed terms like low self-worth and social loser, indicating that the failures were incorporated into the negative self. One participant with borderline personality disorder disclosed a detailed narrative about her education. She talked about how her first teaching job caused more and more intense anxiety, leading her to call in sick. She then said:

> *So it ended up in a failure. I don't know how, that is, it's fucking difficult I think, because it's the most fun thing I ever did, but I couldn't go on, because it was too anxiety provoking . . . . Because it meant so much to me. And because there were too many failures, or too many times recognizing, when I was supposed to come in or was there, too many times recognizing every time I failed, that I couldn't handle it.*

With repeated failures, our participants sometimes talked about losing faith and hope that they would be able to enter the world of school and work. Some also spoke about loss of purpose flowing from giving up jobs and studies, as well as financial problems resulting from an inability to hold jobs or work full time.

Some described their futile efforts as leading to part-time education or employment. A few participants also talked about disability benefits. They often resented this option because they perceived it as a signal that all other possibilities were closed, losing hope. One of our participants with borderline personality disorder grew up in an orphanage and shared chapters about emotionally draining relationships with her romantic partners and family. She managed to complete her education as a teacher and obtain a job but burned out after two years. She described her mental anguish when faced with disability benefits:

> *That I received disability benefits, that was a giant failure to me. That I didn't come back. . . . I had to give up work, I became ill, really ill, completely. I was really sad about that. I am really sad about it. I have kicked myself because I couldn't manage anymore . . . . When you are on disability benefits. The thought that you might as well lie down and die. Because what are you doing here? You are just a big failure anyway. You can't do anything. I get those thoughts like lightening.*

However, some participants also spoke about relief, reduction of stress, and much needed calm, when storying disability benefits: "*When I finally received my disability benefits, I calmed down even more. Now everyone, even the public sector, accepted that I was ill."*

This subtheme nests identity conclusions such as "I am a failure because I can't study/work," "I have no purpose because I can't study/work," and "I am stressed out by study/work." This testifies to the narrative processes underpinning the expansion of the negative self as an indirect result of the difficulties with education and vocation stemming from mental illness. Such identity meanings can turn into self-fulfilling prophesies, hindering individuals in pursuing realistic opportunities for study and work that would foster self-worth and purpose, key aspects of personal recovery.[86]

Loss of Basic Everyday Life and Cognitive Functioning

As we revealed in Chapter 8, relatively few of our participants included losses of basic everyday life and cognitive function as consequences of their mental illness when constructing their narrative identities. They elaborated on these losses less and often they were simply mentioned briefly as an integral part of illness episodes, emphasizing the severity. Our participants would talk about how they were only able to lie in bed, could not do basic things like cooking, follow conversations and read, and had to move in with parents or in psychiatric group homes. The peripheral status of these losses in our analyses does not imply that these functional impairments are insignificant in everyday life. Rather, it suggests that from a life story perspective, they bear less identity meaning than costs to relationships, self, education, and vocation, perhaps because they contribute indirectly through their impact on these domains (e.g., difficulties reading would impact education). However, we note that this finding may also reflect the strengths of our relatively well-functioning sample. To the degree that this subtheme becomes central to narrative identity, it may come with implications such as "I cannot care for myself" and "I cannot even do basic things."

Subthemes Concerning Well-Being, Value, and Meaning from Functional Level

Many of the functional-level subthemes were similar to those presented in Chapters 9 and 10, perhaps because we had these previously developed subthemes in mind while coding. When participants shared well-being stories in the context of education, vocation, and leisure activities, they often portrayed the self as valued, growing, and agentic, and relationships as fostering self-worth and togetherness, as accepting, and as opening doors for giving to others. We display our findings in Figure 11.2. Because many subthemes are familiar from the previous chapters where we analyzed relationships and self with functional level in the background, we provide fewer examples here.

Education and Work as Fostering Well-Being, Value, and Meaning through the Self

Many participants simply talked in general terms about work and education as something they liked without much elaboration. Sometimes participants would employ terms like "*exciting*" and "*love my job*," indicating that engagement and passion were brought into narrative identity through the integration of experiences within these domains.

Many shared stories where education and work experiences were the context for bringing forward the growing and valued self. They talked about learning and gaining self-esteem. Most stories revolved around the agentic self, emphasizing mastery and achievement, such as being good at their work, obtaining high grades, entering and completing education, gaining responsibility, and making their own money. One participant with bipolar disorder suffered from severe depression during high school but shared a chapter about working in her gap year, where she causally links the experience to the growth of her agentic self: "*I worked as a theater assistant. It was a positive experience for me since I got quite a bit of responsibility and projects that I managed and was praised for. It gave me a feeling of being in control of things and competent.*"

Sometimes participants would explicitly relate their achievement to their own and others' low expectations due to their mental illness. As shared by a participant with schizophrenia: "*Just the fact that I have gotten a job and have come this far, right? They wanted to give me disability benefits. Right away.*" Or they employed stories to remind them of their agentic resources, reconnecting to past selves. As one of our participants with borderline personality disorder said: "*At the time I also completed my education as a nurse, and I had steady employment at a nursing home before I got on sick leave. It gave me some strength of will. I know that I can do it.*"

Education and vocation served as the context for constructing stories that allowed the self to emerge as agentic, valued, and growing. The identity meanings these subthemes carry may encompass "I can do well at study/work," "I learn from study/work," "I love to study/work," and for some: "I beat the odds by obtaining this job/education."

Education and Work as Fostering Well-Being, Value, and Meaning through Relationships

The most prominent feature of well-being stories, especially within education, was making friends. Good colleagues and teachers were also frequent figures in well-being stories: "*I became really good friends with those I lived with,*" "*there were a lot of good people in there that I became real good friends with,*" "*loved to work with children and cared for my colleagues,*" "*some good teachers who helped me,*" and "*there were some really nice girls in my study program.*" By including such experiences in narrative identity, the meaning our participants may derive is "I can make friends."

Echoing subthemes from Chapter 9, our participants storied school and work around togetherness: "*The first year at the teachers' college, we were just full speed ahead, partying, and fun*"; acceptance: "*I start boarding school back in, that is four years ago, and again I met some people saying 'you are ok, it is OK to be you'*"; gaining value: "*The teacher who was responsible for the workshop was really amazing. She made me feel that I could do stuff and that I was something special*"; and giving to others: "*I worked there for four months during which we created a theater set up with the pupils. I became intensely absorbed in those children and their processes and development. It touched me deeply. I got a sense that it is possible to make a difference for someone, even if it is just a small one.*" In other words: Several of the relationship subthemes that we derived from our analyses in Chapter 9 may sprout from relationships in schools, study programs, and workplaces; to fellow students, teachers, colleagues, and managers. Extending the positive identity conclusions into the domain of education and work may take the forms "I can feel good when I am with others at school/work," "I feel accepted when I am with people at school/work," "I feel valued by my peers/colleagues," and "I can make a difference to others at work/school." As individuals shape their everyday lives from these identity meanings, they can move toward well-being and personal recovery.

Well-being, Value, and Meaning through Leisure Activities

The stories our participants shared revolved around a range of leisure activities. The most prominent were creative projects, including music, theater, visual art, and writing. In addition, our participants often storied traveling, sports, nature, reading, listening to music, and pets with well-being, value, and meaning. They employed emotional terms such as fun, joy, interest, love, novelty, and calm, indicating passion, engagement, exploration, and relaxation as central components. Implicitly these stories carry the identity meaning of capacity for well-being: "I can experience joy," "I can relax," and "I am passionate about..."

One of our participants with borderline personality disorder started her life story with a happy childhood chapter. She then described her ugly youth and loss of contact with her father as the source of her present problems. In elaborating on a recent positive chapter, she illustrates many of our observations:

> *It means that I started doing what I am doing today and which I love. It was good for me. I developed a lot. Creatively and such. I paint. So it is really, really positive. It was positive for me. I had a good job, I loved what I did. I worked in a nursery home. It was fantastic. Made my own money and could paint as much as I wanted to . . . . It was what made me realize that I like art. I find peace in it and get some things out of the system. It is like my world. It has surely been positive for me; it is one of the things I love most. It has been fantastic. I think it is one of the best ways, you know. People walk by the sea, but when I paint then the same thing happens in my head like when people are walking on the beach and look at the waves. It is my beach . . . . It is the last chapter, so it also holds significance because at the time I started therapy, I also started painting a lot, being productive and expressing things. It has a positive influence on me, it really helps with everything. I also use it for . . . I have a great need to be the best and do everything so well and so on. I also use it to, like, I get a lot of self-esteem from it. It is what makes me feel that there is something I can do. It's because I know I am good at it.*

In constructing this narrative, she links her painting to positive emotions and effects on self-esteem. Like this participant, several others explicitly interpreted creative activities as an opportunity to express their difficult experiences and emotions.

As is clear in the quote, our participants storied leisure activities featuring the self as growing, valued, and agentic. When focusing on relationship subthemes, togetherness and developing friendships most often characterized the stories. In other words, leisure activities served as the context for identity implications coupled with well-being as it scaffolded positive aspects of the self and relationships. Unlike education and vocation, leisure activities featured rarely in stories of identity costs of mental illness.

Well-Being, Value, and Meaning through Living Space

In contrast to the other themes we analyze in this section, well-being stories about living space were rarer and did not strongly feature subthemes detected within the superordinate themes of relationships and self. We detected two patterns in how participants storied living space with well-being. One took the form of calm, safety, and relaxation. A participant with borderline personality disorder said: "*Then I got an apartment, which was the thing that made the major difference, when I was 22 or 23, I think.... I ended up living there for about 8 years and that is the longest time I have ever lived anywhere. It made a world of a difference to me, I think. I had a safe base.*" The other pattern revolved around having their own place, freedom, and self-determination. As one of our participants with schizophrenia reflected about moving into a protected home: "*What meant a lot to me was that you had your own, we had small, terraced houses, we were 12 living in small, terraced houses, and I could have a cat and I just remember that meant everything to me.*" As a part of narrative identity, this subtheme implicates meanings such as "I have a place I can feel safe" and "I can decide over my own space."

Storying Mental Illness and Personal Recovery: Functional-Level Themes in Narrative Identity

The identity meaning many of our participants ascribed to their difficulties pursuing education and working was bleak. They paid a steep price for trying to live a "normal" life as structured by society and cultural norms in terms of stress, anxiety, and relapse. They felt like failures when their mental illness got in the way of school and work, and lost faith and hope when the pattern repeated itself. Lack of purpose and poor finances sometimes followed suit. Some storied reduced hours and the mixed blessing of disability benefits. Healthcare professionals, experts-by-experience, and close others may naturally decide that abandoning the culturally valued milestones of completing education and holding a job will ease the pain and protect identity.

On the other side of the scale, however, are the stories of well-being, value, and meaning. Our participants weaved joy, excitement, calm, and fun into their narrative identities through constructing their selves as valued, growing, and agentic when engaging with school, jobs, and leisure activities. They interpreted themselves as capable of developing friendships and depicted fellow students, teachers, colleagues, and managers in nurturing relationships where they felt valued, accepted, togetherness, and able to give to others. The many positive identity implications arising from narrating experiences in the domains of education, vocation, and leisure activities (e.g., "I can do well at study/work" and "I feel valued by my peers/colleagues") testify to their potential in pursuing personal recovery.

While basic everyday life and cognitive functioning were less often assigned a central place in narrative identity, they included the practical costs of mental illness, such as problems with the basic tasks of cooking, cleaning, and reading as well as independent living. These functional losses were often described as a part of severe mental illness with potential negative identity implications such as "I cannot care for myself." Against this backdrop, some of our participants assigned value, well-being, and meaning to living space. They interpreted it as a space where they could feel safe, calm, and relaxed; and as a space that was their own, where they felt in control.

The main lesson from this chapter is that the costs to identity and identity as a source of well-being unfold within larger socially and culturally structured activities that scaffold narratives of the self and relationships. The implication is that individuals working toward recovery may find resources for desired changes in education, vocation, and leisure activities. At the same time, education and vocation is risky, as falling short of requirements tailored to individuals without mental illness may push the ill self, the negative self, and their fellows to the forefront of the story. Policymakers can help by providing flexible possibilities for education and vocation as well as funding for professionals that offer continuous and personally tailored counseling. Centrally, individuals need to pay close attention to the identity implications involved in pursuing these activities: They can harm or help depending on how they unfold over time and are narrated into identity.

Summary

- Our participants storied their mental illness as causing them to struggle with education and vocation, experiencing stress and anxiety, leading to relapse, educational dropout, sick leave, reduced work capacity, and disability benefits. They interpreted these struggles to mean that they were failures.
- At the same time, education and vocation were also storied with well-being, including engagement, passion, and happiness. These stories were often interweaved with the agentic, valued, and growing self and with relationships characterized by togetherness, gaining self-worth, acceptance, and giving to others.

- Leisure activities included a range of experiences, such as creative projects, traveling, and sports. Our participants shared stories about passion, engagement, and relaxation, featuring the growing, agentic, and valued self as well as togetherness with others.
- Our participants often narrated education, vocation, and leisure activities as paths to friendships.
- They described living space as associated with safety and calm as well as the freedom of their own place.
- As such, education, vocation, leisure activities, and living space provide the context for a variety of positive identity conclusions needed for personal recovery.

CHAPTER 12

Treatment Themes in Narrative Identity

When our participants shared their narrative identities, they depicted their illness as causing a range of costs within the superordinate theme of treatment. We organized these into three subthemes capturing the most frequently shared meanings: unclear and negative diagnoses, inadequate access to needed help, and negative aspects of treatment. We display these in Figure 12.1 and elaborate on them below.

It may be painful for healthcare professionals to read stories testifying that individuals with mental illness perceive their efforts to be harmful. At the same time, most professionals realize that the system they work in does not always foster optimal care due to organizational and financial constraints. They are also acutely aware that while state-of-the-art research provides answers to difficult questions and psychiatric care is improving, there is still much to learn. We hope readers with a professional background will engage with the stories in this spirit.

Many aspects of treatment and care were at the same time narrated into identity as sources of well-being, value, and meaning and we developed three subthemes: diagnosis as helpful, the growing and agentic self in treatment, and beneficial relationships in treatment. We show these in Figure 12.2 and, later in the chapter, we unpack their nuances.

The stories shared by our participants do not speak directly to what works and what does not work in treatment and care of mental disorder. Rather they provide a picture of how treatment and care is experienced from a first-person perspective and how it shapes identity in positive and negative ways. As such, the stories may inspire ideas about how to tailor treatment and care to build narrative identities that foster well-being while avoiding identity damage. Such a minimum-negative-maximum-positive treatment and care may translate into improved outcomes. Naturally, healthcare staff should employ evidence-based effective treatment targeting reduction of symptoms and increase of functional level, well-being, and personal recovery. We suggest that while doing so they

Figure 12.1 Consequences of mental illness for narrative identity: treatment themes

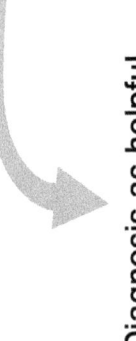

Figure 12.2 Well-being, value, and meaning in narrative identity: treatment themes

pay close attention to how their actions impact the narrative identities of individuals in their care.

Subthemes Concerning Negative Consequences of Treatment

Unclear and Negative Diagnoses

The stories shared by our participants highlighted two negative patterns. The first concerned problems with being diagnosed, spanning from long delays, unrecognized diagnosis, receiving different diagnoses, and even being told that no diagnosis seemed to fit. As shared by one of our participants with schizophrenia: *"I got a hell of a lot of medicine. With all the wrong diagnoses it also meant that I got a lot of wrong medications. Because they couldn't sort out what it [the diagnosis] was, I just got a lot."* The potential identity implication of this subtheme could be along the lines "I am difficult to sort out and therefore to help."

The second pattern concerned negative feelings, such as shock and sadness, accompanying diagnosis of a mental disorder. One of our participants with schizophrenia storied his early life with strong family bonds and school years with friendly peers and teachers. After his high school exam, just before his illness emerged, he was attacked on the street, needing several operations to recover. Concerning his diagnosis, he said:

> Then I got ill in '91 and that was simply a hellish experience. It was. Maybe I put more weight on the diagnosis than I . . . I don't know . . . I thought it was horrible. I thought it was completely horrible. From one day to the next you go from being able to do everything and have all options open and then suddenly the burden.

He interpreted the diagnosis as causing him to lose options, indicating that the diagnosis in itself may sometimes ignite the identity costs we elaborated on in Chapter 10, including the negative self and the bleak, uncertain future self.

Inadequate Access to Needed Help

Our participants described a range of very diverse experiences revolving around the subtheme of inadequate access to needed help. This comprised staff who were storied as not offering treatment and care: *"No one initiated a new therapist for me, so they left me to sink or swim"* or as not helping with practical problems such as living place and work: *"I am sent home from hospital with no place to live.*" There were also staff who provided medicine and psychotherapy that were experienced as ineffective: "*I have seen three psychologists who have not managed to help me very much, I think*" and who were portrayed as not perceiving our participants' needs: "*Then there is a nurse. Or a psychiatrist. I tell them that I have been feeling unwell. Then they say: 'Well, why is that?' Like, well, you have done these things that you know are not good for you and so on. You know, all the time analyzing what you have done wrong.*"

Some stories explicitly or implicitly concerned "the system," such as long waiting times for diagnosis and treatment, lack of treatment due to staff vacation time, shifting staff and financial priorities, and inflexibility in treatment provision. One of our participants disclosed how he had been violent as a part of his schizophrenia, suffered from massive self-harm, and had been hospitalized at a forensic psychiatric ward. He had moved from group home to group home and one of them he described the following way: "*We were a group of drug abusers and externalizers [psychiatric term referring to individuals who display signs of distress outwardly, often in a destructive way] who lived together. It went totally wrong. The staff constantly ran away. We got new staff all the time, no one stayed because it was too hard.*" Later he moved to a new psychiatric group home where he was happier until the following happened: "*Then it simply closed so I have to start from scratch again. I just feel gigantically let down in some way. I had just begun to feel better and now you [the system] are ruining it.*"

From this subtheme, identity conclusions such as "I will not get the help I need" and "no one cares" may emerge. If this becomes central to narrative identity, it may shape a range of behaviors, such as withdrawal and hostility toward staff that reduce possibilities of benefitting from treatment.

Negative Aspects of Treatment

As our participants composed their narrative identities, one subtheme revolved around negative effects of treatment and care, ranging from medicine side effects, disliked effects of psychotherapy, to stressful hospitalizations. Where the subtheme of inadequate access to needed help centers on the absence of help, this subtheme concerns interpretations of harmful impact of treatment. Many participants, often with schizophrenia, but also with bipolar disorder, narrated resented side effects of medicine, unplanned consequences of medicine, or receiving the wrong medical treatment. They talked about weight gains, diabetes, eye diseases, tiredness, poor memory, loss of sexuality, triggering of affective episodes, and feeling like zombies. Some stories depicted healthcare staff as drugging our participants with medicine or as fumbling along as they tried different medical products. While rarer, some of our participants also storied disliked aspects of psychotherapy, including detesting their therapist or the group, the hard work involved, and straining family bonds.

We read many vivid stories of hospitalizations, particularly from participants living with bipolar disorder and schizophrenia. The stories revolved around coercive treatment, not fitting in at the ward, and the stress of living among others with mental illness, including scary behavior and fellow patients sharing advice about self-harm. Some also talked about poor communication with staff. Our participants employed strong emotional language when disclosing negative hospitalization stories: *"shock," "fear," "violent," "the worst experience in my life," "I was scared shitless,"* and *"totally awful."* One of our participants with schizophrenia storied an episode during her hospitalization where she was overcome by extreme anxiety and attempted to jump from a window she had just smashed. A nurse was holding her hand, talking to her, while our participant was sitting in the window sill:

> *Then these big men came over and grabbed me and pulled me inside again.... They take me, both holding me, to the closed ward.... I remember that I talk, shout, with the doctor and she wants to mechanically restrain me and give me an injection, and the mechanical restrain I didn't care about, but I would rather not have the injection. But I get it and then I remember, well I don't remember any more.... Then I remember that I wake up the next morning in an empty ward restrained to a bed with no one around. The door is closed, and I really need to pee, so I shout out, but it takes a very long time before someone hears me.*

Note that some participants shared stories with similar, although less intense, content about psychiatric group homes, such as the stress of coercion, lack of autonomy, surveillance, and living among other individuals with mental illness.

Toxic identity conclusions can arise from this subtheme, including "I am harmed by treatment." Recall that narrative identities reflect subjective interpretations of experiences, not scientific facts. Accordingly, an important task for healthcare staff is to provide care and treatment that foster more adaptive identity implications as these are crucial for sustained engagement in treatment that can support personal recovery.

Subthemes Concerning Well-Being, Value, and Meaning from Treatment

As we pointed out in Chapter 3, treatment directed at reducing symptoms – a core aspect of mental illness diagnoses – may not automatically improve well-being in the process.[82] In principle, our participants could have shared stories where traditional treatment, such as medicine, decreased their symptoms and once symptom free they grew as persons, developed positive relationships, and felt happy and satisfied. Although some participants shared well-being stories within the context of traditional treatment, such as valuing symptom relief, this was not the dominant story line. Still, we would like to share a vivid story from one of our participants with bipolar disorder, which followed this structure:

> *My psychologist at the center was fantastic. He employed cognitive therapy and acceptance and commitment therapy, and I could start sensing that the medicine helped. There was a kind of filter that was removed, and I got more stable energy when I could sleep through the night. I had 10 sessions and when spring came, I really got well. I was no longer depressed. I started to see myself, life, people and the world in a completely different way.*

Note also that general positive statements about treatment ("I got better") may reflect the medicine → symptom reduction → well-being structure. Still, from a first-person perspective, treatment focused on symptoms seems not to suffice in gaining well-being, value, and meaning. This relates back to the idea that mental health and well-being is not simply the absence of illness (see Chapter 4)[95] and the idea that well-being may depend on how illness and its costs are narrated into identity.

Our participants disclosed many diverse well-being stories of treatment and care. Many simply said that treatment had positive effects, they were happy about therapy, and that they felt better as a result of treatment and care. The subthemes developed in Chapters 9 and 10 (relationships and self superordinate themes) influenced our analyses and we grounded the current subthemes in these. Like education, vocation, and leisure activities, treatment provides a context for positive identity conclusions and thriving when it features positive aspects of the self and relationships. We organized the stories into the following subthemes: diagnosis as helpful, the growing and agentic self in treatment, and beneficial relationships in treatment (see Figure 12.2).

Diagnosis as Helpful

As will be clear from the above, some of our participants storied diagnoses with negative consequences. At the same time, some also interpreted it as bringing well-being, value, and meaning. A recurrent message seemed to be that diagnosis contributed to clarity and understanding: "*It isn't just me who has to pull myself together, there are others who feel the same way. When I read about it, I can really recognize the problems and putting some words on it really means a lot to me*"; "*I got a stable diagnosis that suited me and got the right treatment which wasn't just that they couldn't explain my symptoms*"; "*Getting the diagnosis was a relief because it provided an explanation for why I couldn't master it by myself*"; "*It was positive to find out what it was*"; and "*I get the diagnosis bipolar which is a huge relief.*" The identity implications could involve "I can make sense of my experiences," "I am not alone," "I am not weak," and "I can get help with my illness." Coupled with the earlier analyses demonstrating that lack of diagnostic clarity was narrated as problematic, it appears that some of our participants value the meaning a fitting diagnosis provides for difficult experiences (see also Chapter 2), while some also suffer negative identity effects when diagnosed.

The Growing and Agentic Self in Treatment

The growing and agentic self was featured strongly in stories about well-being, value, and meaning in the context of treatment and care. Our participants emphasized the self as learning and developing. Many highlighted a change in their inner world, in their perspective on themselves and their illness, employing terms like understand, think, see, find out, realize, and explain. Note that this differs from positive consequences of mental illness because our participants did not interpret the illness itself as impacting them positively. They appeared as agentic selves in how they sought out treatment and worked to get better. One of our participants with schizophrenia shared this reflection:

> *Especially these last years, where I have had more time and energy to focus so much on treatment, I have become much, much better at knowing myself and knowing what is going on in my mind. Before it was a lot like, I knew I felt bad, but I didn't know why, and I didn't know how or what kinds of thoughts go wrong. I didn't know, but I have become much better at that. I can feel when I get stressed, why, and what I should do about it. A lot of self-development.*

Some also made causal connections between engaging in treatment and growing positive aspects of the self, such as improving self-esteem and becoming stronger. As one of our participants with bipolar disorder said: "*I work with it [her disorder] for many years with hospitalizations in between. The last one in 2015. I get better, I develop some tools and a growing sense of strength and abilities.*" Some mentioned concrete life changes such as obtaining education or vocation and quitting drug habits as a part of their growing self in treatment.

When individuals highlight this subtheme in their narrative identities, it grounds implications such as "When I engage in treatment I get better." Such codas likely contribute to empowerment and taking responsibility for managing the illness, both aspects of personal recovery.[86]

Beneficial Relationships in Treatment

A few participants storied well-being into treatment experiences by accentuating positive contact with peers with mental illness, such as feeling understood, supported, and having a sense of community: "*There was also another patient about the same age as me, so I talked a lot to him. I played chess with him, and table tennis, and we did a lot of things, I think.*"

Many healthcare professionals took on the role as helpers when our participants narrated their identity. These included doctors, psychiatrists, staff at psychiatric group homes, support persons, psychologists, nurses, and social workers. Participants underscored varied key aspects of these relationships, and several of these are similar to the relationship subthemes we developed in Chapter 9. They mentioned help and support from staff, who took their perspective and understood them. They valued it when professionals supported autonomy, provided hope, were direct, and made demands. These characteristics mirror guidelines from patient-centered treatment.[189] Of primary importance here, such stories shape how individuals understand themselves in relation to healthcare staff. One of our participants with schizophrenia disclosed an engaging story encompassing several of these subthemes. She identified a chapter in her youth entitled "*The darkness*" which revolved around hospitalization, countless involuntary mechanical restraints, and living in a psychiatric group home. The staff from her hospital decided to move her to another hospital and here she met a new doctor:

> *I get this totally amazing doctor . . .. God, she had a kind of hope or belief in me. She didn't know me at all, but she just saw a light, I think, and in some*

> way, she transmitted that hope to me . . . . She was really into asking me about what I thought, and I was really poor at answering. Everyone else used to give up when I didn't answer, because I had this long response time and I really had to think and you had to ask the question in twenty different ways, before I could simply get it in and formulate something. But she took the time for it and it just worked very well, because it meant that treatment was centered around things that mattered to me. Like before when decisions were just made over my head, decided that now we do this and now we do that, where she like went "what do you want?," "I would like to go for a walk" and then we worked toward that.

She then talked about her support person whom she described as holding a similar attitude. Later she stated:

> Like today, when I think back upon him and the doctor, I am moved by how much energy they poured into this hopeless project, or that was what it seemed at the time, right . . . . So meeting these two people has meant a lot to me. You know, they may not have made me recover, but they have planted a kind of hope in me, which has clearly been of vital importance to my improvement.

In this narrative, she causally connects various treatment events with growing hope and improving.

When individuals emphasize this subtheme, they may draw identity meanings such as "I am understood and supported by staff" and "I can become better with the help of professionals." In combination with other positive identity implications presented in Chapters 9–11, these may pave the way for personal recovery.

Storying Mental Illness and Personal Recovery: Treatment Themes in Narrative Identity

Many, but not all, of our participants narrated their identities with early vulnerability including physical and psychological violence, parental alcohol abuse, neglect, bullying, and social exclusion. At some point, their illness erupted, the ill self entered the scene with its splintering, chaos, confusion, fear, secrecy, and loss of self-care and self-control. They disclosed how their mental illness flowed into strained and ruptured relationships, guilt, shame, and loneliness with negative implications for their identities. They lost their previous self, feared how their ill self may shape their future, and a negative self moved to the forefront. Education and vocation became an uphill battle, interpreted as signs of personal failure. They needed treatment and care. However, treatment itself came with a price. Our participants narrated frustration when healthcare professionals were perceived to stumble in diagnosing and providing appropriate help within a system that sometimes seemed counterproductive. In their stories, they paid a price of long-lasting and resented side effects of medicine, coercive treatment, and fear during some hospitalizations. These subthemes may give rise to identity conclusions such as "I don't get the help I need" and "I am harmed by treatment."

While our participants told life stories revealing negative treatment effects, they also portrayed healthcare professionals as powerful allies, who took their perspective, understood, nurtured hope, fostered autonomy, were direct, and made demands. Our participants shared narratives about how they grew in the context of treatment and care, learned about themselves and their illness, and developed positively. They described how they sought out treatment and worked with staff to get better. The analyses spotlight an identity perspective of psychiatric care and treatment. What professionals do have implications for how service users see themselves. Do interactions with staff scaffold narrative identities featuring the negative self and the ill self or the agentic and growing self that is needed for well-being and personal recovery?

While some of our participants storied helpful reductions of symptoms from traditional treatments such as medicine, most well-being stories did not follow a medicine → symptom reduction → well-being structure. Our first-person perspective suggests that symptom reduction may be interpreted as valuable, but that healthcare staff can fruitfully supplement this approach with narrative identity interventions if the aim is to assist individuals with mental illness grow well-being. We provide a guide for working with narrative identity toward personal recovery in Chapter 15.

Summary

- Our participants recounted a problematic lack of clarity in diagnoses. While diagnosis provided explanation and understanding, some participants shared stories about negative reactions to diagnosis. As such, when diagnosis is included in narrative identity, it may scaffold both positive and negative identity implications.
- They narrated treatment and care with negative impact, including instances when they were not helped by healthcare staff, side effects of medicine, and hospitalizations with coercive treatment and scary behavior in fellow inpatients. If toxic identity conclusions from these subthemes come to dominate (e.g., "no one cares" and "I am harmed

by treatment"), individuals may withdraw from treatment and become hostile toward staff.
- In parallel, treatment was the context for well-being stories revolving around the subthemes concerning the growing and agentic self, nurtured by healthcare staff who were helpful and understood their perspective, fostered hope, supported autonomy, made demands, and were direct. Identity implications from these subthemes included "I can get help with my illness" and "when I engage in treatment I get better."
- The analyses testify to how narrative identity can be constructed with both positive and negative meanings as a part of psychiatric care and treatment. We suggest that healthcare staff pay attention to how their actions may impact the identity of the individuals in their care as identity is a crucial resource for personal recovery.

CHAPTER 13

Summary and Synthesis

In this book, we set out to answer two main questions: 1) What do life stories reveal about subjective consequences of suffering from mental illness? and 2) What do life stories reveal about experiences bringing well-being when living with mental illness? Based on the assumption that narrative is at the core of how individuals make sense of experience and create identity, we argued that examining life stories provides a valuable first-person perspective on mental illness.[8,9] We analyzed life stories from 118 individuals with severe mental illness and found that they narrated their disorder as leading to cascades of negative consequences within the superordinate themes of relationships, self, functional level, and treatment. As individuals incorporated these costs into their narrative identities, toxic identity implications emerged. In parallel, some individuals storied positive impacts of their illness on relationships and self. Below, we summarize and integrate the findings on consequences for narrative identity emerging from Chapters 9–12 into one model (displayed in Figure 13.1) and discuss how it supplements existing research in psychopathology and personal recovery.

When our participants narrated their identities, they shared a multitude of well-being experiences despite the steep price of mental illness. These stories fell into the same four superordinate themes of relationships, self, functional level, and treatment, which underscores that happiness can grow where mental illness takes the highest toll. Relationships and selfhood ran as intertwined red threads through stories of thriving. Later in the chapter, we synthesize the findings from Chapters 9–12 into one model of how narrative identity may support well-being (displayed in Figure 13.2) and discuss it in relation to personal recovery.

Consequences of Mental Illness for Narrative Identity

As we display in Figure 13.1, individuals living with severe mental illness experience a range of costs that color their narrative identities.

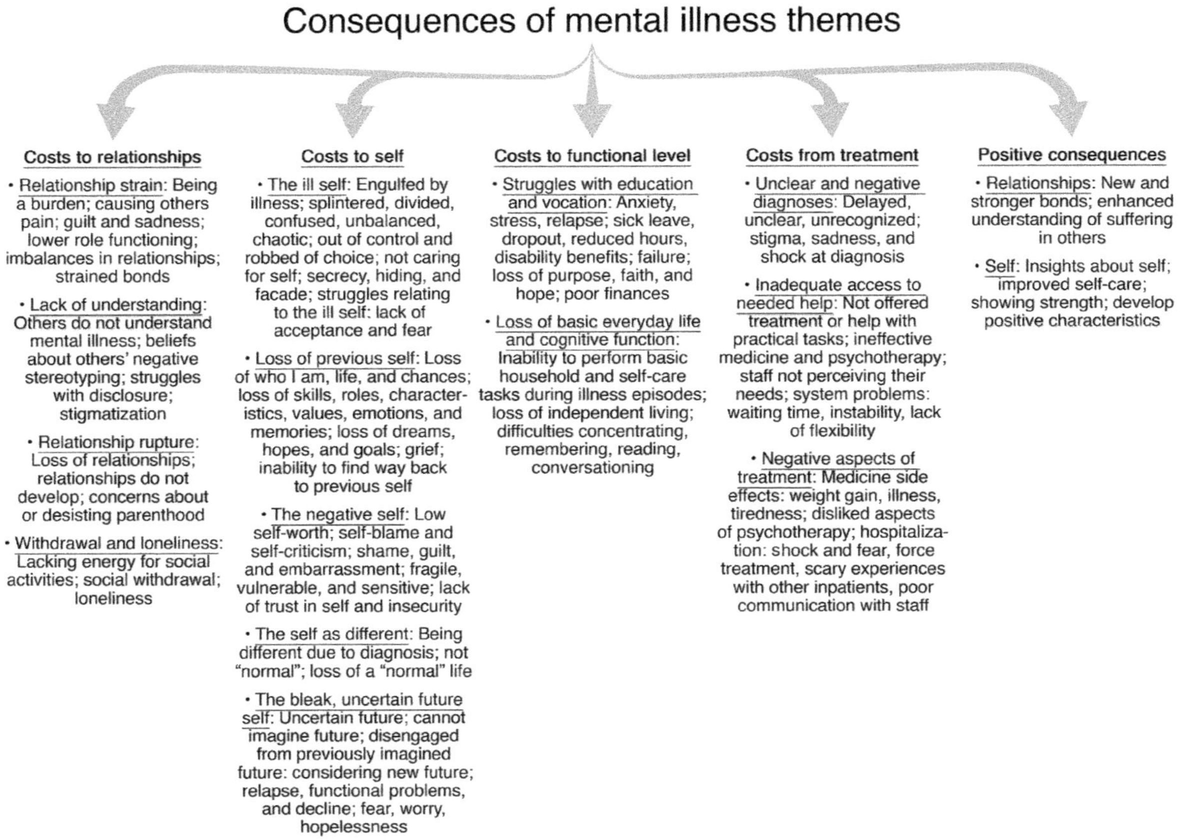

Consequences of mental illness themes

Costs to relationships
- Relationship strain: Being a burden; causing others pain; guilt and sadness; lower role functioning; imbalances in relationships; strained bonds
- Lack of understanding: Others do not understand mental illness; beliefs about others' negative stereotyping; struggles with disclosure; stigmatization
- Relationship rupture: Loss of relationships; relationships do not develop; concerns about or desisting parenthood
- Withdrawal and loneliness: Lacking energy for social activities; social withdrawal; loneliness

Costs to self
- The ill self: Engulfed by illness; splintered, divided, confused, unbalanced, chaotic; out of control and robbed of choice; not caring for self; secrecy, hiding, and facade; struggles relating to the ill self: lack of acceptance and fear
- Loss of previous self: Loss of who I am, life, and chances; loss of skills, roles, characteristics, values, emotions, and memories; loss of dreams, hopes, and goals; grief; inability to find way back to previous self
- The negative self: Low self-worth; self-blame and self-criticism; shame, guilt, and embarrassment; fragile, vulnerable, and sensitive; lack of trust in self and insecurity
- The self as different: Being different due to diagnosis; not "normal"; loss of a "normal" life
- The bleak, uncertain future self: Uncertain future; cannot imagine future; disengaged from previously imagined future; considering new future; relapse, functional problems, and decline; fear, worry, hopelessness

Costs to functional level
- Struggles with education and vocation: Anxiety, stress, relapse; sick leave, dropout, reduced hours, disability benefits; failure; loss of purpose, faith, and hope; poor finances
- Loss of basic everyday life and cognitive function: Inability to perform basic household and self-care tasks during illness episodes; loss of independent living; difficulties concentrating, remembering, reading, conversationing

Costs from treatment
- Unclear and negative diagnoses: Delayed, unclear, unrecognized; stigma, sadness, and shock at diagnosis
- Inadequate access to needed help: Not offered treatment or help with practical tasks; ineffective medicine and psychotherapy, staff not perceiving their needs; system problems: waiting time, instability, lack of flexibility
- Negative aspects of treatment: Medicine side effects: weight gain, illness, tiredness; disliked aspects of psychotherapy; hospitalization: shock and fear, force treatment, scary experiences with other inpatients, poor communication with staff

Positive consequences
- Relationships: New and stronger bonds; enhanced understanding of suffering in others
- Self: Insights about self; improved self-care; showing strength; develop positive characteristics

Figure 13.1 Consequences of mental illness for narrative identity: an overview of themes

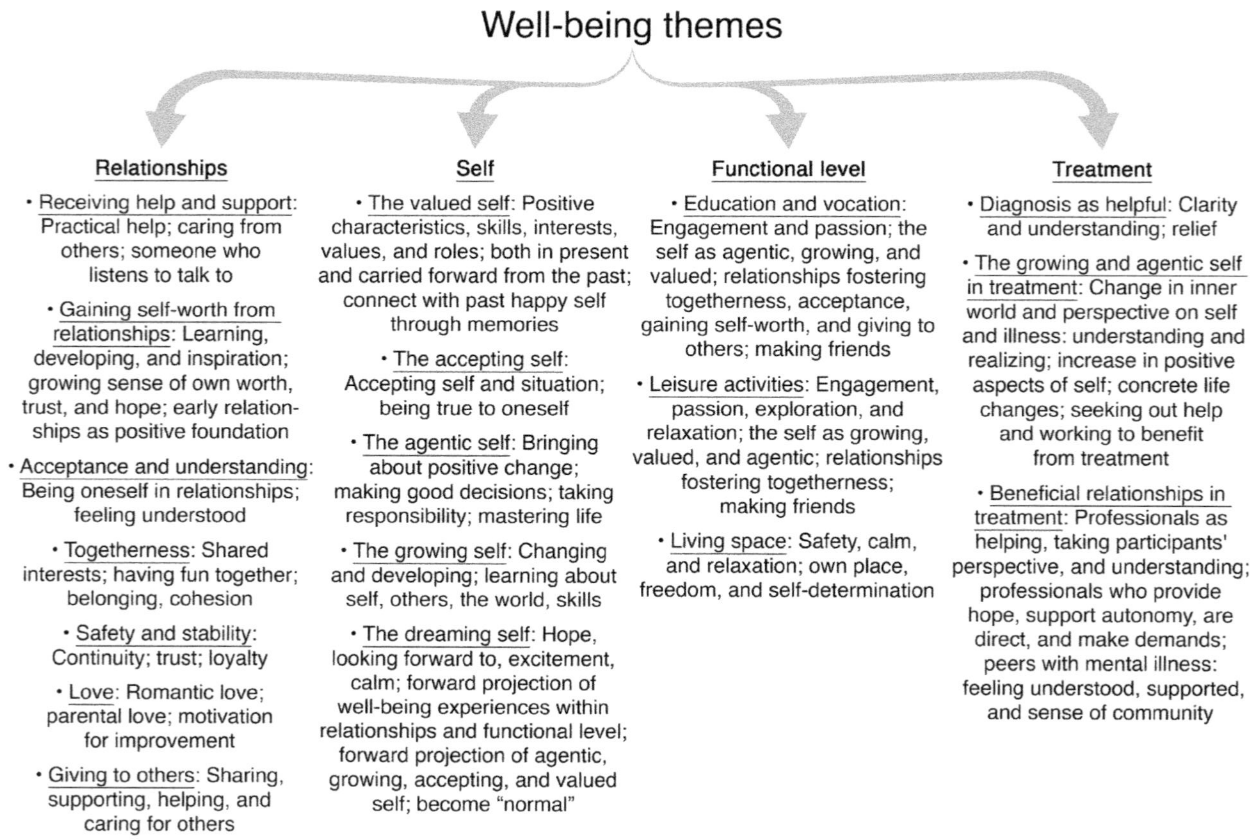

Well-being themes

Relationships

- **Receiving help and support:** Practical help; caring from others; someone who listens to talk to
- **Gaining self-worth from relationships:** Learning, developing, and inspiration; growing sense of own worth, trust, and hope; early relationships as positive foundation
- **Acceptance and understanding:** Being oneself in relationships; feeling understood
- **Togetherness:** Shared interests; having fun together; belonging, cohesion
- **Safety and stability:** Continuity; trust; loyalty
- **Love:** Romantic love; parental love; motivation for improvement
- **Giving to others:** Sharing, supporting, helping, and caring for others

Self

- **The valued self:** Positive characteristics, skills, interests, values, and roles; both in present and carried forward from the past; connect with past happy self through memories
- **The accepting self:** Accepting self and situation; being true to oneself
- **The agentic self:** Bringing about positive change; making good decisions; taking responsibility; mastering life
- **The growing self:** Changing and developing; learning about self, others, the world, skills
- **The dreaming self:** Hope, looking forward to, excitement, calm; forward projection of well-being experiences within relationships and functional level; forward projection of agentic, growing, accepting, and valued self; become "normal"

Functional level

- **Education and vocation:** Engagement and passion; the self as agentic, growing, and valued; relationships fostering togetherness, acceptance, gaining self-worth, and giving to others; making friends
- **Leisure activities:** Engagement, passion, exploration, and relaxation; the self as growing, valued, and agentic; relationships fostering togetherness; making friends
- **Living space:** Safety, calm, and relaxation; own place, freedom, and self-determination

Treatment

- **Diagnosis as helpful:** Clarity and understanding; relief
- **The growing and agentic self in treatment:** Change in inner world and perspective on self and illness: understanding and realizing; increase in positive aspects of self; concrete life changes; seeking out help and working to benefit from treatment
- **Beneficial relationships in treatment:** Professionals as helping, taking participants' perspective, and understanding; professionals who provide hope, support autonomy, are direct, and make demands; peers with mental illness: feeling understood, supported, and sense of community

Figure 13.2 Well-being, value, and meaning in narrative identity: an overview of themes

Many storied how their illness made them feel like a burden to close others, impaired their ability to fulfill social roles (e.g., as parents and friends), and strained relationships. They shared how they lost relationships to their mental illness, doubted their ability to parent, withdrew from social activities, and felt lonely. Mental illness came between our participants and others who had difficulties understanding the impact of the illness or held stigmatizing views. Importantly, this gap between our participants and others also shaded their inner landscape. They imagined and feared others' negative evaluations. These subthemes carried a web of toxic identity conclusions, such as "I am a burden" and "I am alone."

In symphony with these costs to relationships, many participants disclosed stories of how the illness directly affected their selves in negative ways and tinted narrative identity conclusions. They portrayed an ill self, which they struggled to accept, feared, and hid from others. This fear seeped into their future chapters, which, although often hopeful, had the ill self lurking at the edge. They also talked about losing the self they were and the dreams they had before mental illness and turning into someone too fragile and vulnerable with low self-worth. Finally, they narrated how they felt different from others and sensed the opportunity for a desired "normal" life slipping through their hands.

Many of our participants talked about how mental illness overwhelmed them as they were pursuing education or holding jobs. Almost with one voice, they interpreted these problems as a signpost of personal failure. As the story repeated itself, some participants described how they lost faith and purpose. While disability benefits sometimes gave needed respite from the stresses of education and vocation, some participants also detested disability benefits as a message that all hope was lost. The loss of basic everyday life and cognitive functions featured more rarely in the life stories, possibly because the relationship, educational, and vocational problems these losses likely contributed to overshadowed them in the context of creating life stories. Vocation and education more often constituted the context for negative identity meanings such as "I am a failure" and "I have no purpose."

Many of our participants storied aspects of treatment as a burden. Some of our participants with schizophrenia and bipolar disorder graphically depicted detested medicine side effects and strongly negative emotional experiences during hospitalization. Some participants also narrated diagnosis and treatment as lacking clarity and effectiveness, and communication with healthcare staff as problematic. The adverse identity meaning arising from these subthemes could encompass "I will not get the help I need" and "I am harmed by treatment."

While positive consequences were rarer, several participants interpreted their illness as a path to enhanced insight and care for themselves. Some talked about personal growth and the strength gained from coping with psychiatric disorder. Furthermore, their illness fueled understanding of and empathy for others in difficult circumstances, such as fellow sufferers. From these subthemes, identity implications such as "I can manage my illness" and "I can help others who are in pain" may grow.

In the analyses, we zeroed in on each of the four superordinate themes. However, as is very clear from the quotes in Chapters 9–12, costs to relationships, self, and functional level, and consequences from treatment were linked when individuals constructed their narrative identities. The negative self arose from relationship rupture and educational failure. The ill self withdrew from the social world and proved too much to handle for some close others, straining and breaking bonds. The previous self may be lost and difficult to recover when friends from that part of life are estranged. Hospitalization and medicine side effects may contribute to impaired functioning with implications for social, educational, and vocational life. These are just examples to illustrate the interconnectedness in the web of narrative identity costs individuals with mental illness can become caught in.

Our model as depicted in Figure 13.1 complements research under diathesis-stress frameworks, which emphasize vulnerability and stressors as causes of mental illness.[6,58,64] Treatment inspired by diathesis-stress frameworks focuses on alleviating the causes and maintaining processes involved in mental illness with the implicit assumption that if healthcare professionals intervene with these, individuals will return to well-being. Researchers have demonstrated that treatments conducted from this perspective can be effective.[190,191] However, there is a rising awareness that we need to expand understanding and treatment of mental illness to encompass outcomes other than symptom remission and functional level.[2,80]

Our analyses suggest that to advance understanding and treatment of mental illness, researchers and healthcare professionals could move their attention to the damage it does to narrative identity. This aligns with ideas from the personal recovery literature, which highlights the necessity of recovering from the effects of mental illness.[5,73] In Figure 13.1, we provide a list of narrative identity costs that individuals with mental illness may need to tackle to recover. While the nature of these costs is unique and subjective, and as such very different creatures from more objectively established and general processes within diathesis-stress models, they have very real impact on the lives and thriving of individuals with mental illness.

We suggest that these costs may be recognized as such when individuals create narratives grounded in their experiences and that the costs become pervasive when individuals weave their identities to reflect toxic implications. Narrative is a basic mode of understanding that individuals need to comprehend the subjective side of how mental illness impacts them.[9] As a vehicle of insight and identity, life stories can serve as tools to build personal recovery.[8,98] We provide more practical guidance in Chapter 15.

Narrative Identity as a Source of Well-Being, Value, and Meaning When Living with Mental Illness

We integrate our findings on well-being subthemes in narrative identity in Figure 13.2.

As we recounted in the section above, mental illness stole away interpersonal bonds. At the same time, many of our participants narrated well-being, meaning, and value into their identities by portraying close others as supportive, helpful, caring, understanding, and accepting. Further, they thrived when they could give to others and provide needed care, support, and help. They interpreted learning, development, and self-worth as growing from treasured relationships characterized by trust, safety, and stability. They spoke warmly of love and togetherness in shared activities. Our participants harvested well-being and value from relationship stories with family, partners, friends, children, and many others. The adaptive identity implications emerging from these subthemes could include "I gain strength from caring relationships", "I belong", and "I can help and support others."

Education, vocation, and leisure activities provided platforms for narratives featuring peers, colleagues, managers, and others while accentuating friendship, togetherness, acceptance, gaining worth, and giving to others. In juxtaposition to harmful treatment experiences, our participants shared well-being stories depicting connections to healthcare staff and other professionals that were helpful and understanding, took the perspective of our participants, and provided hope, autonomy, and support, while being direct and making demands. Some participants also narrated understanding from and community with peers suffering from mental illness as connected to thriving. From these subthemes, the following meanings may seep into identity: "I can do well at education/work" and "I can get help with my mental illness."

Intertwined with stories interpreting the massive impact mental illness had on the self, we discovered stories featuring selfhood as a rich trove of well-being. Our participants shared valued aspects of their selves, sometimes discovered early in life and sometimes more recently recognized. They experienced thriving when they accepted themselves and their situation; when bringing about desired life changes, taking responsibility, and mastering life; and when learning and developing. These treasured self-images may bloom in tandem with bonds to close others that accept and value them and in broader contexts that nourish such relationships (e.g., education, vocation, and leisure activities). When our participants projected themselves into a future with well-being, they emphasized helpful aspects of relationships and the continued growth of the self as agentic, accepting, and valued. Notably, most participants described a hopeful future narrative identity, while still accommodating the reality of their mental illness. Complementing the negative stories of treatment, our participants gained well-being when they expanded their understanding of themselves, actively sought out help, and worked with healthcare staff and other professionals to benefit from treatment and grew valued aspects of their self. The analyses of these subthemes indicated a rich variety of positive identity conclusions such as "I can learn and grow," "I am X [personal strength]," and "I can handle difficulties."

Stories of well-being emerged both with mental illness as the backdrop but also in versions that did not explicitly feature psychopathology. We highlight this observation because it suggests that working with narrative identity to facilitate well-being could spotlight both mental illness and other parts of life. Individuals are much more than their mental illness. They are parents, friends, creative, caring, students, workers, artists, strong, sociable, and many, many other things. One step in employing storytelling to nurture thriving, gain hope, and grow positive identities could be to bring these other selves more to the forefront. We suspect that the ill self and its dreaded companions (the negative self, the self as different, and the bleak, uncertain future self) occupy center stage in the stories lived by individuals with mental illness, who experience low well-being and struggle to recover. Engaging in narrative identity work to balance these selves with selves that bring well-being, meaning, and value is one pathway to personal recovery. Indeed, the valued, agentic, accepting, growing, and dreaming self we unearthed in our analyses resonate with core aspects of personal recovery.[3,5,86] We provide more details on how to facilitate personal storying toward recovery in Chapter 15.

Summary

- We synthesize the findings from Chapters 9–12 into two models illustrating the consequences of mental illness for narrative identity and narrative identity as a source of well-being when living with mental illness (see Figures 13.1 and 13.2).
- The models complement research conducted under diathesis-stress theories, which center on causes of psychopathology, to suggest that researchers and healthcare professionals could focus on understanding and intervening with the massive impact of mental illness and the costs for narrative identity.
- Further, the models supplement current approaches to personal recovery by providing 1) an overview of the consequences and impact on narrative identity individuals with psychiatric disorder may need to recover from and 2) identifying narrative identity resources that could pave the way for well-being and recovery.

CHAPTER 14

Understanding the Interplay between Narrative Identity and Mental Illness: A Framework

In this chapter, we view our findings from a broader perspective, integrating them with ideas reviewed in earlier chapters. The main purpose of the book so far has been to provide analyses illuminating the impact of psychiatric disorder and resources for well-being from a narrative identity perspective. In this chapter, we expand our focus to also address the question of how narrative identity may be a vulnerability to mental illness. This is the first part of the framework we present. While our life story interviews cannot speak directly to this issue, as vulnerability must be prospectively examined before the eruption of disorder, we draw on ideas from Chapters 5 and 6 to suggest potential pitfalls for narrative identity. In the second and third part of the framework, we draw more directly on the analyses from Chapters 8–12 to illuminate how narrative identity is affected by mental illness and crucial for personal recovery. The purpose of this chapter is to compose a fuller understanding of how narrative identity and mental illness interact. While empirical findings discussed in earlier chapters support parts of the framework, much of it is still speculative awaiting further research. Despite this limitation, we believe our framework will assist researchers, experts-by-experience, and healthcare professionals to appreciate the complex interplay between narrative identity and psychopathology while providing the foundation for working with narrative identity to aid personal recovery. In Chapter 15, we build on this framework to outline our guide for narrative repair.

The Interplay between Narrative Identity and Mental Illness

Our findings can be viewed through different lenses, casting light on the significance of relationships, education, vocation, leisure activities, and treatment from a first-person perspective. Given that our starting point is narrative identity, we expand on our findings from this perspective and present insights on how narrative identity and mental illness interact. While backgrounding the superordinate themes of relationships, functional level, and treatment, these are still a part of the framework. They constitute the contexts for stories of costs (e.g., individuals narrate themselves as failures when illness interrupts education) and well-being (individuals construct stories of the growing self as a part engaging with treatment).

We present our framework employing a transdiagnostic perspective. This is partly for pragmatic reasons since we analyzed the life stories from a transdiagnostic perspective and in general found few differences between groups. Past studies of narrative identity in psychopathology have shown similar patterns across different mental disorders (see Chapter 6).[37,141,148] We further ground this decision in research demonstrating transdiagnostic processes involved in mental disorders (see Chapter 2).[50,53] Still, we acknowledge that our participants do not represent all psychiatric disorders and that our approach was not well suited to detect diagnostic differences. We recognize that diagnostic differences in the interplay between narrative identity and psychiatric disorder may be likely. While we do not elaborate, future studies will hopefully illuminate this issue.

Our framework outlines how narrative identity may be a vulnerability to psychopathology, be affected by mental illness, and be crucial for personal recovery, but we do not claim that narrative identity acts alone. Rather, narrative identity is one piece of the puzzle in comprehending mental illness from a psychological and medical standpoint. A host of other factors, including personality traits, emotion-regulation, attachment patterns, and biological processes, are involved in psychopathology.[6,64,192–194] Narrative identity is nested in the complex human mind and as such in dynamic exchange with other processes. However, we argue that narrative identity may be particularly important from a first-person perspective of individuals coping with mental illness, because they live through multiple life transitions and massive transformations in their inner worlds. Recall the idea that narrative identity moves to the forefront during times of change.[106] To create personal continuity, purpose, and meaning when mental illness periodically disrupts daily life and its associated selves (self as student, self as parent), narratives are essential. Stories are needed to explain how individuals fell into mental illness, what their disorder did to them, how they coped and grew better, why they relapsed, and what was important for finding their way back to thriving again. At the same time, individuals with mental illness sometimes lack tools for composing their lived and told stories. We elaborate on this vulnerability below. Note that while we describe the framework in general terms and believe it will hold explanatory power for many individuals with mental illness, it will not apply equally well to all individuals. The fit will depend on the unique pattern of experiences and interpretations in the person's narrative identity.

Narrative Identity as a Vulnerability to Mental Illness

The first part of our framework concerns narrative identity as a vulnerability to psychiatric disorder. This idea parallels diathesis-stress models.[58] As alluded to in Chapters 6 and 7, we and others have demonstrated that individuals with a range of mental illnesses struggle to story their lives in adaptive ways.[38,41,141,148] The problems may take a variety of forms and depend on diagnoses. When living with mental illness, individuals may tell stories that are less coherent, fail to tie together events organized in time, incorporate plausible explanations for life changes, and lack reflections on how key chapters impacted them. In addition, such life stories place little emphasis on positive meaning, including growth and learning, or may do so in ways poorly anchored in experience. Individuals with psychopathology bring memories and interpretations suffused with powerlessness and social discord to the center stage of their stories at the cost of other memories that would support more adaptive narrative identities. These aspects of narrative identity may constitute vulnerability to mental disorder because they are liabilities when individuals confront life stressors, such as starting education, moving to a new city, and romantic breakup. Equipped with narrative identities that provide little scaffolding for structuring narratives of negative events and with little opportunity for emerging as active protagonists and experiencing the support of others, individuals may more easily fall victim to intense stress. Such stress could trigger cascades of symptoms and functional impairment in biologically and psychologically predisposed individuals.

Vulnerable narrative identities grow out of a variety of past experiences. As reviewed in Chapter 5, close others coauthor narrative identity from childhood and onwards.[118,122] Extensive research documents that troubled early relationships constitute a vulnerability to mental illness.[69,195] One effect of such negative interpersonal experiences could be that it depletes narrative resources. Many of our participants' life stories carried clear evidence of massive relationship issues in childhood and youth. We witnessed stories of parental neglect, silencing of abuse, and social exclusion in school. Due to lack of opportunities for sharing stories, such dearth of social connection could erode capacities for narrating experiences to make sense of them and understand their implications for identity. With depleted narrative resources, negative events may prove overwhelming and defeat order and comprehension, paving the way for chaos "narratives."[11,121]

A second type of vulnerable narrative identity may surface when individuals fall victim to massive traumatic events. Recall our participant from Chapter 3 who protected her mother from being beaten by the alcohol-abusing father and who was placed in foster care. Events such as these are well-known risk factors for psychopathology and associated with a range of processes that can trigger mental illness.[69,196,197] At the same time, traumatic events are raw material for building a negative narrative identity[156] and their harmful impact may double if individuals interact with hostile coauthors who insist on identity-defeating interpretations of blame and inadequacy.

Finally, the local narrative ecology may brim with toxic vicarious life stories,[118] leaving individuals with few story models to assist them in narrating negative events with more adaptive meaning. From such negative narrative ecologies, narrative identity may unfold into versions casting individuals as passive victims, stunted in their growth, and others as unhelpful or even harmful.

We present narrative identity as a possible candidate for preexisting vulnerability that together with other risk factors may trigger mental illness in some individuals. It has been argued that some experience with storying difficult events is needed to craft a resilient narrative identity that can support adaptation in times of stress.[118] We agree with this notion and emphasize that vulnerable narrative identities may emerge from erosion of narrative capacities stemming from neglect, exclusion, and silencing; from overwhelming traumatic events coupled with hostile coauthors and lack of adaptive story models. Such circumstances may lead to narrative identities with little potential for coherence, agency, communion, or positive meaning. Crucially, we do not understand vulnerable narrative identity as stable, it can wax and wane with shifting life events, changes in other aspects of personality, and evolving narrative ecologies. As we expand on in the next section, the eruption of psychopathology may push individuals to spotlight negative meanings of the past to make sense of their illness, shifting their narrative identity toward the ill self, the negative self, and their sources.

Psychiatric Disorder Affects Narrative Identity

The second part of our framework concerns how mental illness disrupts narrative identity and is grounded in the subthemes we discovered when analyzing negative consequences for narrative identity in Chapters 9–12, including the ill self, the negative self, the self as different, loss of previous self, and the bleak, uncertain future self. The disorder may sever the threads of individuals' ongoing narratives, leaving them with little connection to their past story and a future that dissolves as the ill self takes over, teeming with chaos, division, and loss of control, throwing self-care to the wind. In acute crisis, the ill self dominates with lived turmoil, confusion, and splintering, defeating the organizing power of verbal storying.[121] At other times, the ill self may share the scene with the negative self, featured in narrative identity conclusions of how weak, vulnerable, and fragile individuals feel as a result of their mental illness, submerged in self-criticism, self-blame, lack of trust in themselves, accompanied by shame and guilt. These negative identity conclusions may be reinforced when relationships are strained or lost. Individuals may silence the stories of their ill self and hide them from close others and themselves. They may struggle to accept the ill self into their life story and fear its full return in their future chapters. Illness and the costs that may flow from it (educational dropout, inability to work, and loss of independent living) push forward stories featuring the self as different and the negative self. When individuals reflect on how they miss one cultural milestone after another (as represented in the cultural life script, see Chapter 5),[128] they sense opportunities for a wished-for "normal" life escaping.

The previous selves from before mental illness seem lost, as the illness cuts through the fabric of these previous selves. When individuals drop out of education and vocation, suffer ruptured relationships, and struggle with independent living, they risk losing the associated valued, agentic, and growing selves, which may seem forever gone. Following Lars-Christer Hydén,[131] we suggest that individuals may begin narrating their life from the vantage point of severe mental illness, so that the story starts to shift to provide explanations for how they became ill enough to attempt suicide or enter a psychiatric hospital or lose their ability to care for themselves. Healthcare praxis, such as collecting anamneses that emphasize illness-related events, may reinforce this story shift, by telling again and again when symptoms started to occur, identifying potential triggers, and generating reasons for worsening. While detailed information about the illness is essential in tailoring treatment to provide the best possible help, a single-sided zooming in on the illness story may foreground this story at the cost of others. As indicated in our analyses, adverse treatment experiences may foster the growth of negative identity conclusions. Furthermore, the attention of healthcare professionals and others who coauthor the narrative identities of individuals with mental illness, may be subtly guided by negative master narratives of mental illness. As the restitution master narrative may fit mental illness poorly,[121] there is little help for structuring more adaptive illness narratives. Professionals may ask elaborate questions when narratives center on vulnerability, trauma, and deficit and overhear aspects testifying to strengths and resources. After all, they also need the story to make sense of why their patient is in so much pain and diathesis-stress models tell them to look for strain and liability. Such storying pushes the ill self, the negative self, and the self as different to the center of the stage, and fades out the agentic, valued, and growing selves, which are desperately needed for personal recovery. As this told story shapes the lived story, individuals' actions begin to confirm the self-defeating story, feeding back into the told story. As a natural continuity, the bleak, uncertain future self overwhelms narrative identity, potentially leading individuals into a future darker than it needed to be. If individuals enter into mental illness carrying vulnerable narrative identities, the ill self and the negative self find fertile ground for rapid growth.

Some individuals may not experience clear moments of illness eruption. Rather, they narrate their problems as existing for as long as they can remember. Mental illness did not sever an ongoing narrative identity, it is a constant in their stories – a constant that may wax and wane, but with little sense of a self and a life before mental illness. While they may not story the consequences of their psychiatric disorder with loss of a previous self, their narratives could still feature the ill self, the negative self, the self as different, and the bleak, uncertain future self. Likely, their narrative identities would also shift gradually toward emphasizing these selves at the cost of the agentic, valued, accepting, and growing selves.

Narrative Identity as Contributing to Personal Recovery

The third part of our framework concerns how personal recovery can grow from narrative identity and we ground this part in our analyses of sub-themes concerning sources of well-being in Chapters 9–12 (the valued, agentic, accepting, growing, and dreaming selves), while also borrowing from Paul Lysaker's concept of narrative repair (see Chapter 6).[135] When the ill self dominates, lived chaos abounds and verbally narrating experiences is a challenge.[121] Individuals may also shy away from stories even when the ill self subsides. Fear of its return and lack of acceptance can sabotage narrating how mental illness impeded life and robbed personal resources. Nevertheless, individuals need to story their mental illness to gain understanding and acceptance, and to repair the identity damage it did. Notably, this narrative differs in important ways from anamneses and other similar accounts elicited in traditional healthcare. It weights the subjective side of the story, the landscape of consciousness, to integrate it with the factual events, the landscape of action,[9] typically emphasized in clinical interviews. This first step of narrative repair revolves around telling what caused the disorder, what it was like, what its course was, how they felt, and what it did to them and their lives: the costs to relationships, self, educational and vocational achievement, and basic daily and cognitive functioning with their accompanying toxic identity conclusions. The story may also incorporate grief for lost life and previous selves eaten up by the chaos of the ill self.[62] Following Arthur Frank, the focal point in this first step is to narrate suffering.[121] Ideally, this personal illness story provides framing for the pain, it structures the turmoil of guilt, shame, fear, grief, sadness, and anger to become understandable reactions to experiences, and it equips individuals with narrative tools to cope with both continued and remembered suffering in daily life.[11] Based on our analyses, we also suggest that individuals make room in their stories for potential positive impacts of mental illness on relationships and self, but resist the push of our culture to tell redemptive stories if this does not fit their experience.[109] The storying in this first step of narrative repair ignites insights into the narrative identity consequences of mental illness, which point toward the task ahead: searching for pathways to restore or discover a narrative identity which can guide individuals toward a life worth living. As evident in our analyses, storying treatment to foreground the agentic and growing selves that actively seek out help and collaborates with healthcare professionals to recover could be an essential thread in weaving personal illness stories directed at thriving.

The second step in narrative repair is to bring adaptive self-images and well-being experiences (back) into narrative identity. These include the valued self, the accepting self, the agentic self, the growing self, and the associated identity conclusions that surfaced from our analyses in Chapters 9–12. To scaffold this process, individuals can share past chapters and memories, reflecting on these positive selves as they are narrated in the contexts of relationships, education, leisure activities, vocation, and treatment (as evident in Chapters 9–12). These selves may be associated with goals, skills, values, interests, and roles that are either still evident in individuals' daily lives or lie dormant waiting to be recovered. However, delving into the story of who one was before the eruption of mental illness can be a double-edged sword. The chapters may point to a cherished past perceived to be forever gone or it may point to a past that is an active resource today or at least partly possible to recover. Facilitating grieving for losses and at the same time vitalizing treasured aspects of the past,[62] while also balancing these feelings and insights with present chapters, could be important to composing an enriching and sustainable narrative identity that can shape a good life.

The third step in narrative repair is projecting a desirable and realistic personal future flowing from the story work at the first and second step. It is a future that can inspire hope and ease present burdens, as captured by the dreaming self subtheme presented in Chapter 10. Individuals with mental illness may elaborate on this future and consider how they as protagonists in their own lives can bring the hoped-for future story into play through everyday actions with the help of close others and healthcare staff. To be adaptive, we suggest that such reflection needs be grounded in the present and the past rather than crafted as unanchored idealized images. Bring to mind our participant quoted in Chapter 10 who described future chapters of reconciling with her ex-boyfriend and studying medicine with few explanations of how she would bring this future to life. To be lived, the future story needs a beginning in concrete present circumstances and a protagonist ready to maneuver into place events that become stepping-stones toward desired future chapters. Recall also our participant quoted at the beginning of Chapter 5, who was in the process of completing her education, hoping to achieve an active work life. When she decided to get back on track, she knew she could not do it alone and started a study group at a day center. She was maneuvering an event into place that would become a bridge to her end goal of completing her degree.

Narrative repair requires supportive coauthors. Individuals must work continually to defy inaccurate stereotypes and negative master narratives (e.g., vulnerability and trauma leads to mental illness with repeated relapse and difficulties with social roles)[20] and they must resist falling back into the stories of the ill self and negative self they have habitually told and lived. Close others, healthcare professionals, and peers can hinder narrative repair if in conversation and action they feature the ill self and its dreaded fellows (the negative self, the self as different, and the bleak, uncertain future self).

Individuals need a warm narrative ecology for story repair. They require close others and healthcare professionals who through open questions, sensitive observations, and supportive actions emphasize the agentic, accepting, growing and valued selves; a social world that nurtures a recovering narrative identity and help settle the repaired story into place. They will benefit from peers who share their own stories of struggling with mental illness and working to recover; who offer vicarious stories that scaffold adaptive personal storying.[182] In wider circles of the narrative ecology, individuals with psychopathology require master narratives of personal recovery depicting possibilities of living well with or after mental illness. Ideally, society would provide them with healthcare systems structured to facilitate citizen-led treatment and recovery support, with continuous personal and financial support during periods of illness debut, stability, relapse, and recovery; and with flexible opportunities for education and vocation besides the beaten track traveled by individuals who are lucky not to suffer from psychopathology. Such societal support would ease the path to crafting narrative identities that facilitate well-being.

Summary

- We outline an understanding of how narrative identity and mental illness interact.
- This framework comprises ideas about how narrative identity may be a potential vulnerability to psychopathology, how narrative identity is disrupted by mental illness, and how individuals can engage in narrative repair to foster thriving and personal recovery.
- Narrative identity as a preexisting vulnerability emerges from negative narrative ecologies including the absence of coauthors and hostile coauthors, which may erode individuals' capacities for storying negative events in adaptive ways.
- Such vulnerable narrative identities can intensify stress in connection with life events and trigger mental illness in biologically and psychologically predisposed individuals.
- The emergence of psychopathology severs ongoing narrative identities, potentially sowing chaos and turmoil, dissolving the hoped-for future as identified in our subthemes of the ill self and the bleak, uncertain future self.
- The entrance of the ill self into narrative identity is accompanied by the negative self, the self as different, the bleak, uncertain future self as well as the loss of previous self, and narrative identity may begin to shift toward trauma, deficit, and vulnerability to make sense of mental illness.
- Existing healthcare practice, such as anamneses, stressful treatment experiences, negative master narratives as well as loss of relationships, education and vocation possibilities, can speed the growth of this toxic change and push the agentic, accepting, valued, growing, and dreaming selves identified in our analyses as needed for personal recovery, to the back of the story.
- To resist the ill self and its dreaded companions, individuals can engage in narrative repair, which includes working on a personal illness story

that makes sense of and accepts the costs of mental illness while coping with fear of the ill self, loss of previous self, and the negative self.
- Narrative repair also involves constructing vitalizing stories that anchor valued, accepting, growing, and agentic aspects of the self and crafting hopeful, realistic future stories with stepping-stones toward projected, recovering selves (the dreaming self identified in our analyses).

CHAPTER 15

Tools for Narrative Repair

In this last chapter, we propose narrative identity methods for enabling well-being and personal recovery. Grounded in our framework from Chapter 14, we outline a guide for narrative repair (GNaR; see Appendix 8 for a case story). We intend this tool for two main audiences: individuals with mental illness who seek guidance as they reach toward recovery and healthcare professionals who aim to assist them. At the end of the chapter, we discuss how peer workers, who have personal experience with mental illness, can employ storytelling to improve psychiatric care and the valuable dividends for healthcare professionals of listening to narratives.

The Context of Our Guide for Narrative Repair

The idea that narratives can mend broken lives is not new. Scientists and therapists with different backgrounds unite in embracing the healing power of stories.[134,154] We base our guide on the literature reviewed in Chapters 5 and 6 concerning narrative, illness, well-being, and psychotherapy, with much borrowed from Paul Lysaker's concept of narrative repair[135] as well as Michael White and David Epston's narrative therapy.[117] Furthermore, we sought inspiration in other scientifically established approaches, including but not limited to acceptance and commitment therapy,[198] interpersonal and social rhythm therapy,[62] positive psychology interventions,[199] value-confirmation,[200] and mental contrasting.[201] We synthesize these ideas with findings from our life story analyses to arrive at our guide for narrative repair. Specifically, we construct the guide to target the identity problems revealed in our analyses, including struggles with accepting the ill self, the negative self evolving from the ill self, fearing the ill self, the bleak uncertain future self, and loss of previous selves. We further ground the guide in the sub-themes emerging from well-being stories, including the self as valued, accepting, agentic, growing, and dreaming supplemented with the insight that these selves often bloom in the broader contexts denoted by our other superordinate themes (relationships, functional level, and treatment).

We anchor the guide in our core assumption that narratives are a basic mode of understanding oneself, events, and emotions.[9,10] Individuals gain insight into their strengths and values through narration. They let positive emotions, such as love, happiness, and calm into their identities through storytelling. Discovering well-being, value, and meaning is crucial to personal recovery and crafting narratives is a pathway to these bounties. When individuals weave narrative identities, their past, present, and future selves with their associated values, strengths, and memories become patterned into meaningful wholes that individuals can claim ownership of, namely their lived and told stories.

The main purpose of the guide is to facilitate exploration of 1) stories of coping with the losses and challenges emerging in our analyses as narrative identity costs of mental illness (see Figure 10.1) and 2) stories integrating adaptive selves into narrative identity (see Figure 10.2), thus paving the way toward personal recovery. The guide aims to nurture narrative skills that individuals can harness when in remission, when in risk of relapse, and when pursuing of personal recovery. We only address narrative identity as a vulnerability to mental illness when such vulnerabilities interfere with narrative repair. In other words, by targeting identity consequences of mental illness, the guide differs markedly from interventions inspired by diathesis-stress theories, which focus on addressing vulnerabilities.[6,64] More specifically, the guide aims to 1) grow acceptance of and coping with mental illness and the identity costs flowing from it, 2) aid resistance against mental illness overtaking narrative identity by energizing adaptive aspects of identity, and 3) scaffold the construction of hopeful and realistic future narrative identities. These purposes reflect subthemes surfacing in our analyses of personal costs and well-being experiences (see Figures 13.1 and 13.2). As such, we move from insights derived from our open-ended analyses to suggestions for practical narrative intervention.

Asking open questions is key to narrative repair. Narrative identities that are wounded need gentle healing. Individuals with mental illness need to author their own story, anchored in experience, resisting the influences of silencing, hostile audiences, and negative master narratives. Finding their voices is essential. Asking open questions, grounded in scientifically established knowledge about narrative identity and mental illness, can foster exploration of positive identities and possible routes to a good life. We highlight exploration rather than change because individuals require storytelling for comprehension, insight, and discovery. If healthcare professionals and close others push storytellers to narrate their lives and illnesses into preconceived templates, like a stereotyped redemption story of their mental illness, their voices may falter, the authoring may become unsure. At the same time, we suggested in our framework that many individuals emerge from acute illness crises with stories penetrated by the ill self and its dreaded companions, with narrative identities shifting to accentuate traumas and vulnerabilities to make sense of their illness, and with negative identity conclusions flowing from the losses accompanying mental illness (e.g., relationship rupture and educational failure) (see Chapter 14). We developed our guide to counter this malaise of mental illness. Thus, the guide structures narrative repair, while still emphasizing the uniqueness of each individual life story. It emphasizes personal exploration, but change can flow from insights emerging in work with narrative repair.

We developed the full guide for individuals in a stable phase of their illness, out of immediate crisis. However, the guide can be employed flexibly and individuals in various places of their illness and recovery course may benefit (as illustrated in the case story in Appendix 8). We intend it to assist individuals with psychopathology who desire a tool for their work toward personal recovery and healthcare professionals called to accompany individuals on their voyage. Close others may also find the guide helpful if they hope to learn more about how their beloved suffer from psychopathology and strive to recover. Depending on the context, the guide may function to scaffold individual life story work, structure conversations about mental illness and recovery with close others, or inform interventions with trained healthcare professionals. Experienced psychotherapists, especially those with a background in narrative therapy, may find it most meaningful to consider the guide as a supplementary source of inspiration to employ in tandem with their other expertise.

Individuals with mental illness, who recognize the ill self and its fellows all too well, may decide that narrative repair presents opportunities for their individual life story work. We suggest that they employ the guide to scaffold this work. We believe that writing their stories from the platform of the instructions and questions encompassed in the guide can spur the growth of well-being and personal recovery. If individuals feel more comfortable recording their stories while talking from the guide, this is another option. If they have a close other, whom they trust and who is a sensitive, nonjudgmental listener, they can ask them to take on the role as interviewer and witness. In any case, individuals may desire a written document that they can revisit from time to time, a testimony of their narrative repair. Such written or otherwise recorded testimonies could be especially helpful to revive in the context of threatening relapse. The testimonies will serve to remind individuals of narrative identity resources that can be used to cope with and resist negative identity conclusions that may move to the forefront of the story if symptoms and functional impairment resurface.

Still, we believe that there are several advantages to pursuing narrative repair with healthcare professionals trained to listen and employ a therapeutic stance. First, they are experienced witnesses prepared to confront difficult life events and emotions and ready to offer a wide space for listening outside the informal rules of everyday conversation (e.g., turn-taking). They possess sophisticated skills attuning them to hear unsaid things and read between the lines. Such competence is important to scaffold elaboration of unique outcomes testifying to the valued, agentic, growing, accepting, and dreaming selves that are fading as narrative identities lean toward the ill self, the negative self, trauma, and vulnerability.[117] Second, healthcare professionals may be in a better position to dose out narrative repair. Their sensitive listening informs them when to pause questions eliciting expansion of the painful struggle with mental illness and perhaps shift to other parts of the story. Their skills help them decide when and how to offer observations on contradictions or overlooked storylines and when to simply listen.

We suggest that healthcare professionals embracing the trusted role as facilitator of narrative repair think of themselves first as witnesses and listeners, simply equipped with a toolbox of questions they can employ to guide storytelling. Second, they can think of themselves as someone who can see the stories from a different vantage point, offering their observations, while keeping in mind that the author is the story expert. To nurture the budding authorial voice, healthcare professionals need to frame their observations carefully and as stemming from their personal perspective on the story, which by its nature is less complete than the storyteller's vista. Think back to our participant with borderline personality disorder quoted in Chapter 6, who told a story dominated by defeat and discord until she arrived at the last chapter featuring "*the best boss in the world*" and caring colleagues in her new workplace. A healthcare professional attuned to listen between the lines may realize that she elaborated little on her own role in bringing this happy chapter to life and did not feature her agentic and valued self and the associated positive identity conclusions. Possible ways to share such observations could be:

> I note that you only briefly talked about your own role in obtaining the job/developing such good relationships with your boss and colleagues. Would

you like to tell me more about what you did to secure this job/gain these trusting relationships? [scaffolding the agentic self]. What does this say about your strengths and about what is important to you? [scaffolding the valued self]

Crucially, the question is an open invitation to elaborate on this part of the story. The decision to expand is always the storyteller's right. We emphasize this point because open questions can feel directive. Recall our participant quoted in Chapter 12, who felt that healthcare staff were always analyzing all the things she had done wrong ("*Then there is a nurse. Or a psychiatrist. I tell them that I have been feeling unwell. Then they say: 'Well, why is that?' Like, well, you have done these things that you know are not good for you and so on*"). In her experience, the professionals implicitly suggest in their open questions that she accepts responsibility and blame for relapse, which did not fit her own understanding. Rather, she shared this metaphor of personal responsibility with us:

> *I accommodate, of course I do, in relation to stress and reduced work hours and all the things that I know are good for me. At the same time, I compare it to going on a bike ride. I can wear reflexes and lights and all those things but if there is a truck coming at high speed and it has to get by, then it will hit me.*

The intricate art of nondirective questions is difficult and likely most healthcare professionals will fail from time to time. Pay attention, acknowledge that the question may have been overly directive, and reframe if possible. Remember that the primary role is to witness and listen. This approach will likely fall more naturally to healthcare professionals working from patient-centered values, emphasizing patients' perspectives and empowerment.[189]

When healthcare professionals take on the role as facilitator with respect to narrative repair, perhaps with explicit therapeutic goals, the relationship between the professional and the individual with mental illness becomes crucial. Extensive literature documents that therapeutic relationships are central to improvement and that good working alliances characterized by shared goals, empathy, and trust are core features.[202] It is beyond the scope of the present chapter to detail this research and we refer readers to more detailed sources.[203–205] Here, we simply advise healthcare professionals to prioritize the working alliance and seek training and supervision by experienced professionals as needed.

The guide does not comprise a fixed 10-session manual. Rather, it directs attention toward tasks and strategies for narrative repair that can be adapted to circumstances. It is a flexible tool that individuals can employ in full going step-by-step or they can select tasks that seem particularly relevant at the time and perhaps return later to continue the work. We believe that individuals at various stages in the course of illness and recovery can benefit from the guide, but caution against engaging with the full guide when individuals are in acute illness crisis or suicidal, where safety is the primary concern. Individuals and healthcare professionals can adjust the temporal scope to fit a range of contexts (e.g., intensive narrative repair for a week or distributed over months), as long as they allow time for the tasks they have agreed to work on. Individuals can undertake narrative repair independently, with a close other, with a support person in a psychiatric group home, with healthcare staff during hospitalization, or with a psychologist in private practice.

Healthcare professionals and individuals with mental illness can employ our guide in tandem with other approaches, if they agree that the guide is a good supplement to ongoing treatment. Individuals who may find the guide helpful will often be engaged in various treatments, including drug regiments, as they embark on narrative repair. As individuals craft desired future chapters, they may recognize that they need to expand their resources and seek out other interventions, such as social skills training, cognitive rehabilitation, or mindfulness exercises, as stepping-stones toward their hoped-for future. As protagonists in their own stories, individuals with psychopathology can pursue these other interventions and braid their effects into the chapter depicting their climb out of an identity engulfed by illness.

Task 1: Initiating Narrative Repair and Tackling Potential Obstacles

When initiating work on narrative repair (see Figure 15.1 for an overview), experts-by-experience and healthcare professionals may find an introduction helpful.

Here is one suggestion for introducing narrative repair, which can be adapted according to the individual and the context:

> Stories are an important way to understand who we are and the events in our lives. I am here to support you in telling your story. Some people find that it helps them to tell their life story. Maybe it will also aid you in exploring who you are, how your mental illness is a part of your life, and where you would like to go in the future. I have a guide that I can use to assist you. It has four tasks, and we can work with all of them or just some of them depending on your preferences [show Figure 15.1 to help organize the introduction]. The first task is to give an overview of your life story in

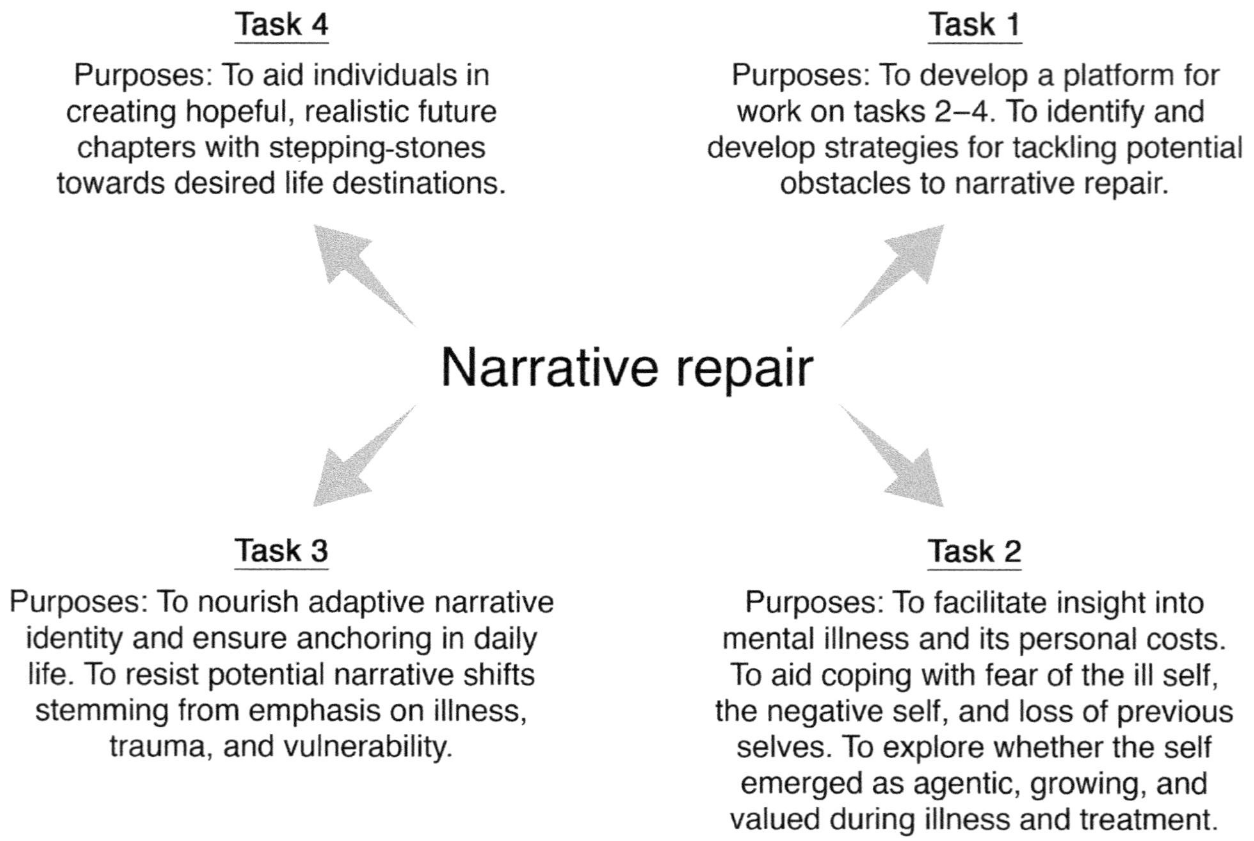

Narrative repair

Task 1

Purposes: To develop a platform for work on tasks 2–4. To identify and develop strategies for tackling potential obstacles to narrative repair.

Task 2

Purposes: To facilitate insight into mental illness and its personal costs. To aid coping with fear of the ill self, the negative self, and loss of previous selves. To explore whether the self emerged as agentic, growing, and valued during illness and treatment.

Task 3

Purposes: To nourish adaptive narrative identity and ensure anchoring in daily life. To resist potential narrative shifts stemming from emphasis on illness, trauma, and vulnerability.

Task 4

Purposes: To aid individuals in creating hopeful, realistic future chapters with stepping-stones towards desired life destinations.

Figure 15.1 Overview of tasks in the guide for narrative repair

order to get a platform for working on the next tasks and identify any difficulties with narrating your life. The second task is to talk about your mental illness and the effects it has on you and your life. The aim of this task is to foster insights into the personal impact of your mental illness, for example negative self-views and losses, and to assist coping with these effects. The third task is to share your life story in general, focusing on the positive parts. The purpose here is to discover and vitalize strengths and values and help bring these into your everyday life. Finally, the fourth task is to describe your future life story, where you would like your story to go. This is important to grow hope while being realistic about how you can change and move toward recovery. There are no right or wrong answers. It is up to you how you tell your story. My role is to listen to your story and help you tell it by asking questions.

We believe it is beneficial for narrative repair that individuals begin by crafting an overview of their life story. They can get a handle on this daunting task by following the instructions below. Here, we suggest two strategies: A free narrative and a narrative structured by chapters, which may be helpful if a free narrative seems overwhelming, too difficult, and/or if the healthcare professional observes that the free narrative loses coherence:

> Are you ready to begin the first task? Then please start by sharing an overview of your life story, from your birth and up to today. It is completely up to you what to include and how to tell your story. The important thing is to try to cover your whole life, from birth to now. You can talk about important events, what they mean to you, and what they say about who you are. In some of the other tasks, you can elaborate more on each part. If you feel ready, you can simply start talking right now.

This can be supplemented with:

> If you think it will be helpful to think of chapters in your life story, you can tell your story chapter by chapter. I have some work sheets that you can use to note the chapters you would like to share (see Appendix 7). Try to give each chapter a title, note important content using key words, and estimate when the chapter started and ended. Take the time you need to get ready to tell your story.

Healthcare professionals can answer questions concerning story focus and form with "It is completely up to you how you tell your story." Standing on the platform of the life story overview, individuals can identify parts of the story revolving around mental illness and parts where mental illness is absent or in the background, easing the path into the second and third tasks. The overview also provides hints to potential obstacles for employing narrative repair to explore possibilities to accept mental illness and cope with its personal costs, energize adaptive identity, and create a hopeful and realistic future. Below, we discuss these obstacles and suggest strategies for tackling them. Note that we suggest a few questions as starting points and recommend that these are followed up by questions and nonverbal gestures to support elaborative storying. Several of the obstacles relate to vulnerable narrative identities as described in our framework in Chapter 14, although they may also represent effects of mental illness. As such, the obstacles can prolong, but need not abort, the journey toward narrative repair.

Obstacle 1: Lack of Coherence. One potential obstacle to narrative repair is incoherence. If stories lack temporal order, causal connections between events, and clear plots they may not enable comprehension and insight. As discussed in our framework, individuals with mental illness may lack narrative skills due to silencing.[122] Furthermore, the chaos of trauma and illness challenges narration.[121] To assist the construction of coherent stories, individuals with mental illness and healthcare professionals can employ chapters to scaffold the temporal structuring of life stories[113] (see Appendix 7). When they have identified and ordered chapters, they can turn to similar strategies for ordering events within chapters (see Appendix 7). Some individuals may find visual aids, like timelines, helpful (see Appendices 3, 7, and 8). During the process of creating temporal structure, individuals can reflect on causal links between chapters and events. Answering the following questions may facilitate such reflections:

> Are there relationships between the two chapters/events you describe? If yes, can you tell me more about how you see this?
>
> Did this chapter/event have effects on later chapters/events? If yes, can you tell me more about these effects?

Obstacle 2: Lack of Balance in Landscapes. Another potential obstacle to narrative repair is an imbalance between the landscape of action and the landscape of consciousness, failing to ignite the full synthesizing power of narrative.[9,117] Some stories list events and happenings with little expansion on their meaning. The protagonist and the author are absent. No one brings about events, no intentions surface. No one reflects on what events did to the protagonist; few emotions and thoughts find their way into the story. Here is an excerpt from a life story that we edited slightly to illustrate this potential problem: "*Then I became ill the first time, mentally ill and had a breakdown and was referred to here and got some medicine. Finished school and was hospitalized here for the first time when I was 16, one and a half months after starting high school.*" On the other side are stories teeming with emotions and thoughts, but with little explanation of events giving rise to this chaotic or bleak inner world:

> I think the chapter was negative. There was little contact with my parents. I had to fight to get their attention. I think I was very lonely, very alone. It may have led to a basic sense of loneliness, I think. Feeling that you are not close to anyone. I am here today with these diagnoses, so it must be a negative way. It is low self-worth that you feel you are not good enough, that you have to fight for attention or for being acknowledged all the time. That you spend your resources in the wrong way.

Both types of stories fail to integrate the double landscapes of action and consciousness, and both call for questions that scaffold the parallel landscape. This includes on the one hand questions that emphasize intentions, emotion, thoughts, and evaluations and on the other hand questions that emphasize actions and concrete circumstances. We list examples of such questions as a part of task 2.

Obstacle 3: Overly Negative Life Stories. A third potential obstacle to narrative repair is overly negative life stories. While the narrative identities of individuals with mental illness naturally contain stressors and strains, stories with an absolute absence of well-being and positive identity conclusions likely reflect a total narrative shift toward identity costs, trauma, and vulnerability or severe depression.[144] The stories neglect contradictory, happier aspects of identity such as the growing and valued selves. In the case of such narrative shifting, attention on unique outcomes and reading between the lines is crucial.[117] For example, professionals can ask questions to invite expansion on experiences of potential well-being just mentioned in passing. One of our participants shared a chapter about a fire in his home and losing his dear kitten. As a part of this chapter, he mentioned in passing going to a sport event with his friends. Individuals with mental illness and healthcare professionals working on narrative repair could delve into this crack in the negative chapter by asking series of elaborative questions inspired by the following:

> I notice that you mentioned going to this sporting event with your friends. Would you like to tell me more about this event? What do sports/your

friendships say about your strengths and about what is important to you? [scaffolding the valued self]

While one purpose of narrative repair is to explore possibilities for resisting negative narrative identities with trauma, loss, and illness at their roots (see Figure 13.1), major depression will likely make the tasks very difficult, because pessimistic thought patterns completely dominate the inner landscape,[63] and individuals may need to delay work on narrative identity until they achieve partial remission. If individuals with milder depression wish to work on narrative repair, they can accommodate their work to the natural variation in mood, planning their story work to take place on good days or good times of the day. Indeed, some of our participants spontaneously mentioned that their stories might look very different on a bad day. Individuals can use their awareness that stories shift with mood, to resist loss of hope on the bad days. Healthcare staff may support this strategy. Listen to one of our participants, who shared a story about how her support person assisted her in holding on to her dream of independent living during the bad days: "*We had a purple box, like you know a soft paper box, and that was for all the good experiences and the positive thoughts. So once in a while when I was, when I felt bad, she pulled it out.*" When working with narrative repair on a bad day, questions can remind individuals of the alternative versions of their stories. By asking such questions, healthcare professionals hold stories reflecting adaptive selves and happiness for individuals with mental illness and enable them to reconnect with these stories and the identity conclusions they carry during times of distress. The professional should take great care to represent the stories as truly as possible. Questions can include explicit references to the two "versions" of narrative identity:

> I have noticed that you tell stories centering on defeat/inadequacy/self-hate today. This seems different from the stories I have heard before [give extended reminding of other stories]. Do you remember these stories? If yes, would you like to talk more about these alternative stories or do you feel that it is important to stay with the stories of defeat/inadequacy/self-hate today?
>
> If focusing on the alternative, more positive stories: How do they make you feel? Do they remind you of other stories? Do these stories make you feel like doing something else than focusing on defeat/inadequacy/self-hate? If yes, what would you like to do instead and how will you go about it? [scaffolding the agentic self]

If focusing on the stories of defeat/inadequacy/self-hate, the professional's main role can be to witness. It may also be helpful to explore the meaning of sharing these stories, but sensitive questioning is crucial in order not to push unwarranted positive meaning onto individuals:

> Why are these stories important to you? What do you hope to gain by telling these stories today? What does this hope say about what is important to you? [scaffolding the dreaming and valued selves]. How can you work toward this important value? Can you think of instances where you acted in accordance with this value? [scaffolding the agentic, growing, and valued selves]

Obstacle 4: Lack of Anchoring. Like the third obstacle, the fourth revolves around the interconnection between experience and narrative identity, albeit in a different manner. We suggest that redemption master narratives, the wish to appear positive or to please their therapist may sometimes push individuals to verbalize interpretations of strengths, learning, and growth that lack resonance in experience (similar to the concept of pseudo-mentalization).[40] We recommend that individuals with mental illness and healthcare professionals continually reflect on how the growing, valued, accepting, and agentic selves are rooted in everyday life. This serves to tighten the connections between narrative identity and experiences. We give examples of such questions in tasks 2–4 (e.g., "Is this learning a part of your life today?" and "How would you go about bringing this learning into your life today?").

Obstacle 5: Lack of Story Ownership. A fifth obstacle to narrative repair is lack of ownership in the story, representing a dearth of agency. This appears as the absence of an "I" that experiences the events, feels the emotions, moves to make changes in life, and authors the story.[11,110] Readers may recall that some of the quotes shared in previous chapters featured such second- or third-person descriptions: a "you" or "one" rather than an "I" (e.g., "*that you feel you are not good enough, that you have to fight to get attention or be recognized*" versus "*that I felt I was not good enough, that I had to fight to get attention or be recognized*"). We think individuals can nurture ownership by telling their stories in first-person language, but we note that some feelings and actions may be difficult to own with the implication that this intervention needs to be very sensitively presented.[110] When healthcare professionals hear stories where the "I" is missing, they can share their observation and invite individuals to reflect on the reasons for the missing "I" or change their narratives into "I"-versions:

> I notice that you told the story using "you/one" rather than "I" [give example]. Why do you think that is? Would you like to share your

story using "I" instead and see what happens? Did you note a change when telling your story using "I"? If yes, please tell me more about what changed.

Obstacle 6: Lack of Memory. The final potential problem for narrative repair concerns lack of raw material for chapters. Some of our participants complained of poor memory. Whether the reason is stress, mental illness, or medicine side effects, individuals can experience gaps in their memory as problematic when pulling together the storylines. If scarce raw material challenges narrative repair, we suggest that individuals employ photographs, music, or objects from the past as reminders.[206] In addition, they can take advantage of the possibility that other people likely created vicarious stories about them.[43] Close others, such as friends and family, or professionals may hold vicarious versions of the protagonists' stories. Individuals need to employ this strategy with caution, as there is a risk that they discover vicarious stories where they do not resonate with how they are portrayed, leading to estrangement. However, warm vicarious versions hold promise. One of our participants grew up in an orphanage and later in her life met a colleague, whose mother had cared for her when she was a child. Listen to her grateful reception of a vicarious story, which began to take shape during a conversation with the colleague:

> *Then my colleague mentions her mother's name and I say: "I know who that is because she tended me in the orphanage. She also cared for me later in the after-school club." Then my colleague looks at me and says: "Are you little [name of participant]?" "What do you mean?" [our participant asked]. "Do you know how jealous and envious I have been of you? My mother and her colleague almost fought about who got to take you home during weekends. My mother", my colleague says, "has a lot of photos with you in her album." Then I got those photos . . . . It was me taking a bath, me eating, me holding a sweet little girl. It is a treasure because I have no photos of my childhood. I looked happy. It has given me, like a bit of calm to hear her version.*

Vicarious stories are colored by those who carry them, and individuals should bear this in mind when receiving the stories and actively seek out close others who they believe will hold loving versions of their stories.[44] Vicarious stories, thoughtfully shared with the protagonist by caring others, may become material for chapters that are almost empty. Healthcare professionals can probe for the possibility of collecting vicarious stories with questions such as:

> I notice you said that you remembered very little about your illness/your childhood and that this lack of memories bothers you. Do you have someone you trust who can tell you what they remember from that chapter

of your life? If yes, do you think it would be helpful to hear their stories? How do you think it may be helpful?

When individuals have collected the stories, healthcare professionals can invite them to elaborate on the memories and their implications:

> Would you tell me about the stories your parent/friend/support person shared with you?
>
> Are the stories helpful in filling in the gaps in your life story and do they help you understand things better? If yes, can you tell me more about how they help you? [scaffolding the growing self]
>
> How do you feel about those stories?
>
> Do the stories and your reactions to them illustrate something about you that you like? Or something about what is important to you? If yes, can you elaborate on this? [scaffolding the valued self]
>
> Do the stories say something about the relationship between you and your close other/professional? If yes, can you elaborate on this? [scaffolding the valued self as emerging in relationships]

Task 2: Narrating Mental Illness to Cope with Fear of the Ill Self, the Negative Self, and Loss of Previous Self

When individuals with mental illness have shared an overview of their life story, they may be ready to elaborate and go deeper. The purpose of this task is to facilitate insight into and acceptance of mental illness and its personal costs, aid coping with fear of the ill self, resist the negative self, and support emotional closure in relation to losses of previous selves and dreams. Furthermore, the task includes exploration of whether the self emerged as agentic, accepting, growing, and valued during illness and treatment thereby giving positive identity conclusions more weight.

We anchor the suggestion to work on a personal illness narrative in a wide range of literatures, including Donald Spence's[134] and Arthur Frank's[121] ideas that illness needs to be storied to defy chaos and incoherence, Mike Slade's[5] concept of personal recovery as encompassing the task to make mental illness comprehensible as well as research demonstrating beneficial effects of narrating traumatic life events, in particular exploring and representing their emotional impact.[11,154] Hence, a key role for professionals is to provide structure and room for difficult stories and to witness. However, there are challenges in this task. Difficult emotions can overwhelm the storyteller and the ill self and the negative self can conquer the story and swallow up meaning. Individuals working independently or with caring others on narrative repair need to pay close attention to their emotional reactions. If these are strong, prolonged, and interfere with daily functioning, narrative repair should be discontinued, and individuals can consider seeking professional help. Healthcare professionals can employ their fine-tuned interpersonal barometers to monitor emotions and may seek out supervision if their own reactions interfere with their therapeutic stance. If the ill self and its dreaded companions begin to dominate meaning, individuals can pause from task 2 and turn to the next task to counter this effect.

Some individuals may prefer to work on task 3 and skip or postpone task 2, if they have elaborated on their illness stories in other contexts, if they feel too vulnerable to return to the stories revolving around their disorder, or if acceptance, negative emotions, and coping in relation to their disorder are not pertinent issues. For individuals who decide to engage with this task, we suggest entering task 2 with the following introduction:

> The second task in narrative repair is to tell the story of your mental illness. Would you like to tell this story now? You can share when it first began, how it unfolded over time, the important moments in your illness story, the effects it had and still has on you and your life, and what you did to cope with your illness and treatment. It is completely up to you what to include and how to tell the story. If you feel ready, you can simply start telling right now.

This can be supplemented with:

> If you think it will be helpful to consider chapters in your illness story, you can tell chapter by chapter when it first began, how it unfolded over time, the important moments, and the effects on you and your life. I have some work sheets that you can use to note the chapters you would like to talk about (see Appendix 7). Take the time you need to get ready to tell your story.

The healthcare professional's main task is to listen and to ask elaborative questions to foster rich descriptions of mental illness and its meaning, including key scenes such as low points and turning points. We include some questions to guide exploration and suggest that open and elaborative follow-up questions are used generously. Here are some questions intended to expand on the landscape of action:

> Would you tell me more about that?
> Who was with you when this happened?

What did you do?

What happened then?

To invite elaboration of the landscape of consciousness, use the questions below:

What are your thoughts about it, then and now?

What does it mean to you, then and now?

How does it make you feel, then and now?

Research indicates beneficial effects of narrating concrete events with shifts between elaboration of emotion and meaning, and professionals can consider moving between questions concerning emotion, thoughts, and meaning when this brings new insights contributing to the aims of task 2.[207] If emotions seem difficult to verbalize or remain absent, a starting point may be to focus on bodily sensations (e.g., tense, lump in throat) and their possible emotional indications.

We reiterate the importance of exploring stories and the professional's main task of supporting difficult storytelling and witnessing. Still, it may be worthwhile to listen for and ask elaborative questions concerning parts of the illness story featuring the subthemes discovered in our analyses on well-being stories, including the valued, growing, accepting, and agentic self as well as relationship stories of support, help, safety, understanding, acceptance, togetherness, love, and giving with the positive identity conclusions they bring forth. These questions target the potential for positive identity change, but need to be asked in the spirit of open exploration to nurture author voices that can be fragile:

> It sounds like you took responsibility/mastered a difficult situation/learned something important/was supported/felt valued/helped someone in need/etc. in this part of the story. Would you like to say more about this part? [scaffolding the agentic, growing, and valued selves]
>
> What does this say about your strengths, values, and resources? [scaffolding the valued self]

To assist individuals in employing these positive identity conclusions to initiate improvements in everyday life, the following questions may be useful for planning concrete actions:

> Would you like to talk about whether these resources, values, and strengths are a part of your life today? [scaffolding the valued self]

If they are not, would you like them to be? [scaffolding the growing and dreaming selves]

If yes, how would you go about bringing these values and strengths into your life today? [scaffolding the agentic, growing, and dreaming selves]

If individuals hesitate in storying the ill self and the negative self, we suggest the questions below as starting points, while continually asking follow-up questions to support exploration and elaboration:

How would you describe yourself when you were most affected by your mental disorder? [exploring the ill self]

How did the mental illness come to be a part of your life and how did it unfold over time? [exploring the ill self]

How do you feel about your mental illness today? [exploring fear and lack of acceptance of the ill self]

Do you fear your mental illness? Please elaborate on what you fear and why [exploring fear of the ill self]

If yes, can you do anything to cope with this fear? Please tell me about what you can do [scaffolding the agentic and growing selves]

Can you recruit help to cope with this fear? Please describe what you can do [scaffolding the agentic and growing selves]

Do you think less of yourself because you have a mental illness? Please elaborate on your thoughts [exploring the negative self]

If yes, would you like to change that? If yes, how would you change it? [scaffolding the agentic and growing selves]

Do you need help to make this change in your life? Will you tell me more about the kind of help you may need and why [scaffolding the agentic and growing selves]

If yes, how can you find this help? [scaffolding the agentic and growing selves]

If the story contains losses flowing from mental illness, as unearthed in our subtheme on loss of previous self, we suggest that the questions below can aid the unfolding of this story and grieving:

I noticed that you feel you lost this part of yourself/this relationship/your hopes for the future. Would you like to say more about this? [exploring loss of previous self]

How did it make you feel back then? And how does it make you feel today? [exploring loss of previous self]

Do you think it is possible to recover this lost self/relationship/future or maybe some part of it? [scaffolding agentic, growing, and valued selves]

If yes, how would you go about that? [scaffolding the agentic and growing selves]

If no, do you think it would be helpful to say goodbye to this lost self/ relationship/future? What may be helpful about saying goodbye? [scaffolding accepting self]

Would you like to try to say goodbye now? Or maybe write a goodbye speech/letter for the next session? If you find it helpful, you can think about what this lost self/relationship/future means to you, what you hope to achieve when saying goodbye, and what this hope says about you [scaffolding the accepting, valued, growing, and dreaming selves].

Task 3: Storying the Past to Revive the Agentic, Accepting, Valued, and Growing Self

The purpose of task 3 is to nourish adaptive narrative identity and ensure anchoring in daily life, resisting the potential narrative shift stemming from an emphasis on the selves emerging from illness (see Figure 10.1), trauma, and vulnerability. The task is based on our findings that meaning, value, and well-being grew out of a range of past and present chapters, which often featured cherished self-images and the self in relation to others (see Figure 13.2). Although most of the questions below target the agentic, growing, accepting, and valued selves, relationships will often enter into the stories as resources for positive identity conclusions. Elaborating on the identity implications of adaptive relationships identified in Chapter 9 may be helpful.

Individuals with mental illness can work on task 3 for as long as they feel that there is material to cover. If time and energy is more limited, individuals and healthcare professionals can decide to focus on the most significant segments of the life story, such as those that capture strong positive emotions, core values, and treasured strengths. We suggest initiating the task with either of these two introductions, depending on whether individuals outlined chapters as a part of task 1:

> This task in narrative repair concerns the parts of your life story that are important to you because they represent parts that were positive. They may

have been positive because they highlight some of your interests and values (such as hobbies, creative projects, sports, travels, volunteer work). They may also be positive because they emphasize some of your strengths (e.g., being persistent, curious, independent) or treasured relationships (e.g., with family, friends, or romantic partners). Finally, they can be positive simply because they were times where you thrived or felt good about yourself. Think back to the overview of your life story. Which parts were positive? Would you like to share more details about these stories now? It is completely up to you what to include and how to tell the stories. If you feel ready, you can simply start telling right now.

This can be supplemented with:

> If you think it will be helpful to return to the chapters in your life story, feel free to do so. Would you like to share more details about these chapters now? It is completely up to you what to include and how to tell the stories. Take the time you need to get ready to tell your story.

Some individuals may find it difficult to identify affirmative aspects of their stories. In such situations, healthcare professionals can remind them of life story parts:

> I recall you told me about an important friendship in high school/your creative projects/a job you were happy with. Would you like to tell me the story of this friendship/creative project/job?

As we outlined under task 2, healthcare professionals prioritize listening and asking elaborative questions using those below as starting points. Reliving memories can be a powerful experience that carries emotions and meaning forward to the present.[116] Individuals with mental illness and healthcare professionals may like to pay special attention to diving into significant memories associated with positive emotions such as joy, pride, calmness, and love. In addition to task 2 questions on the landscapes of actions and consciousness, we suggest eliciting well-being stories with positive identity conclusion using the questions below (depending on the context and time frame some questions can be emphasized):

> What are the important moments or high points in the story/chapter?
>
> What does the story/chapter say about what is important to you? [scaffolding the valued self]
>
> Did you do something to bring about the good things in this story/chapter? If yes, can you tell me more about this? [scaffolding the agentic self]
>
> Did other people do something to bring about the good things in this story/chapter? If yes, can you tell me more about this? [scaffolding positive identity conclusions in the context of supportive relations]

What does the story/chapter say about your strengths/resources/talents/skills? [scaffolding the valued self]

Are these values/resources/strengths/talents/skills also a part of other stories/chapters? If yes, can you tell me how? [scaffolding the valued self]

Individuals may not employ their valued selves in their present day-to-day life and the three questions below may enable planning of concrete actions extending from the valued self:

Would you like to talk about whether these values/resources/strengths/talents/skills are a part of your life today? [exploring whether the valued self is employed in everyday life]

If they are not a part of your life today, would you like them to be? [scaffolding the dreaming self]

If yes, how would you go about bringing these values/resources/strengths/talents/skills into your life today? [scaffolding the valued and agentic selves]

Questions emphasizing the accepting self could include the following:

Is acceptance a part of this story/chapter? [scaffolding the accepting self]

If yes, what did you do to reach acceptance and what effects did acceptance have on you? [scaffolding the accepting and agentic selves]

What does the acceptance part of the story/chapter say about you and what is important to you? [scaffolding the accepting and valued selves]

Questions supporting the growing self could include the following:

Have you changed as a result of this story/chapter or learned something from it? [scaffolding the growing self]

If yes, please elaborate on how you changed and what you learned? [scaffolding the growing self]

To aid individuals in bringing the growing self to bear on everyday life, we suggest the questions below as starting points:

Is this change and learning a part of your life today? [scaffolding the growing self]

If it is not, would you like it to be? [scaffolding the growing and dreaming selves]

If yes, how would you go about bringing this change/learning into your life today? [scaffolding the growing and agentic selves]

Do you need help for this? [scaffolding the growing and agentic self]

> If yes, how would you obtain this help? [scaffolding the growing and agentic self]

To further bolster these adaptive self-images and their impact of daily living, the following task may be helpful:

> Would you like to welcome these changes/learning/values/resources/strengths/talents/skills (back) into your life? You could write a welcome speech/letter for the next session. If you find it helpful, you can think about what these changes/learning/values/resources/strengths/talents/skills mean to you, what you hope will happen when welcoming them back into your life, and how you will keep them in your life from day to day. Try to be very concrete when you consider how to keep them in your life. You can also write about what welcoming them into your life says about you? [scaffolding the growing, valued, agentic, and dreaming selves]

If revisiting these parts of life stories brings emotional reactions to losses caused by illness, individuals and healthcare professionals can turn to the questions we suggested as a part of task 2 to narrate this more fully and hopefully achieve closure.

Visiting places and people of the past connected to brighter parts of their life stories may be powerful reminders reviving memories of happiness, virtues, and strengths.[208] Illustrating this, one of our participants had taken part in a life story intervention led by healthcare professionals.[209] He shared the following:

> *In connection with life story telling, we went back to something called "my place." I chose to revisit the school in [name of village], where I went to school during 6–7th grade . . .. I was with two of the staff at the psychiatric group home, and some other residents who were also in the group. We had to take the bus from Copenhagen to [name of village]. So that was a bit of an event in and of itself. But let's start where we are at the school and I am meeting my old math teacher. The reason for . . . like the place was chosen because it was a central place from my childhood which had a positive effect. At the school, I had some of the few good years during my time in elementary school and high school and I did well in that school. So that is why I chose it. The school is a red building, village-like, small school, went there until 7th grade. So small school, easy and manageable, small setting, and I did well there. It was worse in the larger schools, that's a different story. But it was fun to meet my math teacher there, whose looks hadn't really changed. A few more wrinkles, but otherwise exactly like I remember her . . .. She showed us around in the old classrooms and we talked about stuff. It was like really cozy. She told me what was going on with some of the other pupils, one of them was a doctor and that sort. But the school had not changed, the buildings were the same, everything was the same, the playground was the same, the classrooms also a lot the same. It's funny . . . the*

reason you do it is to strengthen the positive anchor points in your story. It works really well. It was a lovely summer day. It was almost perfect.

Task 4: Storying the Dreaming Self

In task 4, the story turns to the future to aid individuals in creating hopeful and realistic life destinations. We developed this task from our observation that participants were strongly invested in hopeful futures, while suggesting that anchoring in past and present, personal agency, and stepping-stones characterized more realistic and action-supportive future chapters. We borrow insights from Gabriele Oettingen's research that demonstrates that imaging positive futures coupled with ways to tackle obstacles is connected to adaptive action.[201]

Likely, individuals have already touched upon dreams and fears for the future as a part of the other tasks, but here we suggest spotlighting the dreaming self. Some individuals may decide not to engage with this task because they feel that taking their life one day at a time to live in the present is the best strategy (as was evident in our analyses). If this is the case, we suggest closing narrative repair with reflections on how they can bring the healthy selves and positive identity conclusions discovered while working on tasks 2 and 3 to bear in their everyday life. For embarking on the full fourth task, we offer the following introduction:

> This task in narrative repair is about the future parts of your life story. Before you start, it may be helpful to think back to the values, strengths, and hopes discovered during the other tasks, but also insights concerning the costs of your mental illness. This provides the best platform for constructing a hopeful and realistic future life story. Would you like to share your reflections on this?
>
> Would you like to talk about the future you hope will be a part of your life story? It is completely up to you what to include and how to tell the story. If you feel ready, you can simply start telling right now [scaffolding the dreaming self].

Possibly supplemented with:

> If you think it will be helpful to think of chapters in your future life story, you can tell your future chapter by chapter. I have some work sheets that you can use to note the chapters you would like to talk about (Appendix 7). Take the time you need to get ready to tell your story.

We suggest that it will be helpful to first concentrate on the chapters or parts of the future life story closest to the present, because these are more likely to boost adaptive action in the present, creating needed stepping-stones. After individuals have dived into rich elaboration of their future stories/chapters, scaffolded by the questions we outlined under tasks 2 and 3 (e.g., question to unfold the dual landscapes of action and consciousness and to elaborate on values and strengths), we suggest engaging in further reflections, supported by continued open follow-up questions:

> Is the story/chapter a continuation of your present chapters/life story? Or of your more distant past chapters/life story? If it is a continuation of past and present chapters/stories, what is the connection between the future chapter/story and your present/past? [exploring possibilities of connecting with past/present resourceful selves useful for future chapters/stories]
>
> Would you like to talk about how to employ your values/strengths/talents from the present/past to bring this hoped-for future chapter/story to life? [scaffolding the valued, agentic, and dreaming selves]
>
> What are the stepping-stones between your present/past chapter/story and the hoped-for future chapter/story – try to be very concrete? [exploring possibilities of connecting with past/present resourceful selves useful for the future chapters/stories and scaffolding reaching for the hoped-for future through concrete everyday action]
>
> Are there any obstacles on your path toward the hoped-for future?
>
> If yes, would you like to tell me more about these?
>
> Do you have any ideas for dealing with these obstacles? If yes, please tell me how you would go about this and try to be as concrete as possible [scaffolding the agentic and dreaming self]
>
> Do you need help to tackle these obstacles? If yes, can you tell me more about the kind of help you need and how you could go about getting help? [scaffolding the agentic and dreaming self]

Individuals may discover that they identify future life stories with little connection to their past or present chapters and with few or no stepping-stones within reach and this insight may elicit grieving for or other emotional reactions to lost hopes and futures. We suggest that it may then be beneficial to return to the part of narrative repair concerned with loss (task 2).

The bleak, uncertain future self can surface as individuals talk about their hoped-for future. Parts of task 2, where individuals reflect on possible coping strategies to deal with fear of the ill self, may be useful to revisit. We also propose that it can be valuable to craft future stories relocating the feared ill self to a minor role, emphasizing more hopeful parts. One of our participants shared future chapters that radiated acceptance, coping, and hope. She first identified four future chapters on treasured work projects and family challenges. Then she went on to write:

> I continually struggle with episodes of my bipolar disorder. It fluctuates a lot, but luckily with longer intervals between. Now it is present three times a year, twice with depression, once with hypomania. Even when medicated, the depressions sometimes become so severe that I am hospitalized every 5th year and receive ECT treatment. I can almost keep the hypomania on a short leash, so I use the things I have learned to shield myself in these periods. I am luckily still associated with [name of clinic]. Unfortunately, my psychologist has stopped working in 2025 and I only use the place as a security net, therapy as needed. Later on, I get a new psychiatrist, a young woman psychiatrist. It is hard to get used to, but still secure.

She identifies further future chapters on relationships to family and friends and meeting a new partner. Finally, she closes her future story:

> I die the same way as my beloved grandmother. I have planned the memorial and since I am not a member of a church, my friend leads it. I have asked for my ashes to be sailed onto the North Sea and that the whole family be present as it is spread over the ocean which has been one of the most important places in my life.

For narrative repair to nourish personal recovery, the story needs to stay alive after completion of the tasks. Although individuals can always return to narrative repair, the major thrust of this tool is living the story. Individuals must work to set out stepping-stones toward the hoped-for future day after day; welcome and energize the valued, agentic, growing, accepting, and dreaming selves into life day after day; cope with fear of the ill self and resist the negative self with their bleak futures day after day; reflect on the meaning and purpose of all these actions day after day; and slowly but steadily build a narrative identity of personal recovery.

To aid readers who are considering engaging in narrative repair, we include a case story to illustrate how narrative repair may proceed in Appendix 8 (see also another case description[210]). In the future, GNaR needs more systematic testing to examine the effects and expand knowledge about narrative strategies for personal recovery.

Vicarious Stories as Tools for Narrative Repair

Returning to the quote by Arthur Frank's wounded storyteller: "To tell one's own story, a person needs others' stories" (p. xi),[121] we propose that vicarious stories shared by peers can inspire narrative repair. Individuals with mental illness have few master narratives to lean on as they attempt to story a life worth living. The restitution master narrative fits severe mental illness poorly, and illness may cause individuals to fall outside the cultural life script with its designated ages for normative life events such as education and independent living. As they enter psychiatric hospitals, they meet individuals in severe crisis, in relapse, in chronic chaos, living the negative master narrative of mental illness. Like healthcare professionals are confirmed in their bleak views because they mainly see individuals when they are in most pain,[129] individuals with mental illness may come to believe in bad odds as they stay in wards brimming with stories of defeat and downward spiraling. They absorb these vicarious stories, bring them to bear on their own lives, and the bleak, uncertain future self springs to life. They may see their own feared future self, 10 years from now, in those fellow patients, who are living stories of educational dropout, relationship rupture, and loss of independent living. Where do they turn to, to find stories offering alternative paths toward hope?

Stories from peers who have found ways to live good lives with their mental illness may be vehicles for narrative repair. Our participants told well-being stories of sharing experiences with fellow patients, discovering that they were not alone in suffering. To assist narrative repair, peers who have composed their own personal recovery stories are vital.[5,110] Until recently, few such stories were available in the typical hospital ward. Staff and patients may have known such stories, but they were abstract, distant, a weak whisper. However, the psychiatric system is in the middle of an exciting development as it has begun to employ peer workers, that is, individuals who have struggled with psychopathology and recovered, desiring to work with fellow sufferers to support them on their journey to well-being.[5,211] The topic of peer workers in psychiatric healthcare is complex and here we restrict ourselves to suggesting that one crucial function of peer workers is to embody stories of living good lives with, or recovered from, mental illness.

In their mere presence at the ward and in other psychiatric settings, peer workers demonstrate the possibility of personal recovery. They offer alternatives to those bleak future chapters of relapse and decline. If peers are open to sharing their experiences, including the illness and the climb back to thriving, their narratives may grow as vicarious stories in the minds of the individuals they seek to help. Peers need to be careful not to impose their own stories on others, but simply offer their stories in an open manner. Individuals with mental illness then find themselves with multitudes of vicarious stories depicting different versions of psychiatric disorder, a variety of paths toward thriving. Some of those stories may resonate more clearly with their own. They may identify with some peers and not others, underscoring the importance of a rich and varied trove of stories from peers in recovery. Listen to how one of our participants deliberately immersed himself in vicarious stories: "*To keep on the right track, I make sure to get a lot of coaching and hear a lot of people who have fought their way out of illness to get the positive approach and get mechanisms that work. Like all the time being embossed, embossed, embossed.*" Consistent with the quote, research is emerging to suggest that listening to other people's narratives of personal recovery may be beneficial.[182] Furthermore, organizations working to support recovery offer vicarious stories as sources of inspiration.[212,213] Equipped with vicarious stories from peers who have recovered, individuals are not alone in their suffering and they are not alone in discovering a way out.

Individuals can reap vicarious stories of mental disorder and personal recovery from peer workers, from meeting recovered individuals in other contexts, and from books, including the present one. However, just listening to vicarious stories of personal recovery is not enough. To be helpful, individuals need to metabolize vicarious stories of personal recovery into their own stories. We suggest that reflecting on the questions below may aid this process:

> It is sometimes helpful to think about stories of other individuals in similar circumstances. Can you think of stories you have heard from peers that had a positive impact on you?
>
> If yes, would you like to tell me more about this story?
>
> Can you tell me more about your reactions to this story, what it made you feel and what it means to you?
>
> Can you see any parallels between this story and your own story? If yes, please describe these in as much detail as you can.
>
> Are there parts of the story that you think you can employ in your own life? Please tell me more about this.
>
> If yes, how do you go about that in your everyday life? [to scaffold translation into helpful daily action]

We have yet to realize the full potential of vicarious stories for fostering personal recovery. Research on vicarious stories is still in its infancy and we are far from understanding how they may serve as tools to build personal recovery. We introduce vicarious stories as a part of narrative repair because our participants highlighted stories from peers that helped them gain well-being (as identified in Chapter 9).

Can Healthcare Professionals Benefit from Working with Narrative Repair?

We have clarified how individuals with mental illness may open the door to personal recovery by working with their stories. Does narrative repair also promise advantages for healthcare professionals? Rita Charon, whom we briefly introduced in Chapter 6, has argued strongly that listening to patients' stories carries benefits for doctors, nurses, and other healthcare professionals.[132] Writing primarily from the perspective of somatic illness, her insights are still valuable to elucidate the potential positive impact of narrative repair for healthcare professionals.

Charon proposes that healthcare professionals, who elicit and carefully listen to stories, expand their understanding of patients. The stories draw their attention to the complex pattern of illness and problems in patients' lives and increase their appreciation of patients' perspectives, which in turn nurtures empathic responding and paves the way for improved treatment. Similarly, when healthcare professionals embark on the voyage toward narrative repair with individuals they strive to help, they listen to their stories of illness and wellness, witness the chaos, the fear, and the grief, and watch hoped-for futures bloom. They absorb the tales and include them in their stores of narratives from individuals suffering from psychopathology. As they keep these vicarious stories in mind, they deepen their understanding of the person and grow in empathy. Thus, one potential advantage of storytelling is that it facilitates stronger bonds between healthcare professionals and individuals suffering from psychiatric disorder. As such, storytelling can cultivate patient-centered care, a key value in healthcare.[132,214] Knowing the story of how a young woman with schizophrenia excels in artistic pursuits, how important it is to her identity, makes her intense reaction to failure in art school all the more understandable. The healthcare professional who listens carefully to her story perceives that she cannot just try another program or give up education to minimize stress that triggers her illness. The professional recognizes that it is about identity, about meaning and purpose, and that art school is a bulwark against a narrative identity drowning in illness. This empathic appreciation of the meaning the service user ascribes to art school can support the professional in taking helpful action.

Furthermore, vicarious stories of individuals recovering from psychopathology offer reason for optimism to healthcare professionals. Against the backdrop of the bleak statistics on relapse, educational dropout, and social isolation, vivid vicarious stories of personal recovery can transmit hope and meaning to healthcare professionals. But, like individuals with mental illness, healthcare professionals need a wide web of recovery stories, otherwise it becomes all too easy to give in to the negative master narratives and explain the few hopeful stories as exceptions that prove the point.

To illustrate the bounties of vicarious stories for healthcare professionals, we invited an experienced clinical psychologist to write a story of an individual with mental disorder, who lives a good life with mental illness. We also asked that he reflect on what the story meant to him. Here is an excerpt of the extended narrative he shared (note that Tom B. is a fictitious service-user name and that parts of the story have been changed to ensure confidentiality. Tom participated in the preparation of the text and approved the final version):

> *I have worked in hospital psychiatry for 25 years, mostly as a clinical psychologist in the field of psychosis. In the middle of the first decade of 2000, I worked at an outpatient treatment center for incident schizophrenia (CIS). I worked primarily with research, but I was also responsible for some treatment courses. This was where I met Tom B. Tom made a special impression on me because he was an exceptionally smiling and friendly patient, who cooperated extraordinarily well and cared about his treatment. However, as I got to know him better, I found that he also had another side. Behind the smiling appearance Tom was a tormented man with several inner voices, who constantly spoke badly and degradingly about and to him (hallucinations), and with a constant fear that people from TV and groups of elite-soldiers would kill him. On the psychological level, he had very low self-esteem and he constantly felt sad and isolated. Before Tom was referred to the treatment center, he had been admitted to a psychiatric hospital for approximately six months. This was after a suicide attempt, where he had thrown himself into the water from a ferry. In his childhood and adolescence, he had a problematic relationship with a dominant father, and in his school years, he was subjected to severe bullying from his schoolmates. In his youth, he had few friends with whom he often had conflicts. Coincidentally, Tom was randomized to the research project I worked on. I must admit that I do not remember the details of our research interview and cognitive testing. However, I do remember that the interview confirmed my clinical impression of his torment and that the cognitive testing showed that he had more resources than most other patients and a generally high IQ level. A few months after our interview, I had to say goodbye to him, because the time had come for me to process my research data.*
>
> *Twelve years after I met Tom, my workplace was about 175 kilometers away from where we initially met. I had continued in the field of psychosis and was now working with patients characterized by long-term psychiatric challenges. One day, a bit by chance, I saw a notice that a Tom B. would visit the hospital to give a lecture on living and dealing with psychosis. In a Danish context, Tom's name is rather atypical, so I was pretty sure that he was the patient I met*

several years ago. Of course, I did not know if Tom would remember me but if he did, I might be a reminder of a time when he was feeling very bad. This is something that no lecturer likes to confront before or during a presentation, so I was in doubt about whether to go to the lecture. Still, I decided to go. I told myself that I was only one among several healthcare workers he had met, so how likely was it that he would remember me? In addition, I found the topic of his presentation interesting. I decided to arrive just before the presentation started and sneak down to one of the back seats. I really did not want to make him feel uncomfortable. As planned, I arrived late and walked into the auditorium at a brisk pace but had to stop to orient myself. Then it happened: Tom was standing right in front of me. I did not seek it, but we got eye contact, and I saw his face lit up in a smile that I easily recognized. However, something was completely different. When I looked into his eyes, I did not see at all the torment and insecurity that I could easily recall. Instead, I saw an expression that I can best describe as both calm and purposeful. "Isn't it you from CIS?" he said. I confirmed but I could tell from the clock that his lecture was about to start in a few seconds, and said: "How about talking during the break?" He nodded, smiling, and then started a well-articulated, personal, and humorous presentation, which also had a professional weight that made me completely forget our common past. We talked during most of the break and for some time after his excellent presentation. He told me how his life had slowly, but surely stabilized after completing his course at the CIS; how he was contacted by a staff member in a social psychiatric unit, who had motivated him to join a coping with psychosis group and how it had helped him, not just in relation to his hallucinations, but also with respect to his life in general; and not least about how he had met his girlfriend, who had persuaded him to move to the part of the country, where he now lived, and I had my workplace. After our meeting, I felt very happy.

Before I continue and answer the question the authors have asked me, I just want to tell you about Tom's and my relationship today, since we are colleagues. Not on a daily basis but we work in the same organization. I am still a clinical and research psychologist and he is a peer employee. When we meet, sometimes we just greet each other, at other times we stop, talk about work, and how things are going in our lives. As colleagues do.

Then to the real question: What does my story with Tom mean to me? I have had some time to think about this question and will answer it both professionally and personally: One of the professional activities I appreciate most is psychoeducation. The discussion of remission rate, or clinical recovery, is an important part of psychoeducation. However, as a hospital employee, I am handicapped in my clinical experience with both remission and clinical/personal recovery, as I often say goodbye to patients before they reach this part of their lives. Thus, I can talk meaningfully about for example psychosis of which I have several years of clinical experience, but I cannot in the same way talk about remission and recovery. Here my meeting with Tom makes a world of difference. Tom is the living proof to me that what I teach is true: That life with mental illness can take many paths and some of these are associated with shifts and opportunities that one cannot imagine when psychosis seems to tear apart all possibilities for a good life. Now the personal answer: For me, the meeting with Tom is not just a testimony that life with mental illness can change and develop, it is a testimony that life in general, every life, can change. Life contains possibilities that we cannot imagine at all, especially when it hurts, which even my own life does at times. My life, however, has never hurt as much as Tom's did when we met years ago, but on the other hand, I have never been as tough as Tom is. Not many people know this, but Tom and everyone else who has come out on the other side of mental illness are among the coolest persons, for they have fought and won a battle that others can hardly imagine. That is what I learned from meeting Tom.

Clearly, the stories healthcare professionals keep matter to them. Professionals may find it worthwhile to establish systematic procedures for sharing stories of individuals who live good lives with mental illness. Imagine a ward where peer workers invite recovered individuals to tell their stories to both inpatients and staff. Or imagine a ward conference with staff devoted to sharing stories of former patients doing well. These vicarious stories may safeguard against hopelessness and pessimism that can spread from professionals to individuals with mental illness and contaminate personal recovery. Vicarious recovery stories may become intertwined with professionals' own stories of their work life, as they reflect on their supporting role in the recovery story. As such, the stories may bring a sense of meaning and purpose, foster joy and pride, and may counter work-related stress and burnout. Although professionals know the research demonstrating that recovery is a likely outcome, stories have a power in our minds that outshines statistics[215,216] and professionals can thrive when they keep these stories close to heart.

Summary

- Grounded in our framework, we propose a guide for narrative repair.
- The purpose of the guide is to aid acceptance of and coping with mental illness and its narrative identity costs, welcome healthy aspects of the self (back) into narrative identity, and craft a hopeful, realistic future narrative identity.
- Individuals with mental illness working toward well-being and personal recovery can employ the guide independently or in collaboration with healthcare staff.
- The guide comprises four tasks: composing an overview of the life story, telling a personal illness story, elaborating on positive stories and

identity conclusions while anchoring these in everyday life, and narrating a realistic and hoped-for future.
- Vicarious stories from peer workers can scaffold narrative repair in individuals working toward personal recovery.
- Healthcare professionals can grow their empathy and appreciation of the perspectives of individuals with mental illness while assisting narrative repair.
- In addition, healthcare professionals can kindle hope by holding vicarious stories of individuals who live good lives with, or recovered from, psychopathology.
- When recovery stories intertwine with healthcare professionals' own stories of their work life, professionals may gain meaning, purpose, and positive emotions, reducing the risk of work-related stress and burnout.

Conclusion

Too little research has addressed how individuals with severe psychopathology experience the consequences of their illness and what brings well-being in their lives. Anchored in the assumption that individuals make sense of their lives and build identity through narrative, we explored life stories of 118 individuals with severe mental disorder to answer these questions. We found that individuals story their mental illness with a range of costs to relationships, selfhood, and functional level, and that some individuals experienced aspects of treatment as an additional burden. These costs can turn into a web of negative identity conclusions, such as "I am out of control," "I have to hide who I am," "I am a failure with no purpose because I can't work," "I am a burden," "I am too difficult to be with," and "I am harmed by treatment." At the same time, our participants shared well-being stories revolving around relationships as supportive, loving, and nourishing; and the self as mastering, growing, and dreaming. Many of these stories were shared in the broader context of education, vocation, leisure activities, and treatment. As counterweights to the toxic identity implication flowing from costs of mental illness, these well-being stories carried adaptive narrative identities fostering personal recovery: "I can help others who are in pain," "I can love and others can love me," "I can make good decisions," "I can do well at study/work," and "I can become better with the help of others."

Synthesizing a wide range of research with the present findings, we proposed a framework for understanding how narrative identity may be a vulnerability to psychopathology, be wounded by mental illness, and be crucial for personal recovery. Guided by the framework, we suggest working with four tasks of narrative repair that can assist individuals in recovering from psychiatric disorder. Peer workers and other healthcare professionals play crucial roles in supporting narrative repair and may discover benefits from engaging in narrative work.

Our framework and the guide emerged from robust research in narrative identity, mental illness, well-being, personal recovery, and a range of other areas. Still, it would benefit from systematic evaluation and we hope that future research will test and expand our ideas about how narrative identity intertwines with mental illness and personal recovery.

APPENDIX I

My Personal Story of Mental Illness

As a first author, I would like to share my personal story of mental illness. I think such sharing can contribute to lessen the stigmatization connected to mental illness and dissolve maladaptive them versus us thinking. I am not just an academic writer who analyzes stories from individuals with mental illness. I have had mental disorder in my personal life, driving my pursuit to illuminate it scientifically in the present book.

Psychiatric illness has not been a major disruptive force in my personal life. I am lucky that I have not suffered from psychopathology severe enough to require medication or hospitalization. I did have an episode of what I now think was depression when I was about 17. I would wake up in the morning with a heavy mind and body. I would leave math classes in high school and go to the toilet to cry. I would get too drunk at parties and talk about jumping off the balcony. At some point, my close friend told me that she and my other friends were out of their depth, they had no idea how to help me, and that I should see a psychologist. I followed her plea and my depression lifted. I honestly have no idea what helped. Maybe it was the psychologist, maybe Spring came, or maybe the depression had just run its course. However, I do know the price I paid for that episode. It cost me the belief that I was strong. For a long time, I was convinced that I was vulnerable and less capable than other people were. I started to notice instances of mental illness and suicide in my family history and felt that my genes had probably set me up to be susceptible to psychiatric disturbance. Maybe irrationally, I feared that I would have a psychosis once I had children. However, as I gave birth to my oldest and since then my two other children, I did not become psychotic and slowly my fear of developing severe psychopathology waned. Although I tend to turn blue in the dark winter months of Denmark, I have not since suffered from mental illness. However, some of my close others have and with the slightest indication of threatening relapse, the pain and fear springs to life.

APPENDIX 2

The Alternative View of Personality Disorders

Regarding the alternative view of personality disorders represented in the DSM-5, a supplementary chapter (section III) presents a move toward a dimensional model for personality disorders, which encompasses fewer types of disorders, lists other primary characteristics, and includes maladaptive personality traits specifying each disorder.[51] The new ICD-11 will adopt a full dimensional model of personality pathology based on level of self- and interpersonal functioning, with an option to include trait specifiers and/or borderline pattern qualifiers.[52] The disagreements between the two approaches (the traditional, categorical view on diagnoses versus the dimensional perspective introduced in the DSM-5, section III and in the ICD-11) indicate that conceptualizations of personality disorders are currently in flux, further illustrating the plastic nature of the diagnostic systems and their categories.

APPENDIX 3

Life Story Chapters

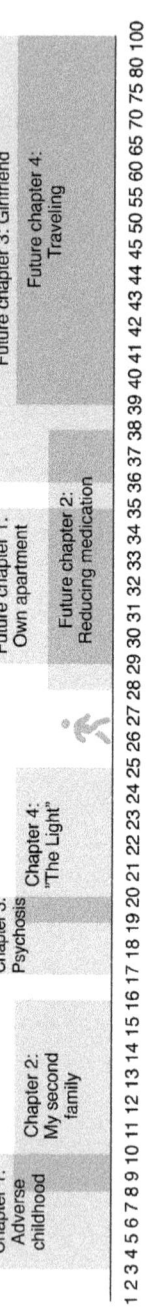

Figure A3.1 Illustration of chapters in a life story

APPENDIX 4

Methodological Details on Studies

Below, we give additional method details on the studies led by Tine Holm, Rikke Amalie Agergaard Jensen, Majse Lind, and Anne Mai Pedersen reviewed in the first sections of Chapter 7. We focus on those aspects of the studies most relevant to the present context. Note that the information below overlaps considerably with earlier published articles and that these sources can be consulted for additional information. For all four projects, life stories were coded for various content, using well-established procedures within the field of narrative identity research.[217] We did not collect information on the religious affiliation or ethnicity of participants but, given the relative homogeneity of the Danish population, most participants were likely Caucasian and would have self-identified as nonreligious.

Tine Holm's Project

Participants

The 24 participants with schizophrenia were recruited from an outpatient clinic at the Department for Psychosis, Aarhus University Hospital, Denmark. They were in a stable phase of their illness and had lived with their diagnosis for an average of 12.04 years (SD = 7.70). Mean level of positive and negative symptoms as assessed with the Scale for the Assessment of Positive/Negative Symptoms was 6.63 (SD = 3.94) and 10.29 (SD = 3.21), respectively. Furthermore, mean level of depression as evaluated by the Common Mental Disorder Questionnaire was 6.46 (SD = 5.42).

The 24 control participants (11 women) were recruited from the local community through flyers and word-of-mouth. They had no history of mental disorder or relatives with a history of schizophrenia and were included to match the clinical group on age (clinical group: M = 36.42 years, SD = 9.85 vs. controls: M = 37.88 years, SD = 10.75) and years of education (clinical group: M = 15.79 years, SD = 3.07 vs. controls

M = 16.17, SD = 1.97). Mean level of depression in controls as evaluated by the Common Mental Disorder Questionnaire was 1.96 (SD = 1.92). The clinical group performed on average around 0.6 standard deviation below the control group on the Brief Assessment of Cognition in Schizophrenia (BACS-composite score: clinical group: M = −0.57, SD = 1.46) indicating that the clinical group was cognitively well-functioning.

Exclusion criteria for both groups were neurological disorder, a history of traumatic brain injury, drug or alcohol dependency, or not speaking Danish fluently.

Materials and Procedure

All the participants received oral and written information about the study and gave informed consent. The research session consisted of two main parts. First, participants were evaluated on symptoms and neurocognition and, second, they shared their life stories, identified life story chapters, and described up to three self-defining memories.

Depression and anxiety were evaluated using 10 questions (e.g., feeling worthless, having panic attacks) from the Common Mental Disorder Questionnaire, which is a self-report measure that has demonstrated good psychometric qualities (CMDQ).[218] Symptoms are rated on 5-point scales (0 = not at all, 4 = extremely) with higher scores reflecting more severe symptomatology.

Symptoms of schizophrenia were evaluated using the Scales for the Assessment of Positive/Negative Symptoms (SAPS/SANS).[219,220] The scales are reliable and valid measures of symptomatology in schizophrenia utilized frequently in clinical and research settings. The severity of each symptom is rated on 6-point scales (0–5) with higher scores reflecting more severe psychopathology. A global score (range 0–5) of each subscale was estimated and a total score for both positive and negative symptoms (range 0–20) was calculated.

Neurocognition was evaluated using the Brief Assessment of Cognition in Schizophrenia (BACS).[221] BACS is a reliable and valid test battery that assesses the aspects of neurocognition most impaired in individuals with schizophrenia.[222] BACS consists of six tests measuring verbal memory, working memory, motor speed, verbal fluency, speed of information processing, and reasoning and problem solving. A weighted composite score was created by calculating the weighted mean of z-scores, separately computed for each subtest relative to the mean and standard deviation of the control group.[221]

For the oral life story, the participants were asked to freely narrate their life stories and given the following instructions:

> In this interview I would like you to tell me your life story. There is no right or wrong way to tell your life story and it can concern all areas of your life. It may include information about what has happened in your past that has shaped who you have become as a person. For example, experiences you have had, your living conditions, or people who have influenced you and your life. It is up to you where to start, what to include and how to organize the story.

Participants were instructed to try to make the story last for approximately 15 minutes and that the interviewer would not comment or ask questions. They were given 5 minutes to consider what they wished to include in the story and a blank sheet of paper to take notes. If participants finished the story before the 15-minute time limit, they were given the following prompt: "There is still some time left, is there anything you would like to add to the story that you have not already described?"

For the life story chapters, participants were asked to think about the life stories that they had described in the first part of the second session and identify up to 10 important chapters in their life stories.[223] They were told that the chapters identified should cover their entire life story and that they were allowed to include ongoing and overlapping chapters. Once participants had identified a chapter, they were asked to give the chapter a title, note their age at the beginning and end of the chapter, and answer several questions, including emotional valence: "How would you describe the emotional content of the chapter?" rated on a seven-point scale from extremely negative to extremely positive. Chronological ordering of chapters was assessed by correlating chapter order (1–10) with reported age at the beginning of the chapter.

For the self-defining memories, participants were asked to identify three self-defining memories following the well-established procedure proposed by Singer and Moffitt (1992).[224] A self-defining memory was described as:

1. At least one year old;
2. A memory from your life that you remember very clearly and that still feels important to you even as you think about it;
3. A memory that helps you to understand who you are as an individual and might be the memory you would tell someone else if you wanted that person to understand you in a more profound way;
4. It may be a memory that is positive or negative, or both, in how it makes you feel. The only important aspect is that it leads to strong feelings;

5. It is a memory that you have thought about many times. It should be familiar to you like a picture you have studied or a song you have learned by heart.

To assess the presence of self-defining memories in relation to the time of diagnosis, the self-reported age of the participants in the memory was plotted relative to the age of the participant at diagnosis.

Coding

The oral life stories and descriptions of self-defining memories were transcribed. The life stories were coded for temporal macrostructure and themes of agency and communion. Before coding, the life stories were segmented into chapters by Tine Holm and each chapter was coded using the criteria outlined below.

Agency was coded if the chapters were related to the need to be in control of one's life, to initiate change, to achieve personal goals, and to feel motivated; communion was coded as the need for intimate relationships (e.g., friendship, romance, sharing, nurturance, and belonging).[146] Each chapter was coded for whether themes were present or absent (0 or 1). If a theme was present, it was evaluated whether it was fulfilled and/or unfulfilled (0 or 1).

Temporal macrostructure was assessed by examining temporal elaborations and contextualization of beginnings and endings of life stories using the coding criteria described by Habermas et al. (2009).[225] In the study, the temporal macrostructure was evaluated based on the content of the first chapter (coded from 0 to 4) and the last chapter (coded from 0 to 3) in the life stories.

All coding was performed by Tine Holm. She trained a co-rater (who was blind to hypotheses) and checked agreement in 20 percent of codes, finding good agreements across all coding categories.

Results

The two groups were compared using a series of t-tests and below we give effect sizes for these comparisons (please see Tables 3 and 1 respectively in the original papers for more details).[35,36] The group with schizophrenia rated their chapters as more negative (d = 0.99) and displayed themes of less fulfillment of agency (d = 1.16) and communion (d = 0.78), but there were no significant differences for chronological ordering of chapters (d = 0.47) nor for temporal macrostructure (ds for beginning and ending = 0.03 and 0.17).

Majse Lind's Project

Participants

The 30 participants were diagnosed with borderline personality disorder (BPD) and had a mean age of 29.50 years (SD = 9.81). They were recruited from two outpatient clinics at the beginning of a treatment course (Aarhus University Hospital and Psychotherapeutic Center Stolpegaard, Copenhagen), including either psychodynamic- or mentalization-based psychotherapy. Exclusion criteria were organic brain disorder or being influenced by alcohol or drugs on the day of testing. At the one-year follow-up, 23 of the participants were retained.

A control group of 30 participants was recruited using word-of-mouth to match the clinical group on age, gender, and level of education. The control participants had a mean age of 29.47 years (SD = 11.50). Exclusion criteria were a BPD diagnosis or a BPD profile on the SCID-II self-report questionnaire, that is, a threshold of five or more BPD symptoms,[51,226] having a parent or sibling with a BPD diagnosis, having organic brain disorder, and being influenced by alcohol or drugs on the day of testing. At the one-year follow-up, 23 of these participants took part.

Materials and Procedure

The participants completed a package of questionnaires at home before the research session, which consisted of completing a test of emotional intelligence and describing up to 10 chapters in first their own and then a parent's life story.

The questionnaire package included the Self-Concept and Identity Measure (SCIM)[227] used to measure disturbed identity, the Toronto Alexithymia Scale (TAS-20)[228] examining the ability to recognize and describe personal emotional states and differentiate them from bodily sensations, the Empathy Quotient (EQ)[229] to assess empathic abilities, and Beck's Depression Inventory-II[230] to assess depression. All scales have demonstrated good psychometric qualities.

The Mayer–Salovey–Caruso Emotional Intelligence Test V2.0 is a frequently used test of emotional intelligence with good psychometric qualities.[231] Participants completed the test on a computer as the first part of the research session.

For personal life stories, participants were given the following instruction:

This part of the study is about your life story. I want you to think about your whole life and identify life story chapters. Chapters are defined as periods in your life, which can last for months or even years. An example of a chapter could be: "my time in primary school." You will be asked to describe every chapter and note how old you were at the beginning and end of every chapter or if the chapter has not yet ended.

They then described each chapter orally and completed three questions concerning emotional tone and meaning-making, while reflecting out loud on their answers. The questions were: 1) "How would you describe this chapter emotionally?"' 2) "Has this chapter influenced how you perceive yourself?"; and 3) "Has this chapter influenced later life story chapters?" The questions were rated on 5-point scales with 1 representing negative emotional tone and negative influences and 5 representing positive emotional tone and positive influences. The same procedure was used at the one-year follow-up study.

For parents' life stories, participants were asked to indicate the parent they chose and answer questions about the relationship. They were then given the same instruction and questions as for personal life stories, adapted to the parent's life story. They were asked to imagine the story and answer the questions from the parent's perspective. The same procedure was used at the one-year follow-up study.

Coding

The interviews were recorded and transcribed. Each chapter in both personal and parents' life stories were then coded for themes of agency, communion, and communion fulfillment as well as complexity in meaning. The coding was similar at baseline and at the one-year follow-up.

Complexity (coded from 0 to 2) refers to elaboration of meaning and was coded using a scale developed by McLean and Thorne (2003)[232] and modified by McLean and Pratt (2006).[233]

Agency and communion themes (coded from 0 to 2) were coded using an adapted version of a coding scale developed by Adler et al. (2012).[146] Agency themes refer to sequences of evaluations and interpretations emphasizing autonomy and empowerment of the individual and communion encompasses themes in life stories focusing on needs for intimacy, love, friendships, closeness, and caring for others.

Communion fulfillment (coded from 0 to 2) was only rated if a communion theme was identified (i.e., if communion was coded 1 or 2), because the purpose of the code is to distinguish between expressed communion needs that were either fulfilled or not fulfilled.

At baseline, all coding was performed by Majse Lind. She trained a co-rater (who was blind to hypotheses) and checked agreement on 13 percent of codes, finding good agreements across all coding categories. At the one-year follow-up, the first 16 interviews were coded by Majse Lind while training a co-rater who was blind to hypotheses. They then independently coded the remaining 30 interviews and examined agreement, which was good.

Results

At baseline, the two groups were compared using a series of t-tests and here we give effect sizes for these comparisons (see Table 3 in the original paper for more details).[40] We found that the group with BPD rated their chapters as more negative (d = 2.41), with more negative meaning (d = 2.28), displayed lower agency (d = 3.03), and lower communion fulfillment (d = 1.97). We found no significant differences for complexity in meaning (d = 0.33) or communion themes (d = 0.31). A similar pattern was evident for their parents' life story chapters: more negative (d = 1.21), with more negative meaning (d = 1.24), displayed lower agency (d = 1.93), lower communion (d = 0.79), lower communion fulfillment (d = 1.69), and lower complexity in meaning (d = 0.88).

Regarding questionnaire measures, the group with BPD rated themselves higher on identity disturbance (d = 2.74), depression (d = 2.03), and alexithymia (d = 2.15), and lower on empathy (d = 1.13), whereas no significant differences were found for the test of emotional intelligence (d = 0.07).[40]

At the one-year follow-up, we tested group differences in change over time for all life story measures. We found a significant interaction, where the group with BPD increased in agency themes from baseline to follow-up (d = 1.63), relative to the control group (d = 0.12) (please see Table 2 in the original paper for more details).[39]

Rikke Amalie Agergaard Jensen's Project

Participants

The 20 participants with schizophrenia had a mean age of 30.85 years (SD = 8.74). They were recruited through advertising the study in support groups and by word-of-mouth and diagnosis was checked by consulting the electronic health journal with the participant as a first part of the research session. All participants with schizophrenia were in a clinically stable phase and received outpatient care. Mean level of positive and negative symptoms as assessed with the Scale for the Assessment of Positive/Negative Symptoms was 4.40 (SD = 3.88) and 5.35 (SD = 3.30), respectively.

The 20 participants with major depressive disorder had a mean age of 32.95 years (SD = 10.56). They were recruited at Aarhus University Hospital, where they received either inpatient or outpatient treatment. Mean level of depression severity as assessed by the Hamilton Rating Scale for Depression was 19.30 (SD = 5.48).

The 20 control participants had a mean age of 31.55 years (SD = 11.32) and were recruited from the local community by advertising the study on flyers and by word-of-mouth.

The three groups were matched on age, gender, and years of education. Participants were excluded if they had a history of traumatic brain injury, drug or alcohol dependency, or if they did not speak Danish fluently. Potential control participants were excluded if they had previously suffered from mental illness, had first-degree relatives suffering from schizophrenia or depression, or scored in ranges indicating mental illness on the Scale for the Assessment of Positive/Negative Symptoms and/or the Hamilton Rating Scale for Depression.

Materials and Procedure

First, written and oral information about the study was shared and informed consent obtained for all participants. The research sessions then consisted of three parts: clinical assessment, life story interview, and neurocognitive testing.

To measure current level of symptoms in participants with schizophrenia and to exclude psychosis in control participants, Rikke Amalie Agergaard Jensen rated participants using the Scale for the Assessment of Positive/Negative Symptoms (SAPS/SANS).[219,220] The scale measures positive and negative symptoms in schizophrenia and has demonstrated good psychometric qualities. Based on ratings of symptom severity, scores on each subscale were estimated and added, yielding a total score for positive and negative symptoms, respectively (0–20).

To assess symptom severity in participants with depression and to exclude depression in control participants, the participants were evaluated with the Hamilton Rating Scale for Depression.[234] The scale has demonstrated good psychometric qualities[235] and items are summed to derive a score ranging from 0 to 28.

The Common Mental Disorder Questionnaire[218] was used as a self-report measure of six symptoms of depression for all three groups. The scale has shown good psychometric qualities.

All participants were interviewed about their psychosocial functioning using the Personal and Social Performance Scale.[236] The scale possesses good measurement qualities and consists of four categories: socially useful activities, personal and social relationships, self-care, and disturbing and aggressive behavior.

For the life story interview, the participants were given the following instruction:[223]

> This part of the study is about your past life story. I would like you to think about your whole life and identify up to five important life story chapters in your past. Chapters are defined as periods in your life, which can last for months or even years. An example of a past chapter could be: "my time in primary school." I will ask you to give each chapter a title, describe the content of the chapter, and note how old you were at the beginning and end of every chapter or if the chapter has not finished yet. Then I will ask you to answer six different questions for each chapter. The first two questions are concerned with the positive/negative emotional tone of the chapter; the two next questions are concerned with whether the chapter illustrates any positive/negative personal characteristics that describe you as a person; and the last two questions are concerned with whether the chapter has caused you to change in a positive/negative way. You may answer from not at all to a very high degree. For each rating, I will ask you to tell me why you rated the chapter as you did. There is no right or wrong way to describe chapters in your life – it is up to you to decide which chapters to include and how to describe them.

For the future chapters, they were given the following introduction:

> Thank you for sharing your past life story chapters with me. In the next part of this interview, I would like you to think about your life as you imagine it in the future and identify up to five important life story chapters in your future. A future life story chapter refers to a period that you imagine you will experience in your future, which can last for months or even years. An example of a future chapter could be "retirement."

The instruction for past chapters was then repeated. For each past/future chapter participants were asked to rate it on six items measuring emotional tone and meaning via self-event connections: 1) "How positive were the events in this chapter?"/ "How positive do you imagine the events in this chapter?"; 2) "How negative were the events in this chapter?"/ "How negative do you imagine the events in this chapter?"; 3) "Does the chapter highlight any positive characteristics that describe who you are as a person?"/ "Do you imagine that the chapter highlights any positive characteristics that describe who you are as a person?"; 4) "Does the chapter highlight any negative characteristics that describe who you are as a person?"/ "Do you imagine that the chapter highlights any negative characteristics that describe who you are as a person?"; 5) "Has the chapter caused you to change in a positive way?"/ "Do you imagine that the chapter will cause you to change in a positive way?"; and 6) "Has the chapter caused you to change in a negative way?"/ "Do you imagine that the chapter will cause you to change in a negative way?"

All participants were assessed on neurocognition with four widely used tests, including 1) Hopkins Verbal Learning Test-Revised,[237] which measures verbal memory; 2) Trail Making Test part B,[238] which measures cognitive flexibility and sustained attention; 3) vocabulary subtest from Wechsler Adult Intelligence Scale (WAIS)[239] assessing verbal ability and IQ; and 4) the d2, which measures concentration.[240]

Coding

The life story interviews were recorded and transcribed. Each chapter was then coded for agency and communion themes.

Agency was coded using a scale of 0–4.[146,241] Highly agentic narratives describe protagonists who can affect their own lives, achieve personal goals, initiate changes on their own, achieve control over the course of their experiences, and feel motivated and empowered.

Communion was coded using a scale of 0–4.[146,241] Communion is concerned with the need for intimate relationships (e.g., friendship, romance, sharing, nurturance, and belonging) or belongingness (e.g., groups or society).

Rikke Amalie Agergaard Jensen trained two raters in coding, a master coder (who was blind to hypotheses) and a reliability coder. The master coded all chapters and the reliability coder independently coded 20 percent of chapters. Agreement was good for both agency and communion.

Results

We used a series of one-way ANOVAs with Bonferroni corrected post hoc test to examine differences between the three groups. Below we report overall effect sizes for these tests (see Tables 1 and 1 respectively in the original papers for more details).[37,38] For past chapters, we found that the two clinical groups scored lower than the control group on positive emotional tone (η^2 = 0.29), positive meaning (η^2 = 0.23), agency themes (η^2 = 0.50), and communion themes (η^2 = 0.25), and higher on negative emotional tone (η^2 = 0.25) and negative meaning (η^2 = 0.39). For future chapters, we found no significant differences between groups on positive emotional tone (η^2 = 0.03), positive meaning (η^2 = 0.09 and η^2 = 0.14), negative emotional tone (η^2 = 0.09), negative meaning (η^2 = 0.04 and η^2 = 0.11). agency themes (η^2 = 0.07), or communion themes (η^2 = 0.03).

In addition, the two clinical groups had lower scores than the control group on psychosocial functioning (η^2 = 0.58) and higher scores on self-reported depression symptoms (η^2 = 0.56; note that the group with depression also scored higher than the group with schizophrenia). The group with depression scored lower than the control group on Trail Making Test B (η^2 = 0.19) and WAIS vocabulary test (η^2 = 0.10), but there were no significant group differences on the remaining tests or between the group with schizophrenia and the control group (η^2 = 0.07, η^2 = 0.03, and η^2 = 0.09).

Anne Mai Pedersen's Project

The participants with bipolar disorder were included from a completed study and enriched with nine additional participants from an ongoing study. Because only the completed study is summarized in the book, we limit ourselves to detailing this study below. Please see our paper in preparation for details on the ongoing study.[242]

Participants

The 15 participants with bipolar disorder had a mean age of 33.87 years (SD = 8.75). They were recruited from the Unit for Mania and Depression at Aarhus University Hospital, where a clinical psychologist confirmed diagnosis. They had on average experienced 15 affective episodes. Exclusion criteria were: 1) concurrent affective episode, 2) severe substance abuse, and 3) severe comorbid disorder, that is, personality disorders or schizophrenia. All participants were clinically remitted at the time of the study, which was confirmed by their scores on the Altman Self-Rating Mania Scale (M = 1.40, SD = 1.84) and their score on the Major

Depression Inventory (M = 6.47, SD = 3.93, although it should be noted that two participants scored in ranges indicating mild to moderate depression).

The 15 control participants had a mean age of 32.80 years (SD = 7.09). They were recruited from the local community by word-of-mouth to match the clinical group on gender and age. Exclusion criteria were: 1) self-reported diagnosis of personality disorder, schizophrenia, or bipolar disorder; 2) self-reported parents' diagnosis of personality disorder, schizophrenia, or bipolar disorder; and 3) that they met criteria for the presence of an affective episode as assessed by the Altman Self-Rating Mania Scale and the Major Depression Inventory.

Materials and Procedure

The participants were given oral and written information about the study and asked to sign an informed consent. The clinical group was given a package of questionnaires at the unit to complete at home or at the clinic. The questionnaire package is described below.

To assess the presence of affective episodes, the participants completed the Major Depression Inventory[243] and the Altman Self-Rating Mania Scale.[244] Both scales possess good measurement qualities.

Life stories were elicited with the following instructions:

> Please think of your life story and identify periods of time comprising chapters in your life story. Chapters refer to periods of months or years. It is important that the chapters cover your entire life story. For each chapter, please describe the main content of the chapter and answer the associated questions. Chapters need not have a clearly defined beginning or ending. You can include parallel chapters, i.e., chapters may refer to the same period in your life. You also may include chapters that are not yet finished. Some describe their life story in just a few chapters, others in many chapters. There is no right or wrong way to divide your life into chapters – it is up to you to decide how many chapters you include.

They were then provided with space to describe up to 10 past chapters.

For future chapters they were given the following instruction: "Please think about your future and identify chapters in your future life story. A chapter in your future life story refers to a period that you imagine you will experience in your future and that will become a part of your future life story." The instructions then repeated the instructions for past chapters and space for describing up to 10 future chapters was provided. For each chapter, participants were asked to answer four questions measuring emotional tone and meaning via self-event connections. These questions were as follows: 1) "To what degree would you describe the chapter as positive/negative?" and 2) "Do you feel that the chapter says something positive/negative about who you are as a person?" In addition, for future chapters they were asked to rate the subjective probability of the chapter with the following item: "How likely do you think it is that this chapter will be a part of your future life?"

To measure well-being, the participants completed two widely used and psychometrically sound scales: 1) Satisfaction with Life Scale,[245] which measures global life satisfaction, and 2) Positive and Negative Affect Scale,[246] which measures positive and negative affect.

Coding

Each chapter was coded for agency and communion themes. Agency was coded using a scale of 0 to 4.[146,241] Highly agentic narratives describe protagonists who can affect their own lives, achieve personal goals, initiate changes on their own, achieve control over the course of their experiences, and feel motivated and empowered.

Communion was coded using a scale of 0 to 4.[146,241] Communion refers to the connection, intimacy, belonging, friendship, love, and caring of the protagonist.

Anne Mai Pedersen trained a co-rater who was blind to hypotheses and both independently coded all chapters. Agreement was good for both agency and communion.

Results

The two groups were compared using a series of t-tests and here we give effect sizes for these comparisons (see Tables 1 and 1 respectively in the original papers for more details).[41,42] Compared to the controls, the group with bipolar disorder rated their past chapters as less positive ($d = 1.60$), more negative ($d = 1.56$), with less positive meaning ($d = 1.12$) and displayed themes of lower agency ($d = 1.36$) and communion ($d = 1.18$). The difference for negative meaning was not significant ($d = 0.52$). For future chapters, we found no significant differences between the two groups on these life story measures, although the differences were in the same direction as observed for past chapters ($ds < 0.72$). However, the group with bipolar disorder rated their future chapter lower on subjective probability compared to the controls ($d = 1.18$).

The group with bipolar disorder reported lower life satisfaction than the control group (d = 2.50). Across both groups, higher life satisfaction was related to past chapters with more positive tone and meaning, less negative tone and meaning, and higher subjective probability of future chapters (rs > 0.41) (see Table 2 in the original paper for additional details).[41]

APPENDIX 5

Detailed Description of Analyses

The text below overlaps with Chapter 7 as this appendix provides elaboration of the overview given in the chapter.

The Coding Manual and Procedure

The analyses contained the following steps (see Figure 7.1 for an overview): 1) we engaged in open reading of the life stories to discover themes within personal impact and sources of well-being, 2) we developed a coding manual for 28 common themes, and 3) we coded all life stories according to the manual. These three steps comprised the initial part of our analyses with the purpose of providing an overview of how frequently our participants narrated different themes concerning consequences and well-being experiences (see Chapter 8). After conducting this initial analysis, we realized that we could paint a more nuanced and richer picture by in-depth analyses of the 28 initially identified themes. Hence, we continued the analyses in two more steps: 4) as a part of step 3, we had marked all segments in the life stories that concerned perceived consequences of psychopathology and sources of well-being; we now created 28 separate documents with these segments, one document for each theme identified in step 3, and analyzed the 28 themes for subthemes. Finally, in step 5) we noted relationships between subthemes across the 28 themes and collapsed these into four superordinate themes. We present these in-depth analyses in Chapters 9–12. Our analyses bear affinity to interpretative phenomenological analysis in the iterative process employed to develop themes and subthemes, discover connections, and collapse into superordinate themes.[167] However, we did not engage in careful case-by-case analyses due to the large number of participants and we were from the beginning oriented toward commonalities in the narratives of our participants.

Steps 1 and 2: In developing the initial coding manual to capture the themes our participants narrated concerning the consequences of mental disorder and well-being experiences, we first read the life stories and extracted all parts that included 1) negative consequences of mental illness, 2) positive consequences of mental illness, and 3) experiences associated with well-being, meaning, and value. Points 1 and 2 were both only coded when participants explicitly interpreted experiences as consequences of their mental illness (e.g., when they made causal connections between the event of mental illness and some outcome and/or aspect of the self), while point 3 was coded both with and without reference to mental illness, except that the experience had to occur after the emergence of mental illness (because we were interested in well-being when living with mental illness). Because positive consequences of illness were often storied with well-being, meaning, and value, many experiences under the second point were also coded as a part of the third point (but not vice versa because many well-being experiences were not interpreted as consequences of mental illness). For example, a participant interpreted her disorder as giving rise to more deeply felt empathy for others in similar circumstances and was happy with this personal growth (a positive consequence *and* a well-being experience). She also shared a chapter about how her marriage had brought her meaning and value (a well-being experience but not a positive consequence). The reason we decided to keep coding of positive consequences as themes separate from other well-being themes is that this analysis speaks directly to several central concepts. First, it helps us illuminate whether our participants construct their psychiatric disorder as a redemption story, where positive impact is caused by the negative experience of illness. Second and relatedly, a sense of having grown from mental illness is viewed as a key component of personal recovery in some models.[3] Coding of well-being experiences, on the other hand, allows a broader view of what our participants interpreted as important to living good lives, whether this was a consequence of their illness or not.

During this stage, we were very inclusive. We prepared documents listing all instances relevant to each of these three issues. We read these documents and developed themes within negative consequences (e.g., mental illness negatively impacting self), themes within positive consequences (e.g., the disorder bringing new insights), and themes within experiences related to well-being, meaning, and value (e.g., social relations as bringing happiness). We discussed the themes in the group and further adapted them into a draft for our coding manual. We checked the draft against the documents with all listed instances and further modified the themes in the coding manual based on an initial coding of 20 life stories (drawn from the four different projects). These themes are displayed in

Table 7.2 and comprise the coding manual that helped us gain an initial overview of common story lines concerning consequences and well-being experiences. As such, this part of the analyses helped establish the frequency of themes in the narrative identities of our participants.

Step 3: When coding the life stories according to this coding manual (see Appendix 6), we read the life stories and marked segments where the themes were present. The themes were not mutually exclusive. If a participant shared an experience revealing several sources of well-being, we coded them all. For example, the following life story segment was coded with both education and positive memories as sources of well-being, since the educational success in itself brought positive feelings and because she actively used the memory of this success to restore self-worth:

> So I am pretty happy about my four A grades because then I can't be that stupid. When my voices say: "You are no good, you can't get anything right, you are stupid and lazy, no one has any use for you, and you should kill yourself because the world would be a better place without you." Then I can simply say, well I did get my four As and I also have other good grades.

We marked all instances of a given theme in each life story. However, we only counted each theme once per participant, ignoring variation in number of instances and elaboration. When we later discuss how often themes were present in the life stories of our participants in Chapter 8, this reflects how many participants voiced stories with a given theme, not how many times or how richly they storied each theme.

One potential pitfall in coding personal consequences was discerning whether descriptions referred to consequences of psychopathology or aspects of the illness itself. For example, amotivation may be an obstacle to educational pursuit and, according to diagnostic manuals such as the DSM-5, this would constitute a symptom and functional impairment inherent to schizophrenia, not a consequence of schizophrenia.[51] In the life story analyses, however, we followed the participants' explanations in deciding whether narratives referred to consequences of their illness. That is, we coded statements as consequences if the participants made causal connections between their mental illness and some outcomes and between mental illness and their self. One could argue that this approach defeats the purpose of illuminating real consequences of psychiatric disturbance, as it blends symptoms, functional impairment, and consequences. However, as acknowledged in the DSM-5, the system represents "a historically determined cognitive schema imposed on clinical and scientific information to increase its comprehensibility and utility" (p. 10).[51] Here, we simply develop a different cognitive schema, a schema embodying what individuals with psychopathology interpret as consequences when they story their identities. Note that we choose to view mental illness as a delimited entity with identifiable consequences, an assumption implicit in the disease model as laid out in Chapter 2. Had we adopted a broader view of psychological problems, the results of our analyses may have yielded different themes. However, many of our participants likely had a similar understanding, given their extensive experience with the psychiatric system where the disease model is influential.[5] Hence, our conceptualization may align with theirs and be consistent with our aim to provide a first-person perspective.

The assumption of mental illness as a circumscribed segment of experience also colored coding themes concerning well-being. We only included experiences taking place after the emergence of mental illness, because our main focus is understanding well-being in the face of psychiatric disorder. The time of emergence of psychopathology was assessed through the life stories. When participants mentioned symptoms, diagnosis, and/or treatment for the first time, we assumed that this marked their perceived beginning of illness and started coding for experiences of well-being after this time. While this is a highly subjective way to assess the starting point of mental illness, we had no good alternative, as we did not collect date of first diagnosis in the four projects. Even if we had collected these data, they might not be accurate reflections of the emergence of mental illness, as it may erupt long before diagnosis, go undiagnosed, or be difficult to locate (as for borderline personality disorder). What we target here is a first-person perspective on illness debut.

We checked the coding of the 28 themes by asking a student assistant to code a subset of the life stories. We first trained with her on 20 life stories, 5 from each of the four projects. When our agreement was good, indicating that we applied the coding manual in similar ways, we independently coded 20 of the life stories, 5 from each of the four projects. This procedure allows some indication of whether our initial coding is heavily one-sided or whether another person may find answers similar to ours when analyzing the life stories. When looking at the life stories we coded separately, we agreed most of the time about whether a theme was present or not (83 percent agreement; kappa = 0.60). Consequently, it is reasonable to assume that the themes we coded would also be visible to other persons, although with the variation that is an intrinsic aspect of comprehending complex material.

Step 4: As noted above, we developed steps 4–5 in our analyses to delve deeper into each of the themes identified in steps 1–3. While the 28 themes identified in the initial analyses provided the starting point for steps 4–5, we moved beyond these initial themes because the in-depth analyses revealed subthemes within each theme (e.g., the subthemes of withdrawal and loneliness as well as relationship strain identified as a part of the theme of negative consequences for social relations) and further that these subthemes sometimes overlapped with subthemes identified within other themes (e.g., the self as agentic emerged as a subtheme for well-being experiences across the themes of work, education, and personal qualities). Moreover, it became apparent to us that four superordinate themes could be used to organize the themes and their subthemes. Below, we elaborate on this process and we share the findings from this part of the analyses in Chapters 9–12.

As a part of step 3, we had marked the passages relevant to the themes of negative and positive consequences as well as well-being experiences. Now we copied and pasted all passages relevant to a given theme into separate documents, yielding 28 documents, one for each theme (see Table 7.2). From here on, we focused on the emergence of subthemes and superordinate themes (see Table 7.3 for an overview). We read each document (e.g., the document on the theme negative consequences for social relations), allowing subthemes to emerge from participants' own words and descriptions. We started by labeling a subtheme based on the first participant in the document. If later participants narrated similar subthemes into their stories, we would count them in the same subtheme, while adding nuances when necessary. When later participants shared stories with new subthemes, we added them to our list of subthemes. Subthemes did not exclude each other; often stories would speak to several subthemes at the same time. Returning to the example cited above, where one of our participants used her positive memories of educational success to counter her critical voices, this illustrates at least three subthemes: 1) self as agentic (she actively uses her memories of educational success to regain self-worth), 2) self as valued (she values herself as an academic achiever), and 3) education and work as fostering well-being through the self (education forms the context for the emergence of this valued and agentic self). Subthemes emerging across several participants were preserved and collapsed into broader subthemes based on considerations of conceptual relations. For example, when analyzing the theme of negative consequences to self and identity, we collapsed stories of self-criticism, self-blame, shame, low self-worth, and lack of trust in self into one subtheme labeled "the negative self." We then reread the documents to check for nuances and omissions and, if we discovered any, we adapted the descriptions of subthemes accordingly. To examine the validity of the subthemes, we relate our findings to other research in Chapters 9–12.

Step 5: During the analyses in step 4, it became clear to us that we could organize themes and subthemes into four superordinate themes: relationships, self, functional level, and treatment. We decided that there was a useful message in presenting stories of consequences and well-being within the same superordinate theme together, showcasing contrasting stories. Similar subthemes emerged across themes within the same superordinate theme (although also across superordinate themes). For example, the subtheme of being different/not "normal" arose across the themes of negative consequences to self, loss of positive states, and goals and dreams. Hence, we use these subthemes rather than the initial 28 themes identified in steps 1–3 to elaborate on each superordinate theme in Chapters 9–12. The organization of the superordinate themes, the themes from Table 7.2, and the subthemes is displayed in Table 7.3.

As will become clear when we present our results, several subthemes discovered under the superordinate themes of relationships and self reappeared in the superordinate themes of functional level and treatment. For example, the self as growing emerged as a subtheme in our analyses of well-being experiences, initially coded under the theme of personal qualities and organized into the superordinate theme of self. However, the subtheme of self as growing often occurred in the context of the initially identified themes of education, work, and treatment and, as a result, we allowed this subtheme to form a part of the superordinate themes functional level and treatment.

We present these in-depth analyses of subthemes and their associated identity conclusions in Chapters 9–12 with one chapter dedicated to each superordinate theme. In these chapters, we emphasize the subthemes rather than the initially identified themes. We provide illustrative examples to allow readers to evaluate the validity of our subthemes and to offer vicarious stories of mental illness for readers to learn from. When selecting quotes, we preferred examples that were elaborate, yet representative of the subtheme. We attempted to present quotes from as many participants as possible, including participants from all four studies and of all genders. We translated quotes from Danish to English and edited them slightly to improve readability. This included deleting some repetitions and filler words that are part and parcel of speech, but not written language. We strove to keep the quotes close to our participants' voices, and hence their tone differs from our written academic language.

APPENDIX 6

Coding Manual

General Coding Rules

When coding the life stories for negative/positive consequences of mental illness and experiences facilitating well-being, meaning and value, keep in mind that none of the categories is exclusive. That is, any statement in the life story can be coded into different categories at the same time. Every time you read a statement that seems relevant, consider whether it is relevant for more than one coding category. If this is the case, please mark both categories in the coding sheet. Notice that you should not count the number of times a given category is present in the life story – it is a simple yes-no coding for each of the categories. So, do not count the number of times a given category is present.

For all three foci, a central issue is that it arises AFTER the beginning of the illness. We are primarily interested in what, according to the person themself, happened after the illness. This means that you may often read initial parts of the life story less thoroughly until the person mentions mental illness for the first time and then start coding from here (but notice that this is not always the case since life stories are not always chronological or the person may not mention mental illness explicitly). Notice that transitions in life stories may be gradual.

When you code the life stories and mark in the coding sheet whether a category is present or not, notice that future chapters can only be coded into two categories: either the category *Thoughts about the future* under negative consequences or the category *Goals and dreams* under well-being/meaning/value. This strategy ensures that future chapters are not coded similarly to past chapters with respect to what contributed to well-being, etc. After all, the future chapters have not yet happened and you cannot know whether they will contribute to well-being, etc., when they take place. Notice that statements under future chapters may refer to the past. In this case, they can be coded under other categories.

Read each life story. Mark the categories that are present in the participant's life story in the coding sheet. Highlight the statement in the margin in the printed life story referring to the category number. Use red for negative consequences, yellow for positive consequences, and green for contributions to well-being, etc.

Coding Consequences of the Illness

Read the life stories and identify negative and positive consequences of the illness. It may be difficult to discern consequences of the illness from the illness in and of itself, like loss of identity in persons with borderline personality disorder or problems with social relations for persons with schizophrenia. As far as possible, only code statements that clearly refer to what the person themself considers consequences of the illness. That is, do not code statements that are simply generally negative or a part of the illness (anxiety, depression, self-harm, negative relationships, negative self-view – but notice that negative self-view and negative relationships may ALSO be described as consequences of the illness – the context decides whether this is the case). The person need not explicitly say "as a consequence of my illness. . ." but the meaning should be quite clear from the context. The understanding of the negative/positive consequences of the illness may include several steps. For example, the illness may make the person unable to work which may lead to feelings of lower self-worth. Notice that consequences by definition occur after the illness is known/diagnosed – they cannot surface before. Regarding evaluating when the illness began, we take the person's own words on this as it is described in the life story. For example, the person may say as a part of the life story "this was when my symptoms started" or "my eating disorder appeared" or mention treatment, self-harm, or suicide attempts (notice that drug abuse is not considered a mental illness, while depression, anxiety, ADHD, eating disorder, mania, etc., are included as mental illnesses). While reading it may sometimes become clear that statements made earlier in the life story are relevant to code as they refer to experiences after the occurrence of mental illness. If this is the case, go back and code the statements. We take the person's words for what constitutes a consequence but notice that if the consequence is clearly an expression of psychosis, it should not be coded.

Negative consequences – remember at all times: BECAUSE OF THE ILLNESS. Notice that it should be clear that the consequence is perceived as negative/as a loss by the person themself. It should not automatically be coded as a negative consequence if it is just something you think probably was negative/a loss – it should be clear from the description.

Work. Unable to work, keep or obtain employment and the accompanying consequences/interpretations (failure, feel like a loser, lose self-esteem, lose purpose). Also include early retirement benefit (disability benefits), work absence due to illness, varying work capacity, difficulties with living up to certain work demands, taking on too much work in relation to illness.

School/education. Unable to complete education or maintain educational activities or attain the desired level of achievement and the accompanying consequences/interpretations (like failure, down upon down, lag behind, feel incompetent and like a fiasco, lose hope), including dropout, obtain lower grades than expected, pursue different education than desired.

Social costs. The illness impacts others negatively, assumptions that others judge one negatively due to illness, the person describes withdrawing from relationships (including family, romantic partners, friends, etc.), relationships are ruptured because others withdraw or the relationship breaks down due to illness, romantic relationships never materialize, unable to have/choose not to have children, relationships suffer due to illness (including role as mother, romantic relationships, parent/friend relationships), loneliness, relationships to others with mental illness associated with problems, lost ability to interact with others.

Self and identity. More negative self-view and identity (including losing self-esteem, someone who breaks down, scared of failure, do not have the right to be here, introverted, self-critical, lose belief in and trust in self, guilt and shame, not trust yourself, ruined self-worth, more vulnerable, difficulties finding balance, not looking after oneself), lost self (lost the person one was, unable to recover who one was), unclear self (not knowing who you are, confusion about who you are), ruined/fragmented self (unable to connect with who one was, see oneself from the sideline, broken, inner world fragmented, fall apart, divided from oneself), empty self, hiding oneself (hide, conceal, keeping up appearances, secrets), seeing yourself as different, alienated, someone who does not fit in, unable to regulate or control oneself, feel older, unable to feel oneself, struggling with seeing oneself as ill.

Stigmatization. Others saying/doing something concerning the person's ability with regard to, for example, work/education due to illness, that others view one in certain ways due to illness, descriptions of being stereotyped due to mental illness.

The loss of positive states. Lost or oppressed hopes, not daring to hope, lost dreams and expectations (like "the normal life," "what the others achieved"), realizing that life did not turn out as one thought it would, lost joy, purpose and meaning, content in life, lose courage, lack purpose, lose desires.

Consequences of treatment. Including medicine (undesirable side effects), hospitalization, mechanical restraint, other treatment as a part of hospitalization, psychiatric group home, diagnosis, psychological consequences of treatment (lose freedom, lose part of one's life, lose self-determination, negative emotions).

Thoughts about the future. For example, the future as negative (including illness-related, for example anxiety about relapse, anxiety about deterioration, anxiety about functional losses (like self-care, living independently), side effects of medicine, anxiety about failure related to education, work, etc.), the future as uncertain (including not knowing what tomorrow will bring, unable to handle the future, difficulties relating to the future, the future is not there).

Loss of cognitive functions. Including memory, concentration, sense of time as well as consequences of these.

Loss of everyday life. Including cooking, managing sleep, living independently, getting out of bed, structuring the day, not having an everyday life, unable to care for oneself.

Other. Coding of other negative consequences.

Positive consequences – remember at all times: BECAUSE OF THE ILLNESS. Notice that it should be clear that the consequence is perceived as positive by the person themself. It should not automatically be coded as a positive consequence if it is just something you think probably was positive – it should be clear from the description.

Insight and self-understanding. Including understand oneself better, recognize limitations better, become good at reflecting on things, grow wiser about oneself, worldly, becoming more aware of oneself, grown calmer.

Shown/grown strength. Including proud of overcoming the illness, be a fighter, show strength, manage the illness.

Improved care for oneself. Including self-compassion, spare oneself, look after oneself, set boundaries, say no, better at asking for help, create balance, change things that were not expedient (job, social circle, etc.).

Concrete relations to others. Including new relationships growing out of illness, enhanced relationship to others.

Caring for others. Including better understanding of others, do not judge, more open, aware of own prejudices, patient, forbearing, help others, recognize the suffering of others.

Other. Coding of other positive consequences.

Coding of What Helped Achieve Value, Meaning, and Well-Being

The overall purpose is to identify what has helped achieve value, meaning, and well-being after the person has had mental illness in their lives. Well-being, value, and meaning should only be coded after some type of illness has appeared. It may be the case that what contributed to well-being, value, and meaning preceded the illness, for example a good relationship with one's parents or one's education. The crucial point is that it contributes to value, meaning, and well-being AFTER the appearance of illness (whether it is after the appearance of illness is determined in the same way as for coding consequences of the illness). While reading it may sometimes become clear that statements made earlier in the life story are relevant to code as they refer to experiences after the occurrence of mental illness. If this is the case, go back and code the statements.

Note that value, meaning, and well-being are quite broad. Descriptions to look out for while reading include the following: mention of positive emotions, positive self-evaluations, what makes life/everyday life better, or other words signaling that the person experienced something as positive. Note, however, that we are NOT interested in what improved the illness/the symptoms or reduced the negative impact of something. That is, statements about for example what made the depression lift are not of interest, while statements concerning what the person experienced as positive besides illness/in spite of illness is the focus point. So, for example, if the person says "the treatment made my suicide thoughts disappear" then this is NOT relevant to code, but if the person says "the treatment reduced my hallucinations and then my relationship to my family improved," then it is relevant to code because "my relationship to my family improved" equals value/well-being/meaning.

For each life story consider whether it includes the following categories described in ways that are positively evaluated. That is, it has impacted the person in a positive way or is in itself connected with positive states (joy, calm, love) or generally described in terms that we in our culture associate with something positive (security, meaning, self-esteem, etc.). Remember that the same sentence/statement can easily be scored into more than one category. Generally, the categories do not exclude each other. Aim to assign codes only if it is clear that well-being/meaning/value occurred after the appearance of mental illness (symptoms surfaced and/or diagnosis given according to the person's own account, but note that drug abuse is not included as a mental illness).

Social relations. Concrete relations, family, friends, groups, children, pregnancy, etc. The social relations are described as giving love, safe environment, support, someone to share things with/common interests, meaning, something to fight for, stability, make one take responsibility, understanding, acceptance, good advice, value, to be special to someone.

School/education. The school itself as well as teachers and pupils, etc. These are described as giving self-esteem, experiences of success, courage to try something new, network, social advantages (friendships, community, attentive teachers, etc.), fixed boundaries, be a part of something larger, grow more social/extraverted, something to be passionate about, learn something, possibility of starting over again, mastery, strength of will, independence, gain direction and goals.

Work. The job itself as well as colleagues, etc. These are described as giving self-esteem, experiences of success, courage to try something new, network, fixed boundaries, be a part of something larger, contributing, grow more social/extraverted, something to be passionate about, learn something, earn own money, possibility of starting over again, mastery, strength of will, independence, make a difference, gain direction and goals, gain meaning.

Leisure, including sport, nature, traveling, pets, and creative activities. These are described as being meaningful, calming, give self-understanding, network, lower stress, forget about being ill, be good at something, take responsibility, getting out and about.

Aspects of treatment. Treatment generally (including mentioning the treatment location), doctors/nurses/psychologists, etc., fellow patients, psychiatric group homes, hospitalization, medicine, being diagnosed, psychotherapy, "the system," contact persons, persons involved in treatment described as giving hope, listening to the person, supporting, helping, accepting, hold on/set boundaries/be consistent.

Personal characteristics/inner processes. These are described as contributing to positive experiences, for example acceptance/be true to oneself/being oneself, stubbornness, to fight, take responsibility, choosing, seeking out treatment or other indications of self-determination, to have goals and dreams and hopes, to be creative, social competences, empathy, good at talking to others, regain self-worth and independence, find oneself, learn something. Note that the central part is that it is described as exactly a personal characteristic and not tied to a concrete activity. For example, "being creative" is not the same as "playing music" (which is coded under leisure).

Place/living space. This is described as one's own place, something one can decide over, independent living, a good place to be. Should be coded when the description concerns qualities and things about the place itself (and not, for example, social aspects). Note that it may also include concrete things as a part of one's living space, such as having one's own furniture.

Contact to others with mental illness. This is described as being something for others, to obtain help from and be inspired by others with mental illness, take responsibility, acquire self-determination, do something for others with mental illness, for example giving lectures or volunteering in support organizations.

Positive memories. When participants describe that some experiences give strength, hope, self-esteem, or other positive states/characteristics <u>when they remember them</u>. That is, it is explicitly described that it is the memory of or thinking back to the experience that yields the positive effects.

Goals and dreams. Often from future chapters but may also surface in the life stories generally. These are described in ways that clarify that they contribute with something positive in the present or that they may yield something positive in the future when it takes place, for example hope and joy, self-esteem, love, communion, peace, etc.

Other. Coding of other experiences contributing to well-being, meaning, and value.

APPENDIX 7

Worksheets for Chapters

Identifying Chapters

Chapter title_____

Key words/sentences, for example important people, places, activities, emotions, meanings, thoughts

_____
_____
_____
_____
_____
_____
_____

Age at chapter start_____
Age at chapter end_____

Placing Chapters on a Timeline to Help Organize the Life Story

This is a timeline of your life. Try to mark each chapter with a box and a title. Feel free to include both past, present, and future chapters.

Birth	10	20	30	40	50	60	70	80	90	100

Placing Memories on the Chapter Timeline to Help Organize Chapter Content

This is a timeline of chapter: _____

Try to mark the important memories in this chapter with a box and a title. If your chapter reaches into the future, feel free to mark future events you imagine as part of the chapter.

Chapter beginning ―――――――――――――――――――――――――― Chapter end

APPENDIX 8

The Guide for Narrative Repair in Practice: A Case Story

I (Tine Holm) previously worked as a clinical psychologist in a psychiatric inpatient unit at Aarhus University Hospital in Denmark. The ward specializes in treatment for individuals with dual diagnoses, that is, comorbid severe mental illness (primarily psychosis spectrum disorders) and substance abuse problems. The service users often have histories of neglect, interpersonal violence, or other traumas. Many suffer from severe and persistent psychotic symptoms not completely alleviated by medication and most display severe cognitive deficits. Some have little insight into their illness and have periods of nonadherence to their medical treatment. Most have years or even decades of frequent relapses and hospitalizations. In short: They represent a particularly vulnerable group of individuals with severe mental illness. My primary tasks were to provide individual and group therapy, psychoeducation, and to assess symptoms and cognitive functions.

I started working with life stories based on the guide for narrative repair (GNaR). As I write this, I have employed the guide in psychotherapy with six individuals. I have used the structured approach with life story chapters because all individuals had cognitive difficulties and struggled to narrate their lives in a free format. I introduce visual aids where we start out by drawing a timeline extending from their birth until their present age (see example at the end of Appendix 7). Then we add chapters with titles (e.g., "childhood" and "school") with each chapter depicted in its own color. In a couple of cases, we have also constructed models of the future, where the timeline extends from the present and into the subjective future (see example at the end of this appendix). Sometimes we apply pictures of objects and symbols (e.g., a ball for one individual whose major interest was basketball) or textboxes with self-statements such as "I have always enjoyed cooking." I use PowerPoint to construct the visual models of the story and update the model after each session. The patients are offered a print with the newest version of their story in each session and are encouraged to add material between the sessions. However, so far no one has done so, and perhaps this indicates that they rely heavily on the structure provided in the sessions. It is my impression that the visual model of the story provides a powerful tool for scaffolding memory and structuring communication. As we build the story across the sessions, it becomes more of a shared and creative activity and less like traditional "talk therapy." We have a common point of reference that focuses our conversations, and this seems to be less intimidating for some of the service users who are socially anxious or have difficulties trusting others. The sessions typically last no longer than 20–30 minutes, which is the time I have found that most of them can fully concentrate on the task. We always start by repeating what we talked about in the previous sessions, and I point out the most recently included chapters or episodes to facilitate memory and set the stage for the current session.

In the sections, I present a case, Linda, to illustrate how GNaR can be employed to collaboratively support personal recovery, when individuals are severely affected by mental illness. The case is based on an anonymized synthesis of my experiences with service users.

Linda was 28 years old when we met, and she had been diagnosed with paranoid schizophrenia in her early 20s. She had delusions about persecution and grandeur as well as auditory and tactile hallucinations. Her psychotic symptoms were present on a daily basis, although not constantly, and did not decrease sufficiently even when she received antipsychotic medicine. She usually wore layers of clothing including a red jacket and boots, also when sleeping, possibly to obtain a sense of safety. She had severe cognitive impairments, including poor memory, slow reaction time when processing information, and difficulties with planning and problem solving. Linda also suffered from a severe chronic somatic illness. She had very limited insight into her psychiatric disorder and would for example say that she considered herself "*a completely normal and healthy young woman*". Periodically, she would cease taking medication both for her somatic and psychiatric illness, possibly because she considered it unnecessary or because she simply forgot. When she discontinued antipsychotics, she would soon become very ill, sometimes leading to involuntary hospitalization and medication. As part of this pattern, she had many negative encounters with police officers who typically brought her to the hospital. Furthermore, observations indicated that her nonadherence to medical treatment undermined her functional level, which deteriorated dramatically every time she was hospitalized. Linda would sometimes state that she did not have a clear sense of who she was and where she was heading in her life, and I suggested working with her life story as a way to support her sense of self and to give her a direction for the future.

Linda and I spent several sessions identifying raw material for her story and developing a visual overview. We began by drawing a timeline and identified early life story chapters (e.g., where she lived in the beginning of her life). Then we moved on to describe subsequent chapters. In the first few sessions, Linda struggled to identify chapters and order them chronologically. However, as we continued our work, she seemed to find it easier to bring her past to mind, perhaps suggesting that familiarity with the task and the identified material scaffolded her memory. As described in Chapter 5, chapters organize life stories and employing chapters as starting points may be especially beneficial when memory problems are a part of the clinical picture. Furthermore, the visual model of her story provided an overview and may have eased the strain on her memory. She did not have to hold on to information, rather it was available to her visually and I would write or draw details as she shared them. After the fourth session, all years in her life story were covered by one or more chapters. I asked her how she felt about working with her life story and she said: "*It is good to see that my past is not empty, but rich. I can tell that I have achieved some things in my life and that gives me confidence.*"

In contrast to many of the stories included in this book, Linda's life story initially contained no negative experiences. This was remarkable considering that she lived with a severe somatic illness as well as a diagnosis of schizophrenia that had led to repeated hospitalizations. However, the exclusion of illness also made sense considering her lack of illness awareness. Possibly, she omitted illness experiences from her life story, because they threatened her self-image as normal and healthy. The purpose of task 2 in GNaR is to facilitate insight into and acceptance of mental illness with its personal costs, and I felt this was a critical part of our sessions. I faced the challenge of inviting Linda to confront the illness-related parts of her past, which she had been avoiding for years. It was a dilemma. On the one hand, I knew that focusing on illness could bring negative selves to the forefront of her story and that realizing the severity of her condition might cause her pain. On the other hand, not accepting illness as a part of her life story had devastating consequences. For example, her lack of illness insight would repeatedly result in resisting medical treatment, which was life-threatening for her. Thus, I decided it was central to explore the possibility of including illness in her life story, while ensuring that this would not be at the expense of the stories that she viewed as positive or "normal."

I did not ask Linda to tell the story of her somatic and mental illnesses as suggested in task 2 in the GNaR since my impression was that it would be too confrontational and difficult for her. Instead, I carefully asked questions about her illness, such as how old she was when she was diagnosed and how many times she had been hospitalized. These details were then included in the story she had already produced. We did this while also emphasizing and elaborating on the happier parts of Linda's life story that remained the same despite illness (e.g., her interest in music and theater). In the GnaR, narrating periods of life where illness was absent or in the background constitutes a separate task (task 3). However, with Linda I found it helpful to work on task 2 and 3 simultaneously because it seemed to have a synergistic effect on her life story construction. Emphasizing the parts of her life that stood out as positive or untouched by illness likely made it easier for her to accept illness experiences into the story. The first couple of times we talked about her mental illness, especially episodes concerning coercive treatment, she would quite naturally become angry and agitated. However, after a while the intensity of her anger faded and in some of the final sessions she talked about these incidents in a much calmer way. In my view, one of the main reasons we succeeded in incorporating aspects of her illness into the story was that we did not start out with this aim. Instead, the first five to six sessions were devoted to telling her story as she remembered it and I highlighted that it was completely up to her how to narrate her life. I think this signaled to Linda that my goal was not to convince her that she was ill. I accepted her narrative and, as a result, she became much less guarded and more open to other perspectives on her life story.

Illustrating insights from research on narrative identity in individuals with severe mental illness (see Chapter 6) and our framework presented in Chapter 14, Linda's narrative skills were impaired. She tended to list events in her life story without expanding on their meaning or causally and thematically linking different periods. She rarely engaged in autobiographical reasoning when sharing experiences. Her failure to reflect on the causes and consequences of her past could become an obstacle to narrative repair. Indeed, it may explain her low level of illness insight. Without the ability to narrate experiences and interpret them in relation to who you are, how can anyone recognize themselves as suffering from a mental illness? The GNaR includes questions to scaffold causal reasoning, e.g., "Are there any relations between the two chapters/events you describe?" or "What does it mean to you, then and now?" However, I found these questions to be too demanding for Linda. Therefore, I decided to employ more concrete ways of evaluating past experiences supported by visual aids. For each chapter, I asked her whether it was mainly positive or negative and we assigned pluses and minuses to the visual model of the story. Then I invited her to elaborate on her reasons for assigning a plus or a minus and she was mostly able to do this. I also applied a modified version of the 20 statements test (the IAM Task),[247] with instructions to generate 4–10 sentences starting with "I am...." The statements help activate self-images related to traits, roles, and hobbies. We generated a couple of self-images together: "*I am a woman*" and "*I am an older sister,*" and she then identified four or five on her own. We went through each of the self-images and tried to link them to her life story. We explored whether they were represented in the story and when they first appeared. I chose this method to scaffold Linda's autobiographical reasoning by connecting her current self-images to her past experiences. As such, it provided an understanding of how her life story had shaped who she was, and how she had directed her story.

This work with Linda's life story seemed to grow her narrative skills and she engaged in more complex autobiographical reasoning as we moved through the sessions. Around our 10th session, she recognized a pattern across her latest chapters. She noticed how every psychiatric hospitalization was preceded by periods of working long hours at various part-time jobs and not taking her medication regularly. This was a breakthrough. Up until then she had insisted that the police brought her to the hospital for no apparent reason other than to persecute her. Around the same time, she started questioning whether it was a good idea for her to live independently. She mentioned that if she moved to a residential home it could help her break the pattern of involuntary hospitalizations. Not only did she begin to detect larger patterns in her life story, she utilized this knowledge to consider life choices concerning living space. It was not an easy or orderly process. Linda would sometimes recognize her illness and need of health care while at other times insisting that she was "normal" and able to manage on her own. However, considering how her past choices were connected to her mental illness was to me a sign that she was beginning to take charge of her life and recovery.

The final task in the GNaR is to story a hoped-for and realistic future. Linda was hesitant about this part because she feared it would be much harder to construct a story of the future. She also seemed uncertain about how realistic the story should be and initially struggled to claim ownership of her projected future as depicted in the visual model. She said: "*I am afraid to include events and periods in this model of my future because what if they do not come true? Maybe I will be disappointed if I look at the model at some point in the future and see all the things I have not achieved.*" She had fears and doubts about working on her future life story and I reassured her that it was completely okay if her story changed and did not turn out exactly how she imagined it.

We applied the same visual template as for her past story, with the timeline extending from the present into the future. Linda could not decide which age to set as the end point, so we used the average life expectancy of women in Denmark. Paralleling our work on constructing her past story, we identified future chapters, while referencing her past story model. We started out by discussing which of her past chapters located close to the present she wanted to continue in her future. We also grounded her hoped-for future events in some of the hobbies and traits she had identified using the "I am" test (e.g., going to a concert with one of her favorite bands, which was related to her interest in music).

When we initiated our work on her future story, Linda was undecided about whether she wished to continue living independently in her apartment or whether she would rather move into a residential home. She valued living by herself and being able to make decisions about her own life, such as when to get up and what to have for dinner. She also emphasized living in a city that she knew well. She had familiarized herself with the layout of Aarhus and knew exactly where to get groceries, which bus to take when visiting her family, etc. The thought of moving to a residential home with people she did not know and in another city worried her. Thus, initially she wanted her first future chapter to be a continuation of her past chapter about living independently in Aarhus. Later she changed her mind and decided it would be best for her to live in a residential home where she could get the help she needed (e.g., with taking her medication). We created a future chapter entitled "*living in a residential home*," the first chapter in her future story. I asked Linda what to do about the future "*living independently in Aarhus*" chapter. Did she wish to replace it with the new chapter? Linda asked if we could create another future chapter labeled "*moving back to Aarhus*" in a more distant future. She could then consider the chapter in the residential home a steppingstone that could lead her to return to Aarhus at a time when she was ready to live independently again.

We also spent time talking about what role her illnesses might play in her future. These conversations mimicked the ones we had about her illness when building her past life story. We discussed her illness while at the same time emphasizing parts of her future not touched by her ailments.

Linda decided that her future would hold a chapter about illness. Unlike the past pattern, she hoped that living in a residential home would prevent repeated hospitalizations and that she would be able to manage her illness with medical treatment and counseling in an outpatient clinic.

For our final session, I printed the two most recent models of Linda's life story, her past and her future stories (see Figures A8.1 and A8.2 at the end of this appendix). She said that she valued our conversations and seemed proud of her accomplishments. I suggested that she could bring the life story models to her new home and share them with healthcare workers to tell them about herself. Shortly thereafter Linda moved into a residential home and started living her new story. I visited her once and she showed me around while we talked about the activities she was engaged in and the friends she had made. While I cannot know how Linda's future will unfold, it seemed like a good beginning.

Linda's story is important to me. Her life story moved me and expanded my understanding of her. This was vital for me to support her recovery. I realized the potential of life stories as a tool to address the complex phenomenon of illness insight, which is much more than the acceptance of a simple fact. Rather, it involves piecing together past and present experiences, emotions, views of others, and reflections about the causes and consequences of changes in life. I will remember Linda's story because our sessions were successful in the sense that she was able to engage with all the tasks in the guide and our sessions seemed to nurture her identity and recovery. It may not always work out like that. For one of the service users I invited into narrative repair, we had to discontinue our sessions because he was too clinically unstable. That said, my impression is that the GNaR holds promise as an approach to support personal recovery, also among severely affected individuals, but systematic examination of its effects is of course needed.

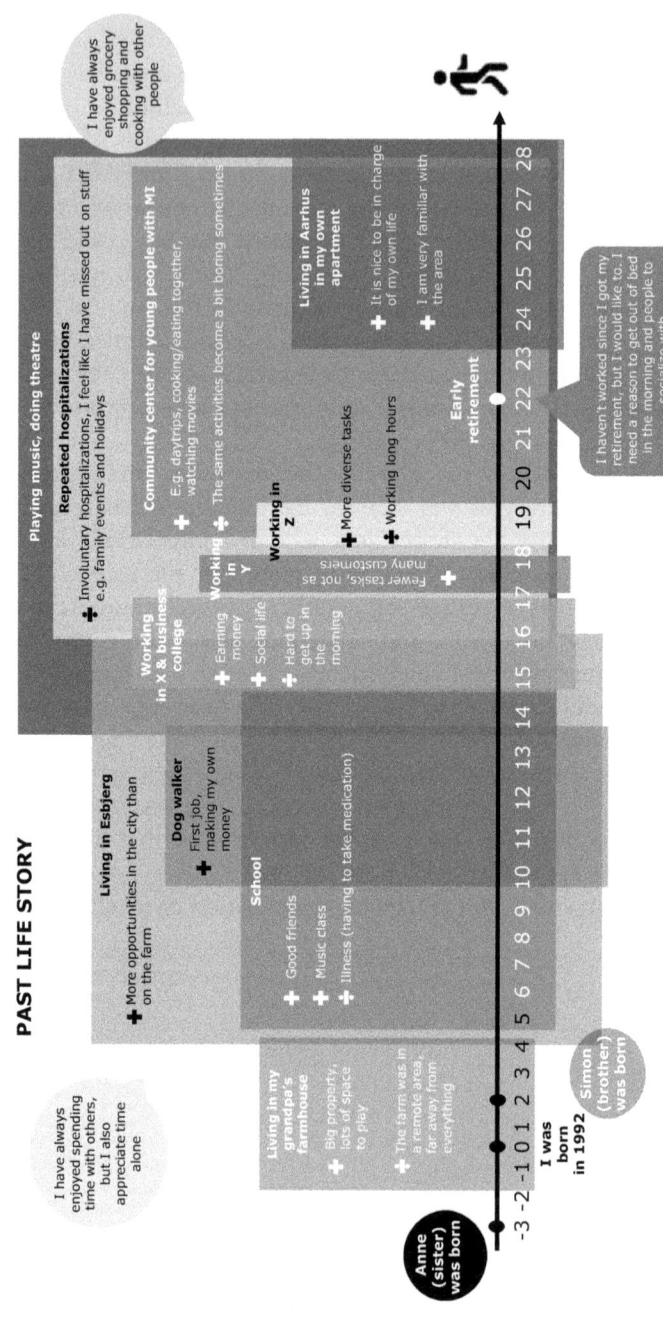

Figure A8.1 Illustration of past chapters in the case story
Note: In these two figures, MI refers to mental illness.

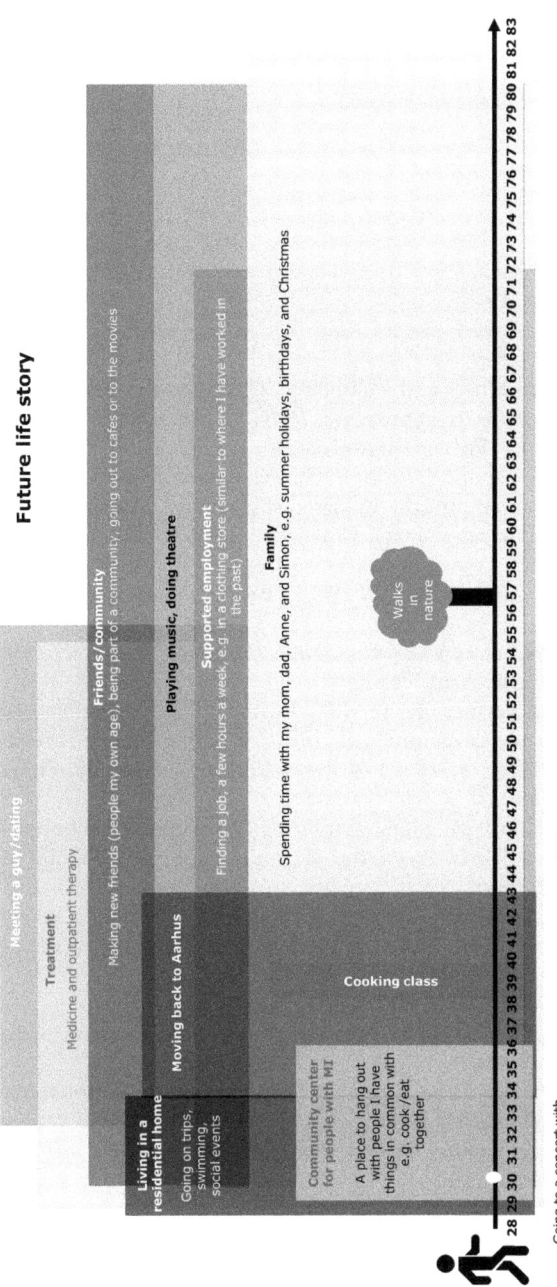

Figure A8.2 Illustration of future chapters in the case story

References

1. Saks, E. R. (2007). *The center cannot hold: My journey through madness.* Hachette Books.
2. Slade, M. (2010). Mental illness and well-being: The central importance of positive psychology and recovery approaches. *BMC Health Services Research, 10,* 26. https://doi.org/10.1186/1472-6963-10-26
3. Andresen, R., Oades, L., Caputi, P. (2003). The experience of recovery from schizophrenia: Towards an empirically validated stage model. *Australian and New Zealand Journal of Psychiatry, 37*(5), 586–594. https://doi.org/10.1046/j.1440-1614.2003.01234.x
4. McNally, R. J. (2011). *What is mental illness?* Belknap Press of Harvard University Press.
5. Slade, M. (2009). *Personal recovery and mental illness: A guide for mental health professionals.* Cambridge University Press.
6. Walker, E., Mittal, V., Tessner, K. (2008). Stress and the hypothalamic pituitary adrenal axis in the developmental course of schizophrenia. *Annual Review of Clinical Psychology, 4,* 189–216. https://doi.org/10.1146/annurev.clinpsy.4.022007.141248
7. Bateman, A., Fonagy, P. (2010). Mentalization based treatment for borderline personality disorder. *World Psychiatry, 9*(1), 11–15. https://doi.org/10.1002/j.2051-5545.2010.tb00255.x
8. McAdams, D. P., McLean, K. C. (2013). Narrative identity. *Current Directions in Psychological Science, 22*(3), 233–238. https://doi.org/10.1177/0963721413475622
9. Bruner, J. (1990). *Acts of meaning.* Harvard University Press.
10. Polkinghorne, D. E. (1988). *Narrative knowing and the human sciences.* State University of New York Press.
11. Habermas, T. (2019). *Emotion and narrative: Perspectives in autobiographical storytelling.* Cambridge University Press.
12. Wurtzel, E. (1995). *Prozac nation: Young and depressed in America, a memoir.* Quartet Books Limited.
13. Haig, M. (2015). *Reasons to stay alive.* Canongate Books.
14. Jamieson, K. R. (1995). *An unquiet mind: A memoir of moods and madness.* Vintage Books.

15. Weinberger, D. R. (1987). Implications of normal brain development for the pathogenesis of schizophrenia. *Archives of General Psychiatry*, *44*(7), 660–669. https://doi.org/10.1001/archpsyc.1987.01800190080012
16. Lysaker, P., Lysaker, J. (2008). *Schizophrenia and the fate of the self.* Oxford University Press.
17. Kessler, R. C. (2012). The costs of depression. *Psychiatric Clinics of North America*, *35*(1), 1–14. https://doi.org/10.1016/j.psc.2011.11.005
18. Laursen, T. M., Munk-Olsen, T., Nordentoft, M., Mortensen, P. B. (2007). Increased mortality among patients admitted with major psychiatric disorders: A register-based study comparing mortality in unipolar depressive disorder, bipolar affective disorder, schizoaffective disorder, and schizophrenia. *Journal of Clinical Psychiatry*, *68*(6), 899–907. https://doi.org/10.4088/jcp.v68n0612
19. Javaras, K. N., Zanarini, M. C., Hudson, J. I., Greenfield, S. F., Gunderson, J. G. (2017). Functional outcomes in community-based adults with borderline personality disorder. *Journal of Psychiatric Research*, *89*, 105–114. https://doi.org/10.1016/j.jpsychires.2017.01.010
20. Corrigan, P. W., Kleinlein, P. (2005). The impact of mental illness stigma. In P. W. Corrigan (Ed.), *On the stigma of mental illness: Practical strategies for research and social change* (pp. 11–44). American Psychological Association. https://doi.org/10.1037/10887-001
21. Michalak, E. E., Murray, G., Young, A. H., Lam, R. W. (2008). Burden of bipolar depression: Impact of disorder and medications on quality of life. *CNS Drugs*, *22*(5), 389–406. https://doi.org/10.2165/00023210-200822050-00003
22. Bluck, S., Habermas, T. (2000). The life story schema. *Motivation and Emotion*, *24*(2), 121–147. https://doi.org/10.1023/A:1005615331901
23. Brown, N. R., Schopflocher, D. (1998). Event clusters: An organization of personal events in autobiographical memory. *Psychological Science*, *9*(6), 470–475. https://doi.org/10.1111/1467-9280.00087
24. Conway, M. A., Singer, J. A., Tagini, A. (2004). The self and autobiographical memory: Correspondence and coherence. *Social Cognition*, *22*(5), 491–529. https://doi.org/10.1521/soco.22.5.491.50768
25. Alea, N., Bluck, S. (2003). Why are you telling me that? A conceptual model of the social function of autobiographical memory. *Memory*, *11*(2), 165–178. https://doi.org/10.1080/741938207
26. Pasupathi, M. (2001). The social construction of the personal past and its implications for adult development. *Psychological Bulletin*, *127*(5), 651–672. https://doi.org/10.1037/0033-2909.127.5.651
27. McAdams, D. P. (1996). Personality, modernity, and the storied self: A contemporary framework for studying persons. *Psychological Inquiry*, *7*(4), 295–321. https://doi.org/10.1207/s15327965pli0704_1
28. McLean, K. C., Pasupathi, M., Pals, J. L. (2007). Selves creating stories creating selves: A process model of self-development. *Personality and Social Psychology Review*, *11*(3), 262–278. https://doi.org/10.1177/1088868307301034

29. Habermas, T., Bluck, S. (2000). Getting a life: The emergence of the life story in adolescence. *Psychological Bulletin, 126*(5), 748–769. https://doi.org/10.1037/0033-2909.126.5.748
30. Dunlop, W. L. (2021). Everything you wanted to know about redemptive stories* (*but were afraid to ask). *Journal of Research in Personality, 92*, 104078. https://doi.org/10.1016/j.jrp.2021.104078
31. Adler, J. M., Lodi-Smith, J., Philippe, F. L., Houle, I. (2016). The incremental validity of narrative identity in predicting well-being: A review of the field and recommendations for the future. *Personality and Social Psychology Review, 20*(2), 142–175. https://doi.org/10.1177/1088868315585068
32. Singer, J. A. (1997). *Message in a bottle: Stories of men and addiction.* Free Press.
33. Ridgway, P. (2001). ReStorying psychiatric disability: Learning from first person recovery narratives. *Psychiatric Rehabilitation Journal, 24*(4), 335–343. https://doi.org/10.1037/h0095071
34. Holm, T., Pillemer, D. B., Bliksted, V., Thomsen, D. K. (2017). A decline in self-defining memories following a diagnosis of schizophrenia. *Comprehensive Psychiatry, 76*, 18–25. https://doi.org/10.1016/j.comppsych.2017.03.014
35. Holm, T., Thomsen, D. K., Bliksted, V. (2018). Themes of unfulfilled agency and communion in life stories of patients with schizophrenia. *Psychiatry Research, 269*, 772–778. https://doi.org/10.1016/j.psychres.2018.08.116
36. Holm, T., Thomsen, D. K., Bliksted, V. (2016). Life story chapters and narrative self-continuity in patients with schizophrenia. *Consciousness and Cognition: An International Journal, 45*, 60–74. https://doi.org/10.1016/j.concog.2016.08.009
37. Jensen, R. A. A., Thomsen, D. K., Bliksted, V. F., Ladegaard, N. (2020). Narrative identity in psychopathology: A negative past and a bright but foreshortened future. *Psychiatry Research, 290*, 9. https://doi.org/10.1016/j.psychres.2020.113103
38. Jensen, R. A. A., Thomsen, D. K., Lind, M., Ladegaard, N., Bliksted, V. F. (2021). Storying the past and the future: Agency and communion themes among individuals with schizophrenia and depression. *Journal of Nervous and Mental Disease, 209*(5), 343–352. https://doi.org/10.1097/NMD.0000000000001302
39. Lind, M., Jørgensen, C. R., Heinskou, T., Simonsen, S., Bøye, R., Thomsen, D. K. (2019). Patients with borderline personality disorder show increased agency in life stories after 12 months of psychotherapy. *Psychotherapy, 56*(2), 274–284. https://doi.org/10.1037/pst0000184
40. Lind, M., Thomsen, D. K., Bøye, R., Heinskou, T., Simonsen, S., Jørgensen, C. R. (2019). Personal and parents' life stories in patients with borderline personality disorder. *Scandinavian Journal of Psychology, 60*(3), 231–242. https://doi.org/10.1111/sjop.12529
41. Pedersen, A. M., Nielsen Straarup, K., Thomsen, D. K. (2018). Narrative identity in female patients with remitted bipolar disorder: A negative past and

a foreshortened future. *Memory, 26*(2), 219–228. https://doi.org/10.1080/09658211.2017.1344250

42. Pedersen, A. M., Straarup, K., Thomsen, D. K. (2022). "My life disappeared in illness": Bipolar disorder and themes in narrative identity. *Memory, 30*(5), 1–12. https://doi.org/10.1080/09658211.2022.2051555

43. Thomsen, D. K., Pillemer, D. B. (2017). I know my story and I know your story: Developing a conceptual framework for vicarious life stories. *Journal of Personality, 85*(4), 464–480. https://doi.org/10.1111/jopy.12253

44. Panattoni, K., Thomsen, D. K. (2018). My partner's stories: Relationships between personal and vicarious life stories within romantic couples. *Memory, 26*(10), 1416–1429. https://doi.org/10.1080/09658211.2018.1485947

45. Holm, T., Thomsen, D. K., Huling, K. S., Fischer, M. W., Lysaker, P. H. (2020). Narrative identity, metacognition, and well-being in patients with schizophrenia or HIV. *Journal of Nervous and Mental Disease, 208*(12), 958–965. https://doi.org/10.1097/NMD.0000000000001238

46. Thomsen, D. K., Panattoni, K., Allé, M. C., Bro Wellnitz, K., Pillemer, D. B. (2020). Vicarious life stories: Examining relations to personal life stories and well-being. *Journal of Research in Personality, 88*, 17. https://doi.org/10.1016/j.jrp.2020.103991

47. Engel, G. L. (1977). The need for a new medical model: A challenge for biomedicine. *Science, 196*(4286), 129–136. https://doi.org/10.1126/science.847460

48. Wade, D. T., Halligan, P. W. (2004). Do biomedical models of illness make for good healthcare systems? *British Medical Journal, 329*(7479), 1398–1401. https://doi.org/10.1136/bmj.329.7479.1398

49. Double, D. (2002). The limits of psychiatry. *British Medical Journal, 324*(7342), 900–904. https://doi.org/10.1136/bmj.324.7342.900

50. Caspi, A., Houts, R. M., Belsky, D. W., et al. (2014). The p factor: One general psychopathology factor in the structure of psychiatric disorders? *Clinical Psychological Science, 2*(2), 119–137. https://doi.org/10.1177/2167702613497473

51. American Psychiatric Association. (2013). *Diagnostic and statistical manual of mental disorders: DSM-5* (5th ed.). American Psychiatric Publishing.

52. World Health Organization. (2018). *International statistical classification of disease and related health problems* (11th ed.). World Health Organization.

53. Harvey, A. G., Watkins, E., Mansell, W., Shafran, R. (2004). *Cognitive behavioural processes across psychological disorders: A transdiagnostic approach to research and treatment.* Oxford University Press.

54. Plana-Ripoll, O., Pedersen, C. B., Holtz, Y., et al. (2019). Exploring comorbidity within mental disorders among a Danish national population. *JAMA Psychiatry, 76*(3), 259–270. https://doi.org/10.1001/jamapsychiatry.2018.3658

55. Regier, D. A., Narrow, W. E., Clarke, D. E., et al. (2013). DSM-5 field trials in the United States and Canada, Part II: Test-retest reliability of selected categorical diagnoses. *American Journal of Psychiatry, 170*(1), 59–70. https://doi.org/10.1176/appi.ajp.2012.12070999

56. Kessler, R. C., McGonagle, K. A., Zhao, S., et al. (1994). Lifetime and 12-month prevalence of DSM-III-R psychiatric disorders in the United States: Results from the National Comorbidity Survey. *Archives of General Psychiatry*, *51*(1), 8–19. https://doi.org/10.1001/archpsyc.1994.03950010008002
57. Paris, J., Gunderson, J., Weinberg, I. (2007). The interface between borderline personality disorder and bipolar spectrum disorders. *Comprehensive Psychiatry*, *48*(2), 145–154. https://doi.org/10.1016/j.comppsych.2006.10.001
58. Ingram, R. E., Luxton, D. D. (2005). Vulnerability-stress models. In B. L. Hankin, J. R. Z. Abela (Eds.), *Development of psychopathology: A vulnerability-stress perspective* (pp. 32–46). Sage Publications. https://doi.org/10.4135/9781452231655.n2
59. Davis, J., Eyre, H., Jacka, F. N., et al. (2016). A review of vulnerability and risks for schizophrenia: Beyond the two hit hypothesis. *Neuroscience and Biobehavioral Reviews*, *65*, 185–194. https://doi.org/10.1016/j.neubiorev.2016.03.017
60. Goodwin, F. K., Jamieson, K. R. (2007). *Manic-depressive illness: Bipolar disorders and recurrent depression* (2nd ed.). Oxford University Press.
61. Geddes, J. R., Miklowitz, D. J. (2013). Treatment of bipolar disorder. *Lancet*, *381*(9878), 1672–1682. https://doi.org/10.1016/s0140-6736(13)60857-0
62. Frank, E., Swartz, H. A., Kupfer, D. J. (2000). Interpersonal and social rhythm therapy: Managing the chaos of bipolar disorder. *Biological Psychiatry*, *48*(6), 593–604. https://doi.org/10.1016/s0006-3223(00)00969-0
63. Beck, A. T. (1976). *Cognitive therapy and the emotional disorders*. International Universities Press.
64. Beck, A. T., Bredemeier, K. (2016). A unified model of depression: Integrating clinical, cognitive, biological, and evolutionary perspectives. *Clinical Psychological Science*, *4*(4), 596–619. https://doi.org/10.1177/2167702616628523
65. Bateman, A. W., Fonagy, P. (2004). Mentalization-based treatment of BPD. *Journal of Personality Disorders*, *18*(1), 36–51. https://doi.org/10.1521/pedi.18.1.36.32772
66. Winsper, C. (2018). The aetiology of borderline personality disorder (BPD): Contemporary theories and putative mechanisms. *Current Opinion in Psychology*, *21*, 105–110. https://doi.org/10.1016/j.copsyc.2017.10.005
67. Bateman, A., Fonagy, P. (2016). *Mentalization-based treatment for personality disorders: A practical guide*. Oxford University Press.
68. Musliner, K. L., Mortensen, P. B., McGrath, J. J., et al. (2019). Association of polygenic liabilities for major depression, bipolar disorder, and schizophrenia with risk for depression in the Danish population. *JAMA Psychiatry*, *76*(5), 516–525. https://doi.org/10.1001/jamapsychiatry.2018.4166
69. Caspi, A., Moffitt, T. E. (2018). All for one and one for all: Mental disorders in one dimension. *American Journal of Psychiatry*, *175*(9), 831–844. https://doi.org/10.1176/appi.ajp.2018.17121383

70. Hayes, S. C., Luoma, J. B., Bond, F. W., Masuda, A., Lillis, J. (2006). Acceptance and commitment therapy: Model, processes and outcomes. *Behaviour Research and Therapy*, *44*(1), 1–25. https://doi.org/10.1016/j.brat.2005.06.006
71. Millier, A., Schmidt, U., Angermeyer, M. C., et al. (2014). Humanistic burden in schizophrenia: A literature review. *Journal of Psychiatric Research*, *54*, 85–93. https://doi.org/10.1016/j.jpsychires.2014.03.021
72. Lysaker, P. H., Davis, L. W., Bryson, G. J., Bell, M. D. (2009). Effects of cognitive behavioral therapy on work outcomes in vocational rehabilitation for participants with schizophrenia spectrum disorders. *Schizophrenia Research*, *107*(2–3), 186–191. https://doi.org/10.1016/j.schres.2008.10.018
73. Davidson, L., Roe, D. (2007). Recovery from versus recovery in serious mental illness: One strategy for lessening confusion plaguing recovery. *Journal of Mental Health*, *16*(4), 459–470. https://doi.org/10.1080/09638230701482394
74. Bellack, A. S. (2006). Scientific and consumer models of recovery in schizophrenia: Concordance, contrasts, and implications. *Schizophrenia Bulletin*, *32*(3), 432–442. https://doi.org/10.1093/schbul/sbj044
75. Bellack, A. S., Drapalski, A. (2012). Issues and developments on the consumer recovery construct. *World Psychiatry*, *11*(3), 156–160. https://doi.org/10.1002/j.2051-5545.2012.tb00117.x
76. Zanarini, M. C., Frankenburg, F. R., Reich, D. B., Fitzmaurice, G. (2012). Attainment and stability of sustained symptomatic remission and recovery among patients with borderline personality disorder and axis II comparison subjects: A 16-year prospective follow up study. *The American Journal of Psychiatry*, *169*(5), 476–483. https://doi.org/10.1176/appi.ajp.2011.11101550
77. Murray, G., Leitan, N. D., Thomas, N., et al. (2017). Towards recovery-oriented psychosocial interventions for bipolar disorder: Quality of life outcomes, stage-sensitive treatments, and mindfulness mechanisms. *Clinical Psychology Review*, *52*, 148–163. https://doi.org/10.1016/j.cpr.2017.01.002
78. Ng, F. Y. Y., Townsend, M. L., Miller, C. E., Jewell, M., Grenyer, B. F. S. (2019). The lived experience of recovery in borderline personality disorder: A qualitative study. *Borderline Personality Disorder and Emotion Dysregulation*, *6*, 10. https://doi.org/10.1186/s40479-019-0107-2
79. Rush, A. J., Aaronson, S. T., Demyttenaere, K. (2019). Difficult-to-treat depression: A clinical and research roadmap for when remission is elusive. *Australian & New Zealand Journal of Psychiatry*, *53*(2), 109–118. https://doi.org/10.1177/0004867418808585
80. Leonhardt, B. L., Huling, K., Hamm, J. A., et al. (2017). Recovery and serious mental illness: A review of current clinical and research paradigms and future directions. *Expert Review of Neurotherapeutics*, *17*(11), 1117–1130. https://doi.org/10.1080/14737175.2017.1378099
81. Harrison, G., Hopper, K., Craig, T., et al. (2001). Recovery from psychotic illness: A 15- and 25-year international follow-up study. *The British Journal of Psychiatry*, *178*, 506–517. https://doi.org/10.1192/bjp.178.6.506

82. Valiente, C., Espinosa, R., Trucharte, A., Nieto, J., Martínez-Prado, L. (2019). The challenge of well-being and quality of life: A meta-analysis of psychological interventions in schizophrenia. *Schizophrenia Research, 208*, 16–24. https://doi.org/10.1016/j.schres.2019.01.040
83. www.google.com/url?sa=t&rct=j&q=&esrc=s&source=web&cd=&ved=2ah UKEwi4u9bP2a30AhXW_rsIHWzwBxkQFnoECAMQAQ&url=https%3A %2F%2Fwww.regeringen.dk%2Fmedia%2F1294%2Fligevaerd__nyt_fokus _for_indsatsen_for_mennesker_med_psykiske_lidelser.pdf&usg=AOvVaw 1XcaR7cJPvoQXHYkUyEBI8.
84. Anthony, W. A. (1993). Recovery from mental illness: The guiding vision of the mental health service system in the 1990s. *Psychosocial Rehabilitation Journal, 16*(4), 11–23. https://doi.org/10.1037/h0095655
85. Davidson, L., Sells, D., Songster, S., O'Connell, M. (2005). Qualitative studies of recovery: What can we learn from the person? In R. O. Ralph, P. W. Corrigan (Eds.), *Recovery in mental illness: Broadening our understanding of wellness* (pp. 147–170). American Psychological Association. https:// doi.org/10.1037/10848-007
86. Leamy, M., Bird, V., Le Boutillier, C., Williams, J., Slade, M. (2011). Conceptual framework for personal recovery in mental health: Systematic review and narrative synthesis. *The British Journal of Psychiatry, 199*(6), 445–452. https://doi.org/10.1192/bjp.bp.110.083733
87. Hancock, N., Scanlan, J. N., Honey, A., Bundy, A. C., O'Shea, K. (2015). Recovery Assessment Scale – Domains and Stages (RAS-DS): Its feasibility and outcome measurement capacity. *Australian and New Zealand Journal of Psychiatry, 49*(7), 624–633. https://doi.org/10.1177/0004867414564084
88. Corrigan, P. W., Salzer, M., Ralph, R. O., Sangster, Y., Keck, L. (2004). Examining the factor structure of the Recovery Assessment Scale. *Schizophrenia Bulletin, 30*(4), 1035–1041. https://doi.org/10.1093/ oxfordjournals.schbul.a007118
89. Corrigan, P. W., Ralph, R. O. (2005). Introduction: Recovery as consumer vision and research paradigm. In R. O. Ralph, P. W. Corrigan (Eds.), *Recovery in mental illness: Broadening our understanding of wellness* (pp. 3–17). American Psychological Association. https://doi.org/10.1037/10848-001
90. Diener, E., Oishi, S., Lucas, R. E. (2003). Personality, culture, and subjective well-being: Emotional and cognitive evaluations of life. *Annual Review of Psychology, 54*, 403–425. https://doi.org/10.1146/annurev.psych.54.101601 .145056
91. Ryan, R. M., Deci, E. L. (2001). On happiness and human potentials: A review of research on hedonic and eudaimonic well-being. *Annual Review of Psychology, 52*, 141–166. https://doi.org/10.1146/annurev.psych .52.1.141
92. Ryff, C. D. (2014). Psychological well-being revisited: Advances in the science and practice of eudaimonia. *Psychotherapy and Psychosomatics, 83*(1), 10–28. https://doi.org/10.1159/000353263

93. Diener, E., Sapyta, J. J., Suh, E. (1998). Subjective well-being is essential to well-being. *Psychological Inquiry*, *9*(1), 33–37. https://doi.org/10.1207/s15327965pli0901_3
94. Bauer, J. J. *The transformative self: Personal growth, narrative identity, and the good life*. Oxford University Press.
95. World Health Organization. (2005). *Promoting mental health: Concepts, emerging evidence, practice*. World Health Organization.
96. Karow, A., Naber, D., Lambert, M., Moritz, S. (2012). Remission as perceived by people with schizophrenia, family members and psychiatrists. *European Psychiatry*, *27*(6), 426–431. https://doi.org/10.1016/j.eurpsy.2011.01.013
97. Demyttenaere, K., Donneau, A.-F., Albert, A., Ansseau, M., Constant, E., van Heeringen, K. (2015). What is important in being cured from depression? Discordance between physicians and patients. *Journal of Affective Disorders*, *174*, 390–396. https://doi.org/10.1016/j.jad.2014.12.004
98. Roe, D., Lysaker, P. H. (2012). The importance of personal narratives in recovery from psychosis. In J. Geekie, P. Randal, D. Lampshire, J. Read (Eds.), *Experiencing psychosis: Personal and professional perspectives* (pp. 5–14). Routledge/Taylor & Francis Group.
99. Roe, D., Davidson, L. (2005). Self and narrative in schizophrenia: Time to author a new story. *Journal of Medical Humanities*, *31*(2), 89–94. https://doi.org/10.1136/jmh.2005.000214
100. Singer, J. A., Blagov, P., Berry, M., Oost, K. M. (2013). Self-defining memories, scripts, and the life story: Narrative identity in personality and psychotherapy. *Journal of Personality*, *81*(6), 569–582. https://doi.org/10.1111/jopy.12005
101. McAdams, D. P. (1993). *The stories we live by: Personal myths and the making of the self*. Guilford Press.
102. Carr, D. (1997). Narrative and the real world: An argument for continuity. In L. P. Hinchman, S. K. Hinchman (Eds.), *Memory, identity, community: The idea of narrative in the human sciences* (pp. 7–25). State University of New York Press.
103. Skowronski, J. J., Walker, W. R. (2004). How describing autobiographical events can affect autobiographical memories. *Social Cognition*, *22*(5), 555–590. https://doi.org/10.1521/soco.22.5.555.50764
104. Polkinghorne, D. (2004). Ricoeur, narrative and personal identity. In C. Lightfoot, C. Lalonde, M. Chandler (Eds.), *Changing conceptions of psychological life* (pp. 27–48). Lawrence Erlbaum Associates Publishers.
105. Dunlop, W. L., Guo, J., McAdams, D. P. (2016). The autobiographical author through time: Examining the degree of stability and change in redemptive and contaminated personal narratives. *Social Psychological and Personality Science*, *7*(5), 428–436. https://doi.org/10.1177/1948550616644654
106. Habermas, T., Köber, C. (2015). Autobiographical reasoning in life narratives buffers the effect of biographical disruptions on the sense of

self-continuity. *Memory*, *23*(5), 664–674. https://doi.org/10.1080/09658211.2014.920885

107. McAdams, D. P. (2001). The psychology of life stories. *Review of General Psychology*, *5*(2), 100–122. https://doi.org/10.1037/1089-2680.5.2.100
108. Dunlop, W. L., Tracy, J. L. (2013). Sobering stories: Narratives of self-redemption predict behavioral change and improved health among recovering alcoholics. *Journal of Personality and Social Psychology*, *104*(3), 576–590. https://doi.org/10.1037/a0031185
109. McAdams, D. P. (2006). *The redemptive self: Stories Americans live by*. Oxford University Press.
110. Maruna, S. (2001). *Making good: How ex-convicts reform and rebuild their lives* (1st ed.). American Psychological Association.
111. McCoy, T. P., Dunlop, W. L. (2017). Down on the upside: Redemption, contamination, and agency in the lives of adult children of alcoholics. *Memory*, *25*(5), 586–594. https://doi.org/10.1080/09658211.2016.1197947
112. Conway, M. A., Justice, L. V., D'Argembeau, A. (2019). The self-memory system revisited: Past, present, and future. In J. H. Mace (Ed.), *The organization and structure of autobiographical memory* (pp. 28–51). Oxford University Press. https://doi.org/10.1093/oso/9780198784845.003.0003
113. Thomsen, D. K. (2009). There is more to life stories than memories. *Memory*, *17*(4), 445–457. https://doi.org/10.1080/09658210902740878
114. Thomsen, D. K., Jensen, R. A. A., Mehlsen, M. Y. (2019). One-year stability in life story chapters and memories among emerging, middle-aged, and older adults. *Journal of Research in Personality*, *82*, 11. https://doi.org/10.1016/j.jrp.2019.103860
115. Pillemer, D. B. (1998). *Momentous events, vivid memories*. Harvard University Press.
116. Singer, J. A., Salovey, P. (1993). *The remembered self: Emotion and memory in personality*. The Free Press.
117. White, M., Epston, D. (1990). *Narrative means to therapeutic ends*. W.W. Norton & Company Ltd.
118. McLean, K. C. (2016). *The co-authored self: Family stories and the construction of personal identity*. Oxford University Press.
119. Pillemer, D. B., Steiner, K. L., Kuwabara, K. J., Thomsen, D. K., Svob, C. (2015). Vicarious memories. *Consciousness and Cognition: An International Journal*, *36*, 233–245. https://doi.org/10.1016/j.concog.2015.06.010
120. Merrill, N., Fivush, R. (2016). Intergenerational narratives and identity across development. *Developmental Review*, *40*, 72–92. https://doi.org/10.1016/j.dr.2016.03.001
121. Frank, A. W. (2013). *The wounded storyteller: Body, illness, and ethics* (2nd ed.). The University of Chicago Press.
122. Fivush, R. (2019). *Family narratives and the development of an autobiographical self: Social and cultural perspectives on autobiographical memory*. Routledge.

123. Fivush, R., Habermas, T., Waters, T., Zaman, W. (2011). The making of autobiographical memory: Intersections of culture, narratives and identity. *International Journal of Psychology, 46*(5), 321–345. https://doi.org/10.1080/00207594.2011.596541
124. Goodman, N. (1978). *Ways of worldmaking*. Hackett.
125. Hammack, P. L. (2008). Narrative and the cultural psychology of identity. *Personality and Social Psychology Review, 12*(3), 222–247. https://doi.org/10.1177/1088868308316892
126. Thorne, A., McLean, K. C. (2003). Telling traumatic events in adolescence: A study of master narrative positioning. In R. Fivush, C. A. Haden (Eds.), *Autobiographical memory and the construction of a narrative self: Developmental and cultural perspectives* (pp. 169–185). Lawrence Erlbaum Associates Publishers.
127. McLean, K. C., Syed, M. (2016). Personal, master, and alternative narratives: An integrative framework for understanding identity development in context. *Human Development, 58*(6), 318–349. https://doi.org/10.1159/000445817
128. Berntsen, D., Rubin, D. C. (2004). Cultural life scripts structure recall from autobiographical memory. *Memory & Cognition, 32*(3), 427–442. https://doi.org/10.3758/BF03195836
129. Cohen, P., Cohen, J. (1984). The clinician's illusion. *Archives of General Psychiatry, 41*(12), 1178–1182. https://doi.org/10.1001/archpsyc.1984.01790230064010
130. Pasupathi, M., Mansour, E., Brubaker, J. R. (2007). Developing a life story: Constructing relations between self and experience in autobiographical narratives. *Human Development, 50*(2–3), 85–110. https://doi.org/10.1159/000100939
131. Hydén, L.-C. (1997). Illness and narrative. *Sociology of Health & Illness, 19*(1), 48–69. https://doi.org/10.1111/j.1467-9566.1997.tb00015.x
132. Charon, R. (2006). *Narrative medicine: Honoring the stories of illness*. Oxford University Press.
133. Schafer, R. (1992). *Retelling a life: Narration and dialogue in psychoanalysis*. BasicBooks.
134. Spence, D. P. (1982). *Narrative truth and historical truth: Meaning and interpretation in psychoanalysis*. W.W. Norton.
135. Lysaker, P. H., Lysaker, J. T., Lysaker, J. T. (2001). Schizophrenia and the collapse of the dialogical self: Recovery, narrative and psychotherapy. *Psychotherapy: Theory, Research, Practice, Training, 38*(3), 252–261. https://doi.org/10.1037/0033-3204.38.3.252
136. Lysaker, P. H., Wickett, A., Davis, L. W. (2005). Narrative qualities in schizophrenia: Associations with impairments in neurocognition and negative symptoms. *Journal of Nervous and Mental Disease, 193*(4), 244–249. https://doi.org/10.1097/01.nmd.0000158376.53165.de
137. Allé, M. C., Potheegadoo, J., Köber, C., et al. (2015). Impaired coherence of life narratives of patients with schizophrenia. *Scientific Reports, 5*, 12934.

138. Berna, F., Bennouna-Greene, M., Potheegadoo, J., Verry, P., Conway, M. A., Danion, J.-M. (2011). Impaired ability to give a meaning to personally significant events in patients with schizophrenia. *Consciousness and Cognition: An International Journal*, 20(3), 703–711. https://doi.org/10.1016/j.concog.2010.12.004

139. Raffard, S., D'Argembeau, A., Lardi, C., Bayard, S., Boulenger, J.-P., Van der Linden, M. (2010). Narrative identity in schizophrenia. *Consciousness and Cognition: An International Journal*, 19(1), 328–340. https://doi.org/10.1016/j.concog.2009.10.005

140. Lysaker, P. H., Ringer, J. M., Buck, K. D., et al. (2012). Metacognitive and social cognition deficits in patients with significant psychiatric and medical adversity: A comparison between participants with schizophrenia and a sample of participants who are HIV-positive. *Journal of Nervous and Mental Disease*, 200 (2), 130–134. https://doi.org/10.1097/NMD.0b013e3182439533

141. Cowan, H. R., Mittal, V. A., McAdams, D. P. (2021). Narrative identity in the psychosis spectrum: A systematic review and developmental model. *Clinical Psychology Review*, 88, 102067. https://doi.org/10.1016/j.cpr.2021.102067

142. Gallagher, S. (2000). Philosophical conceptions of the self: Implications for cognitive science. *Trends in Cognitive Sciences*, 4(1), 14–21. https://doi.org/10.1016/s1364-6613(99)01417-5

143. Parnas, J., Henriksen, M. G. (2014). Disordered self in the schizophrenia spectrum: A clinical and research perspective. *Harvard Review of Psychiatry*, 22(5), 251–265. https://doi.org/10.1097/hrp.0000000000000040

144. Dalgleish, T., Hill, E., Golden, A.-M. J., Morant, N., Dunn, B. D. (2011). The structure of past and future lives in depression. *Journal of Abnormal Psychology*, 120(1), 1–15. https://doi.org/10.1037/a0020797

145. Habermas, T., Ott, L.-M., Schubert, M., Schneider, B., Pate, A. (2008). Stuck in the past: Negative bias, explanatory style, temporal order, and evaluative perspectives in life narratives of clinically depressed individuals. *Depression and Anxiety*, 25(11), E121–E132. https://doi.org/10.1002/da.20389

146. Adler, J. M., Chin, E. D., Kolisetty, A. P., Oltmanns, T. F. (2012). The distinguishing characteristics of narrative identity in adults with features of borderline personality disorder: An empirical investigation. *Journal of Personality Disorders*, 26(4), 498–512. https://doi.org/10.1521/pedi.2012.26.4.498

147. Adler, J. M., Clark, L. A. (2019). Incorporating narrative identity into structural approaches to personality and psychopathology. *Journal of Research in Personality*, 82, 6. https://doi.org/10.1016/j.jrp.2019.103857

148. Lind, M., Adler, J. M., Clark, L. A. (2020). Narrative identity and personality disorder: An empirical and conceptual review. *Current Psychiatry Reports*, 22(12), 67. https://doi.org/10.1007/s11920-020-01187-8

149. Adler, J. M. (2012). Living into the story: Agency and coherence in a longitudinal study of narrative identity development and mental health over

the course of psychotherapy. *Journal of Personality and Social Psychology, 102* (2), 367–389. https://doi.org/10.1037/a0025289
150. Korte, J., Bohlmeijer, E. T., Cappeliez, P., Smit, F., Westerhof, G. J. (2012). Life review therapy for older adults with moderate depressive symptomatology: A pragmatic randomized controlled trial. *Psychological Medicine, 42*(6), 1163–1173. https://doi.org/10.1017/s0033291711002042
151. Roe, D., Hasson-Ohayon, I., Mashiach-Eizenberg, M., Derhy, O., Lysaker, P. H., Yanos, P. T. (2014). Narrative enhancement and cognitive therapy (NECT) effectiveness: A quasi-experimental study. *Journal of Clinical Psychology, 70*(4), 303–312. https://doi.org/10.1002/jclp.22050
152. McAdams, D. P., Reynolds, J., Lewis, M., Patten, A. H., Bowman, P. J. (2001). When bad things turn good and good things turn bad: Sequences of redemption and contamination in life narrative and their relation to psychosocial adaptation in midlife adults and in students. *Personality and Social Psychology Bulletin, 27*(4), 474–485. https://doi.org/10.1177/0146167201274008
153. Baerger, D. R., McAdams, D. P. (1999). Life story coherence and its relation to psychological well-being. *Narrative Inquiry, 9*(1), 69–96. https://doi.org/10.1075/ni.9.1.05bae
154. Pennebaker, J. W., Seagal, J. D. (1999). Forming a story: The health benefits of narrative. *Journal of Clinical Psychology, 55*(10), 1243–1254. https://doi.org/10.1002/(sici)1097-4679(199910)55:10
155. Frattaroli, J. (2006). Experimental disclosure and its moderators: A meta-analysis. *Psychological Bulletin, 132*(6), 823–865. https://doi.org/10.1037/0033-2909.132.6.823
156. Berntsen, D., Rubin, D. C. (2006). The centrality of event scale: A measure of integrating a trauma into one's identity and its relation to post-traumatic stress disorder symptoms. *Behaviour, Research and Therapy, 44*(2), 219–231. https://doi.org/10.1016/j.brat.2005.01.009
157. Gehrt, T. B., Berntsen, D., Hoyle, R. H., Rubin, D. C. (2018). Psychological and clinical correlates of the Centrality of Event Scale: A systematic review. *Clinical Psychological Review, 65*, 57–80. https://doi.org/10.1016/j.cpr.2018.07.006
158. Boydell, K. M., Stasiulis, E., Volpe, T., Gladstone, B. (2010). A descriptive review of qualitative studies in first episode psychosis. *Early Intervention in Psychiatry, 4*(1), 7–24. https://doi.org/10.1111/j.1751-7893.2009.00154.x
159. Warwick, H., Mansell, W., Porter, C., Tai, S. (2019). "What people diagnosed with bipolar disorder experience as distressing": A meta-synthesis of qualitative research. *Journal of Affective Disorders, 248*, 108–130. https://doi.org/10.1016/j.jad.2019.01.024
160. Kean, C. (2009). Silencing the self: Schizophrenia as a self-disturbance. *Schizophrenia Bulletin, 35*(6), 1034–1036. https://doi.org/10.1093/schbul/sbp043
161. Agnew, G., Shannon, C., Ryan, T., Storey, L., McDonnell, C. (2016). Self and identity in women with symptoms of borderline personality:

A qualitative study. *International Journal of Qualitative Studies on Health and Well-being*, *11*, 9. https://doi.org/10.3402/qhw.v11.30490

162. Lally, S. J. (1989). "Does being in here mean there is something wrong with me"? *Schizophrenia Bulletin*, *15*(2), 253–265. https://doi.org/10.1093/schbul/15.2.253

163. Cornford, C. S., Hill, A., Reilly, J. (2007). How patients with depressive symptoms view their condition: A qualitative study. *Family Practice*, *24*(4), 358–364. https://doi.org/10.1093/fampra/cmm032

164. Shepherd, S., Depp, C. A., Harris, G., Halpain, M., Palinkas, L. A., Jeste, D. V. (2012). Perspectives on schizophrenia over the lifespan: A qualitative study. *Schizophrenia Bulletin*, *38*(2), 295–303. https://doi.org/10.1093/schbul/sbq075

165. Michalak, E. E., Yatham, L. N., Kolesar, S., Lam, R. W. (2006). Bipolar disorder and quality of life: A patient-centered perspective. *Quality of Life Research*, *15*(1), 25–37. https://doi.org/10.1007/s11136-005-0376-7

166. Kvale, S. (1997). *Interview: En introduktion til det kvalitative forskningsinterview [Interviews: An introduction to qualitative research interviewing]*. Hans Reitzel.

167. Smith, J. A., Osborn, M. (2015). Interpretative phenomenological analysis. In J. A. Smith (Ed.), *Qualitative psychology A practical guide to research methods* (3rd ed., pp. 25–52). Sage Publications.

168. Christiansen, N. F., Petersen, K. (2001). The dynamics of social solidarity: The Danish welfare state, 1900–2000. *Scandinavian Journal of History*, *26*(3), 177–196. https://doi.org/10.1080/034687501750303846

169. Zuckerman, P. (2017). Why are Danes and Swedes so irreligious. *Nordic Journal of Religion and Society*, *22*, 55–69. https://doi.org/10.18261/ISSN1890-7008-2009-01-04

170. Tennen, H., Affleck, G. (2002). Benefit-finding and benefit-reminding. In C. R. Snyder, S. J. Lopez (Eds.), *Handbook of positive psychology* (pp. 584–597). Oxford University Press.

171. Tedeschi, R. G., Calhoun, L. G. (2004). Posttraumatic growth: Conceptual foundations and empirical evidence. *Psychological Inquiry*, *15*(1), 1–18. https://doi.org/10.1207/s15327965pli1501_01

172. Tedeschi, R. G., Calhoun, L. G. (1996). The Posttraumatic Growth Inventory: Measuring the positive legacy of trauma. *Journal of Traumatic Stress*, *9*(3), 455–472. https://doi.org/10.1002/jts.2490090305

173. Baumeister, R. F., Leary, M. R. (1995). The need to belong: Desire for interpersonal attachments as a fundamental human motivation. *Psychological Bulletin*, *117*(3), 497–529. https://doi.org/10.1037/0033-2909.117.3.497

174. Easterbrook, M. J., Kuppens, T., Manstead, A. S. R. (2016). The education effect: Higher educational qualifications are robustly associated with beneficial personal and socio-political outcomes. *Social Indicators Research*, *126*(3), 1261–1298. https://doi.org/10.1007/s11205-015-0946-1

175. Newman, D. B., Tay, L., Diener, E. (2014). Leisure and subjective well-being: A model of psychological mechanisms as mediating factors. *Journal of*

Happiness Studies, *15*, 555–578. https://doi.org/10.1007/s10902-013-9435-x

176. Sarason, I. G., Levine, H. M., Basham, R. B., Sarason, B. R. (1983). Assessing social support: The Social Support Questionnaire. *Journal of Personality and Social Psychology*, *44*(1), 127–139. https://doi.org/10.1037/0022-3514.44.1.127
177. Erikson, E. H. (1968). *Identity: Youth and crisis*. Norton.
178. Bretherton, I. (1991). Pouring new wine into old bottles: The social self as internal working model. In M. R. Gunnar, L. A. Sroufe (Eds.), *Self processes and development* (pp. 1–41). Lawrence Erlbaum Associates Publishers.
179. Jørgensen, C. R. (2010). Invited essay: Identity and borderline personality disorder. *Journal of Personality Disorders*, *24*(3), 344–364. https://doi.org/10.1521/pedi.2010.24.3.344
180. Flynn, D. (2010). Narratives of melancholy: A humanities approach to depression. *Medical Humanities*, *36*(1), 36–39. https://doi.org/10.1136/jmh.2009.002022
181. Markus, H., Nurius, P. (1986). Possible selves. *American Psychologist*, *41*(9), 954–969. https://doi.org/10.1037/0003-066X.41.9.954
182. Rennick-Egglestone, S., Morgan, K., Llewellyn-Beardsley, J., et al. (2019). Mental health recovery narratives and their impact on recipients: Systematic review and narrative synthesis. *Canadian Journal of Psychiatry*, *64*(10), 669–679. https://doi.org/10.1177/0706743719846108
183. Bandura, A. (2006). Toward a psychology of human agency. *Perspectives on Psychological Science*, *1*(2), 164–180. https://doi.org/10.1111/j.1745-6916.2006.00011.x
184. Berntsen, D., Bohn, A. (2010). Remembering and forecasting: The relation between autobiographical memory and episodic future thinking. *Memory & Cognition*, *38*(3), 265–278. https://doi.org/10.3758/mc.38.3.265
185. Thomsen, D. K., Lind, M., Pillemer, D. B. (2017). Examining relations between aging, life story chapters, and well-being. *Applied Cognitive Psychology*, *31*(2), 207–215. https://doi.org/10.1002/acp.3318
186. McClintock, S. M., Husain, M. M., Greer, T. L., Cullum, C. M. (2010). Association between depression severity and neurocognitive function in major depressive disorder: A review and synthesis. *Neuropsychology*, *24*(1), 9–34. https://doi.org/10.1037/a0017336
187. Mesholam-Gately, R. I., Giuliano, A. J., Goff, K. P., Faraone, S. V., Seidman, L. J. (2009). Neurocognition in first-episode schizophrenia: A meta-analytic review. *Neuropsychology*, *23*(3), 315–336. https://doi.org/10.1037/a0014708
188. Wingo, A. P., Harvey, P. D., Baldessarini, R. J. (2009). Neurocognitive impairment in bipolar disorder patients: Functional implications. *Bipolar Disorders*, *11*(2), 113–125. https://doi.org/10.1111/j.1399-5618.2009.00665.x
189. Scholl, I., Zill, J. M., Härter, M., Dirmaier, J. (2014). An integrative model of patient-centeredness – A systematic review and concept analysis. *PLoS ONE*, *9*(9), e107828. https://doi.org/10.1371/journal.pone.0107828

190. Haddad, P. M., Correll, C. U. (2018). The acute efficacy of antipsychotics in schizophrenia: A review of recent meta-analyses. *Therapeutic Advances in Psychopharmacology*, 8(11), 303–318. https://doi.org/10.1177/2045125318781475
191. Hofmann, S. G., Asnaani, A., Vonk, I. J., Sawyer, A. T., Fang, A. (2012). The efficacy of cognitive behavioral therapy: A review of meta-analyses. *Cognitive Therapy and Research*, 36(5), 427–440. https://doi.org/10.1007/s10608-012-9476-1
192. Aldao, A., Nolen-Hoeksema, S., Schweizer, S. (2010). Emotion-regulation strategies across psychopathology: A meta-analytic review. *Clinical Psychology Review*, 30(2), 217–237. https://doi.org/10.1016/j.cpr.2009.11.004
193. Stovall-McClough, K. C., Dozier, M. (2008). Attachment states of mind and psychopathology in adulthood. In J. Cassidy, P. R. Shaver (Eds.), *Handbook of attachment: Theory, research, and clinical applications* (2nd ed., pp. 715–738). Guilford Press.
194. Widiger, T. A., Smith, G. T. (2008). Personality and psychopathology. In O. P. John, R. W. Robins, L. A. Pervin (Eds.), *Handbook of personality: Theory and research* (3rd ed., pp. 743–769). Guilford Press.
195. Gilbert, R., Widom, C. S., Browne, K., Fergusson, D., Webb, E., Janson, S. (2009). Burden and consequences of child maltreatment in high-income countries. *Lancet*, 373(9657), 68–81. https://doi.org/10.1016/s0140-6736(08)61706-7
196. Morrison, A. P., Frame, L., Larkin, W. (2003). Relationships between trauma and psychosis: A review and integration. *British Journal of Clinical Psychology*, 42(4), 331–353. https://doi.org/10.1348/014466503322528892
197. Ball, J. S., Links, P. S. (2009). Borderline personality disorder and childhood trauma: Evidence for a causal relationship. *Current Psychiatry Reports*, 11, 63–68. https://doi.org/10.1007/s11920-009-0010-4
198. Hayes, S. C., Strosahl, K. D., Wilson, K. G. (2012). *Acceptance and commitment therapy: The process and practice of mindful change* (2nd ed.). Guilford Press.
199. Bolier, L., Haverman, M., Westerhof, G. J., Riper, H., Smit, F., Bohlmeijer, E. (2013). Positive psychology interventions: A meta-analysis of randomized controlled studies. *BMC Public Health*, 13, 119. https://doi.org/10.1186/1471-2458-13-119
200. Howell, A. J. (2017). Self-affirmation theory and the science of well-being. *Journal of Happiness Studies*, 18(1), 293–311. https://doi.org/10.1007/s10902-016-9713-5
201. Oettingen, G. (2012). Future thought and behaviour change. *European Review of Social Psychology*, 23(1), 1–63. https://doi.org/10.1080/10463283.2011.643698
202. Flückiger, C., Del Re, A. C., Wampold, B. E., Horvath, A. O. (2018). The alliance in adult psychotherapy: A meta-analytic synthesis. *Psychotherapy*, 55(4), 316–340. https://doi.org/10.1037/pst0000172

203. Rogers, C. R. (1961). *On becoming a person: A therapist's view of psychotherapy*. Houghton Mifflin.
204. Norcross, J. C., Lambert, M. J. (2018). Psychotherapy relationships that work III. *Psychotherapy*, *55*(4), 303–315. https://doi.org/10.1037/pst0000193
205. Zilcha-Mano, S. (2017). Is the alliance really therapeutic? Revisiting this question in light of recent methodological advances. *American Psychologist*, *72*(4), 311–325. https://doi.org/10.1037/a0040435
206. Kirk, M., Rasmussen, K. W., Overgaard, S. B., Berntsen, D. (2019). Five weeks of immersive reminiscence therapy improves autobiographical memory in Alzheimer's disease. *Memory*, *27*(4), 441–454. https://doi.org/10.1080/09658211.2018.1515960
207. Angus, L. (2012). Toward an integrative understanding of narrative and emotion processes in emotion-focused therapy of depression: Implications for theory, research and practice. *Psychotherapy Research*, *22*(4), 367–380. https://doi.org/10.1080/10503307.2012.683988
208. Knez, I. (2014). Place and the self: An autobiographical memory synthesis. *Philosophical Psychology*, *27*(2), 164–192. https://doi.org/10.1080/09515089.2012.728124
209. Gústafsson, J. (2014). *Livshistoriefortællinger - nøglen til livet: En inspirations- og praksisbog [Life stories – the key to life]* (1st ed.). Frydenlund.
210. Lind, M., Simonsen, S., Dunlop, W. L. (2021). Incorporating narrative repair in the treatment of avoidant personality disorders: A case in point. *Journal of Clinical Psychology*, *77*(5), 1176–1188. https://doi.org/10.1002/jclp.23152
211. Davidson, L., Chinman, M., Kloos, B., Weingarten, R., Stayner, D., Tebes, J. K. (1999). Peer support among individuals with severe mental illness: A review of the evidence. *Clinical Psychology: Science and Practice*, *6*(2), 165–187. https://doi.org/10.1093/clipsy.6.2.165
212. www.researchintorecovery.com/neon.
213. www.scottishrecovery.net/resources/.
214. Sands, S. A., Stanley, P., Charon, R. (2008). Pediatric narrative oncology: Interprofessional training to promote empathy, build teams, and prevent burnout. *Journal of Supportive Oncology*, *6*(7), 307–312.
215. Oschatz, C., Marker, C. (2020). Long-term persuasive effects in narrative communication research: A meta-analysis. *Journal of Communication*, *70*(4), 473–496. https://doi.org/10.1093/joc/jqaa017
216. Baumeister, R. F., Zhang, L., Vohs, K. D. (2004). Gossip as cultural learning. *Review of General Psychology*, *8*(2), 111–121. https://doi.org/10.1037/1089-2680.8.2.111
217. Adler, J. M., Dunlop, W. L., Fivush, R., et al. (2017). Research methods for studying narrative identity: A primer. *Social Psychological and Personality Science*, *8*(5), 519–527. https://doi.org/10.1177/1948550617698202
218. Christensen, K. S., Fink, P., Toft, T., Frostholm, L., Ørnbøl, E., Olesen, F. (2005). A brief case-finding questionnaire for common mental disorders:

The CMDQ. *Family Practice*, *22*(4), 448–457. https://doi.org/10.1093/fampra/cmi025
219. Andreasen, N. C. (1984). *Scale for the assessment of positive symptoms (SAPS)*. University of Iowa.
220. Andreasen, N. C. (1984). *Scale for the assessment of negative symptoms (SANS)*. University of Iowa.
221. Keefe, R. S. E., Goldberg, T. E., Harvey, P. D., Gold, J. M., Poe, M. P., Coughenour, L. (2004). The Brief Assessment of Cognition in Schizophrenia: Reliability, sensitivity, and comparison with a standard neurocognitive battery. *Schizophrenia Research*, *68*(2–3), 283–297. https://doi.org/10.1016/j.schres.2003.09.011
222. Keefe, R. S. E., Poe, M., Walker, T. M., Harvey, P. D. (2006). The relationship of the Brief Assessment of Cognition in Schizophrenia (BACS) to functional capacity and real-world functional outcome. *Journal of Clinical and Experimental Neuropsychology*, *28*(2), 260–269. https://doi.org/10.1080/13803390500360539
223. Thomsen, D. K., Berntsen, D. (2008). The cultural life script and life story chapters contribute to the reminiscence bump. *Memory*, *16*(4), 420–435. https://doi.org/10.1080/09658210802010497
224. Singer, J. A., Moffitt, K. H. (1992). An experimental investigation of specificity and generality in memory narratives. *Imagination, Cognition and Personality*, *11*(3), 233–257. https://doi.org/10.2190/72A3-8UPY-GDB9-GX9K
225. Habermas, T., Ehlert-Lerche, S., de Silveira, C. (2009). The development of the temporal macrostructure of life narratives across adolescence: Beginnings, linear narrative form, and endings. *Journal of Personality*, *77*(2), 527–560. https://doi.org/10.1111/j.1467-6494.2008.00557.x
226. First, M. B., Spitzer, R. L., Gibbon, M., Williams, J. B. W. (1997). *User's guide for the structured clinical interview for DSM – IV Axis II personality disorders – SCID II*. American Psychiatric Press.
227. Kaufman, E. A., Cundiff, J. M., Crowell, S. E. (2015). The development, factor structure, and validation of the Self-Concept and Identity Measure (SCIM): A self-report assessment of clinical identity disturbance. *Journal of Psychopathology and Behavioral Assessment*, *37*(1), 122–133. https://doi.org/10.1007/s10862-014-9441-2
228. Bagby, R. M., Taylor, G. J., Parker, J. D. A. (1994). The twenty-item Toronto Alexithymia Scale: II. Convergent, discriminant, and concurrent validity. *Journal of Psychosomatic Research*, *38*(1), 33–40. https://doi.org/10.1016/0022-3999(94)90006-X
229. Baron-Cohen, S., Wheelwright, S. (2004). The Empathy Quotient: An investigation of adults with Asperger syndrome or high functioning autism, and normal sex differences. *Journal of Autism and Developmental Disorders*, *34*(2), 163–175. https://doi.org/10.1023/B:JADD.0000022607.19833.00
230. Beck, A. T., Steer, R. A., Brown, G. K. (1996). *Manual: Beck Depression Inventory*. Hartcourt & Brace.

231. Mayer, J. D., Salovey, P., Caruso, D. R. (2000). *The Mayer, Salovey, and Caruso Emotional Intelligence Test: Technical manual*. MHS.
232. McLean, K. C., Thorne, A. (2003). Late adolescents' self-defining memories about relationships. *Developmental Psychology*, *39*(4), 635–645. https://doi.org/10.1037/0012-1649.39.4.635
233. McLean, K. C., Pratt, M. W. (2006). Life's little (and big) lessons: Identity statuses and meaning-making in the turning point narratives of emerging adults. *Developmental Psychology*, *42*(4), 714–722. https://doi.org/10.1037/0012-1649.42.4.714
234. Hamilton, M. (1960). A rating scale for depression. *Journal of Neurology, Neurosurgery & Psychiatry*, *23*, 56–61. https://doi.org/10.1136/jnnp.23.1.56
235. Bech, P., Paykel, E., Sireling, L., Yiend, J. (2015). Rating scales in general practice depression: Psychometric analyses of the Clinical Interview for Depression and the Hamilton Rating Scale. *Journal of Affective Disorders*, *171*, 68–73. https://doi.org/10.1016/j.jad.2014.09.013
236. Morosini, P. L., Magliano, L., Brambilla, L., Ugolini, S., Pioli, R. (2000). Development, reliability and acceptability of a new version of the DSM-IV Social and Occupational Functioning Assessment Scale (SOFAS) to assess routine social functioning. *Acta Psychiatrica Scandinavica*, *101*(4), 323–329.
237. Brandt, J. (1991). The Hopkins Verbal Learning Test: Development of a new memory test with six equivalent forms. *Clinical Neuropsychologist*, *5*(2), 125–142. https://doi.org/10.1080/13854049108403297
238. Lezak, M. D., Howieson, D. B., Loring, D. W. (2004). *Neuropsychological assessment* (4th ed.). Oxford University Press.
239. Wechsler, D. (2008). *Wechsler Adult Intelligence Scale – Fourth edition (WAIS-IV): Administration and scoring manual*. Pearson.
240. Brickenkamp, R. (2006). *d2-testen – en vurdering af opmærksomhed og koncentration: Dansk vejledning – administration, scoring og normer [The d2 test of attention and concentration: Danish guidelines – administration, scoring and norms]*. Hogrefe Psykologiske Forlag.
241. McLean, K. C., Syed, M., Pasupathi, M., et al. (2020). The empirical structure of narrative identity: The initial Big Three. *Journal of Personality and Social Psychology*, *119*(4), 920–944. https://doi.org/10.1037/pspp0000247
242. Pedersen, A. M., Straarup, K. N., Holm, T., Thomsen, D. K. (in preparation). Past and future lives with chronic illness: Narrative identity in bipolar disorder and diabetes mellitus.
243. Bech, P., Rasmussen, N. A., Olsen, L. R., Noerholm, V., Abildgaard, W. (2001). The sensitivity and specificity of the Major Depression Inventory, using the Present State Examination as the index of diagnostic validity. *Journal of Affective Disorders*, *66*(2–3), 159–164. https://doi.org/10.1016/S0165-0327(00)00309-8
244. Altman, E. G., Hedeker, D., Peterson, J. L., Davis, J. M. (1997). The Altman Self-Rating Mania Scale. *Biological Psychiatry*, *42*(10), 948–955. https://doi.org/10.1016/S0006-3223(96)00548-3

245. Diener, E., Emmons, R. A., Larsen, R. J., Griffin, S. (1985). The Satisfaction with Life Scale. *Journal of Personality Assessment*, *49*(1), 71–75. https://doi.org/10.1207/s15327752jpa4901_13
246. Watson, D., Clark, L. A., Tellegen, A. (1988). Development and validation of brief measures of positive and negative affect: The PANAS scales. *Journal of Personality and Social Psychology*, *54*(6), 1063–1070. https://doi.org/10.1037/0022-3514.54.6.1063
247. Kuhn, M. H., McPartland, T. S. (1954). An empirical investigation of self-attitudes. *American Sociological Review*, *19*, 68–76. https://doi.org/10.2307/2088175

Index

acceptance
  and mental illness, 3–4
  and personal recovery, 47
  in qualitative studies, 82
  in relation to the developed framework, 192–193
  in relation to the guide for narrative repair, 199, 211, 215
  in relation to the life story analyses, 126, 136, 144, 147, 151, 162
  and well-being, 49
acceptance and commitment therapy, 35, 198
Adler, Jonathan, 76–77
agency
  in narrative therapy, 73
  themes in bipolar disorder, 90
  themes in borderline personality disorder, 76, 86
  themes as increasing in psychotherapy, 77, 86
  themes in major depressive disorder, 89
  themes in narrative identity, 82
  themes in psychopathology, 134
  themes in relation to the guide for narrative repair, 209
  themes in relation to well-being, 78, 144
  themes in schizophrenia, 86, 89
Andresen, Retta, 47, 49, 106
Anthony, William, 46
autobiographical reasoning, 60
autobiography
  Elizabeth Wurtzel, 3
  Elyn Saks, 1, 4
  Kay Redfield Jamison, 3–4, 66
  Matt Haig, 3, 5
  Susanna Kaysen, 3

Baerger, Dana, 79
Bateman, Anthony, 33–34
Beck, Aaron, 32
benefit-finding, 106
Berntsen, Dorthe, 64, 80

bipolar disorder
  diathesis-stress model of, 31
  in DSM-5, 18–19
  interpersonal and social rhythm therapy, 32, 35
  and narrative identity, 90
  recovery from, 43
Bleuler, Paul, 133
Bluck, Susan, 60
borderline personality disorder
  diathesis-stress model of, 33
  in DSM-5, 19, 21
  mentalization-based therapy, 34
  and narrative identity, 76, 86
  recovery from, 42
Bredemeier, Keith, 33
Bruner, Jerome, 54–55

Carr, David, 56, 69
Caspi, Avshalom, 24, 26, 35
centrality of event scale, 80
chaos "narrative", 15, 57, 69, 76, 78, 134, 190, 193, 206, 211
Charon, Rita, 71–72, 224
CHIME, 47, 122
chronic illness management, 45
clinical recovery
  in relation to DSM-5, 44
  versus personal recovery, 42
clinician's illusion, 65, 222
cognitive function, 85, 89, 156
communion
  themes in bipolar disorder, 90
  themes in borderline personality disorder, 76, 86
  themes in major depressive disorder, 89
  themes in narrative identity, 76
  themes in psychopathology, 114
  themes in relation to well-being, 78, 122
  themes in schizophrenia, 86, 92
comorbidity, 24

comorbidity (cont.)
    definition of, 24
    in our samples, 25
    as supporting the transdiagnostic approach, 24
constructivist thinking, 91
contamination, 78
Corrigan, Patrick, 38
Cowan, Henry, 75
cultural life scripts, 64, 142
    as master narratives, 63–64
    and mental illness, 222
    in relation to the developed framework, 192
    in relation to the life story analyses, 110, 138, 140
cultural stories, 63
culture, 63

Dalgleish, Tim, 76
Davidson, Larry, 47, 51
diathesis-stress models
    advantages of, 35
    general description of, 28
    and the guide for narrative repair, 199
    neural diathesis-stress model, 31
    in relation to the developed framework, 190, 193
    in relation to the life story analyses, 36, 184
    stress, 29
    in relation to narrative identity, 76
    transdiagnostic, 35
    treatment grounded in, 29
    vulnerability, 29
Diener, Ed, 49
disease model, 2, 16
DSM-5
    advantages of, 17
    as a cognitive schema, 17, 251
    influence on research, 17
    limitations of, 22
    taxonomy, 16
Dunlop, William L., 59

empowerment, 47
    in relation to the life story analyses, 144, 150, 176
epistemology, 91
Epston, David, 73–74, 198
expressive writing paradigm, 80

first-person
    perspective valuable for research, 9
    perspective in studies of mental illness, 81
    perspective in the life story analyses, 133, 180
Fivush, Robyn, 61–62

Fonagy, Peter, 33–34
Frank, Arthur, 62, 69–70, 72, 76, 80, 92, 134, 138, 194, 211, 221
Frank, Ellen, 31–32, 137
functional level, 48, 156
    in DSM-5, 20
    objective measure of, 43
    in relation to well-being, 44, 50
future life story chapters, 89, 195, 219
future self, 134, 140, 151, 171
    in relation to the developed framework, 194

grief
    and the guide to narrative repair, 220
    and interpersonal and social rhythm therapy, 32
    in relation to the developed framework, 194
    in relation to the life story analyses, 137
guide for narrative repair, 198
    advantages for healthcare professionals, 224
    coping with fear of ill self, 214
    coping with the bleak, uncertain future self, 220
    coping with grief, 214
    coping with self-stigmatization, 214
    and diathesis-stress models, 199
    flexibility in use, 200, 202
    identifying potential obstacles, 206
    instruction for task 1, 205
    instruction for task 2, 212
    instruction for task 3, 215
    instruction for task 4, 219
    introducing, 203
    lack of anchoring as an obstacle, 209
    lack of balance in landscapes as an obstacle, 206
    lack of coherence as an obstacle, 206
    lack of memory as an obstacle, 210
    lack of story ownership as an obstacle, 209
    nondirective questions, 202
    overly negative life story as an obstacle, 207
    peer workers, 222
    and personal recovery, 199
    in relation to other interventions, 203
    the role of healthcare professionals, 201
    severe depression as an obstacle, 208
    sources of inspiration, 188, 198
    storying the valued, accepting, agentic, and growing self, 216
    use of vicarious stories, 210, 221, 223
    use of vicarious stories from peers, 223
    visit a place from positive past, 218

Habermas, Tilmann, 60, 80
Harvey, Allison, 25

Hayes, Steven, 35
hermeneutic perspective, 91
hope, 47
   and the guide to narrative repair, 199, 219
   and personal recovery, 46, 48
   and recovery stories, 224
   in relation to the developed framework, 195
   in relation to the life story analyses, 109, 138, 151, 154, 176
   and restitution narrative, 70
   as a theme in qualitative studies, 82
Hydén, Lars-Christer, 71–72, 195

ICD-11, 16
identity engulfment, 82, 134
Ingram, Rick, 28
intergenerational narratives, 61
International Study of Schizophrenia, 44
interpersonal and social rhythm therapy, 32, 35, 38, 137, 198
interpretative phenomenological analysis, 91, 249

Kessler, Ronald, 24, 37
Kvale, Steinar, 91

Lally, Stephen, 82, 134
landscape of action, 55, 194, 206, 212
landscape of consciousness, 55, 193, 206, 213
Leamy, Mary, 47
Leonhardt, Bethany, 44
life story analyses
   assumptions, 91
   development of themes, 92, 249
   effects of cultural context, 97
   effects of data-collection method, 98
   effects of researcher background, 98
   sample overrepresented women, 95
   sample as well-functioning, 97
life story chapters, 59, 85–86, 89–90, 194, 205, 212, 216
Lind, Majse, 76
Luxton, David, 28
Lysaker, Paul, 38, 75, 193, 198
major depressive disorder
   diathesis-stress model of, 32
   in DSM-5, 19, 21
   and narrative identity, 76, 89
   recovery from, 43
Markus, Hazel, 140
master narratives, 63–64, 222
   destructive, 65
   medical, 70
   and mental illness, 64, 73, 192, 195, 199, 221
   in narrative therapy, 73
   and personal recovery, 195
   in relation to the developed framework, 192
   in relation to the guide for narrative repair, 209
   in relation to the life story analyses, 138, 142
McAdams, Dan, 56, 58, 79
McLean, Kate, 61–63, 79
McNally, Richard, 22
mental contrasting, 198
mental disorder
   DSM-5 definition, 16
mental illness
   disease model, 16, 174
   models of, 46
   and self-disorders, 133
mentalization, 33, 86
   across mental disorders, 34
   mentalization-based therapy, 35
   pseudo-mentalization, 209
Michalak, Erin, 38, 82, 106
Millier, Aurélie, 37
Moffitt, Terrie, 35
Murray, Greg, 43
Musliner, Katherine, 35

narrative
   the body in illness narratives, 72
   communicating illness experience, 71
   and emotion, 56, 80, 194
   future imagination, 56, 58
   and intentionality, 55
   and language, 57
   and meaning, 55
   and memory, 56, 58
   as structuring illness experience, 69, 71, 211
   as temporally organized, 54
   told versus lived, 56–57
narrative ecology, 61, 63
   of mental illness, 65–66, 112, 191, 195
narrative identity, 8
   chapters in, 59
   as coauthored, 62
   coherence in, 60
   coherence and well-being, 79
   definition of, 58
   hostile coauthors, 62, 191, 199
   imagined future events, 59–60
   key scenes in, 60
   and master narratives, 64
   meaning and purpose, 59
   meaning and well-being, 78
   and memory, 59–60
   in narrative ecology, 61
   negative, 76, 191–192

narrative identity (cont.)
  negative events, 79
  and psychotherapy, 77, 86
  resilient, 191
  scaffolded by caregivers, 62
  self-continuity, 58
  self-event connections, 60, 65
  shapes action, 59
  silencing, 62, 190, 199
  and trauma, 77, 80, 190
  as vulnerability to mental illness, 76, 190
  and well-being, 78
narrative medicine, 71, 224
narrative repair, 75, 188, 193, 198
  and supportive coauthors, 195
narrative therapy, 73, 198
narrative truth, 72
Nash, John, 8, 63
Ng, Fiona, 43

Oettingen, Gabriele, 219

Paris, Joel, 26
partnership model of treatment, 45
Pasupathi, Monisha, 62, 65
paternalistic treatment approach, 45, 50, 69
patient-centered treatment, 176, 202, 224
peer support, 122
peer workers, 195, 221
Pennebaker, James, 80
personal recovery
  definition of, 46
  key tasks, 47
  key themes, 47
  as narrative in nature, 51
  partnership model of treatment, 45
  policymaking, 44
  in relation to the developed framework, 193
  in relation to disability, 45
  in relation to illness management, 45
  in relation to the life story analyses, 50, 102, 109, 131, 147, 163, 176, 184, 186
  in relation to well-being, 48
  stages, 47
  versus clinical recovery, 42, 47
  versus paternalistic approach to treatment, 45
PhD project
  Anne Mai Pedersen, 10, 88–89
  Majse Lind, 10, 86–87
  Rikke Jensen, 10, 87, 89
  Tine Holm, 10, 85, 87
Pillemer, David, 61
Plana-Ripoll, Oleguer, 24
Polkinghorne, Donald, 54, 57
positive psychology interventions, 198

post-traumatic growth, 106
psychological well-being, 49
psychotherapy
  and narrative, 72, 75
  and narrative identity, 77, 86
  narrative therapy, 73
  psychoanalysis and narrative, 72

qualitative methodology, 81
quantitative methodology, 81
quest narrative, 70

recovery movement, 9, 43–44
recovery stories, 224
redemption
  benefit-finding and post-traumatic growth, 106
  definition of, 59
  as master narrative, 63, 121
  in the movie *A Beautiful Mind*, 63
  and personal recovery, 106
  in relation to the developed framework, 194
  in relation to the life story analyses, 106, 121, 142
  in relation to quest narrative, 70
  stories in recovering alcoholics, 59
  and well-being, 78
Reese, Elaine, 62
Regier, Darrel, 23
remission, 42, 48
restitution narrative, 70, 141, 192, 222
Ridgway, Priscilla, 46
Roe, David, 47, 51
Rubin, David, 64
Rush, Augustus, 43
Ryff, Carol, 49

schizophrenia
  clinical recovery from, 43
  costs of, 37
  diathesis-stress model of, 6, 30
  in DSM-5, 18–19
  and narrative identity, 75, 85, 89
  recovery from, 42–43
self-defining memories, 85
self-stigmatization
  definition of, 38
  and personal recovery, 47
  in relation to the life story analyses, 102, 118, 134, 139
Singer, Jefferson, 60
Slade, Mike, 42, 45–48, 211
Smith, Jonathan, 91
Spence, Donald, 72–74, 211
stereotypes, 38, 64

stigmatization, 50
  cost of mental illness, 7
  definition of, 38
  as preventing sharing of stories, 107
  in relation to the life story analyses, 102, 118, 139
  schizophrenia, 37
subjective well-being, 49
Syed, Moin, 63

therapeutic relationship, 202
Tracy, Jessica, 59
transdiagnostic
  approach in the developed framework, 189
  approach to narrative identity problems, 76
  argument for approach in the life story analyses, 26
  shared cognitive disturbances, 25
  versus categorical approach, 22, 26
trauma, 29, 63, 75, 77, 80, 190, 206, 211

unique outcomes, 74, 201, 207

Valiente, Carmen, 44
value-confirmation, 198
vicarious life stories, 61, 191, 195, 210
  in borderline personality disorder, 86
  and healthcare professionals, 224
  and peer workers, 142, 222
  in relation to the life story analyses, 125, 142
  in relation to personal life stories, 62, 222

Walker, Elaine, 30–31, 34
White, Michael, 73–74, 198
WHO definition of health, 49
working alliance, 202

Zanarini, Mary, 46

For EU product safety concerns, contact us at Calle de José Abascal, 56–1°, 28003 Madrid, Spain or eugpsr@cambridge.org.

www.ingramcontent.com/pod-product-compliance
Ingram Content Group UK Ltd.
Pitfield, Milton Keynes, MK11 3LW, UK
UKHW021526080625
459375UK00020B/330